D0442879

"Fred Kiel's premise, that good character and strong principles are an essential part of a successful leader's tool kit, may seem obvious. But the sad truth, writ large over the years, is that too often character gets dismissed as superfluous. The science that Kiel has put behind his premise, combined with the tools for how to become a 'Virtuoso leader,' should be required reading for today's and tomorrow's CEOs."

—**JIM BERRIEN,** Partner, Bentley, Farrell, Ahl & Berrien

"Business leaders have an obligation to deliver more than a rising stock price and profits. *Return on Character* demonstrates *how* to identify, choose, and become a 'Virtuoso leader' and *why* character-based leadership actually yields better returns. This book provides the road map for the kind of leaders we must have today and tomorrow."

—**GARY C. BHOJWANI,** Chairman, Allianz of America

"In my experience, the global leaders who obtain the best results are indeed like the ones whom Fred Kiel has identified as 'Virtuoso leaders.' It's great to have this confirmed with hard financial metrics."

—**PAUL J. FRIBOURG,** Chairman and CEO, Continental Grain Company

"As a leader, I always struggled meeting the demands of leadership while still being the person I wanted to be. In *Return on Character*, Fred Kiel provides the data that proves leading with high character is not only possible—it's necessary."

—**DEAN HAGER,** former CEO, Kroll Ontrack

"I intuitively knew that Fred Kiel's groundbreaking research was true—but I did not expect to have it so soundly confirmed with hard data. This book finally provides the justification for boards to embrace scientifically validated character assessment as part of their evaluation of senior management teams."

—**RICHARD J. HARRINGTON,** former President and CEO, Thomson Reuters

"Kiel's research addresses the real heart of the matter and biggest challenge for all leaders. A crucial must-read for anyone seeking a leadership role."

—**THOMAS HERRON,** former CEO, TriStar Centennial Medical Center

"Kiel's book makes the case that moral leadership pays off for the company's bottom line. More important, the book provides a methodology for leaders and companies to develop talent and institutionalize moral leadership across the organization."

—**VERN KIMBALL,** CEO, Calgary Stampede

"Return on Character is brilliant, important, and timeless. The research needed to be done, and the story needed to be told. Fred Kiel finally proves that the presence of moral character is very profitable."

—**DOUG LENNICK,** cofounder and CEO, Think2Perform

"Uniquely combining art, science, and soulfulness, Fred Kiel provides business leaders with a compelling case for true human decency. It drives profits, it rewards people, and it does good. Every person leading—or hoping to lead—an organization should read this book."

—**DANIEL McCARTHY,** Principal, Gallarus Ventures, LLC

"At a time of low public estimation of the moral compass of the business sector, Fred Kiel offers us three reasons for hope: first, that this low moment has created a yearning for great character in leadership; second, in his proof that great character isn't just morally preferable but that it offers better returns; and third, that leaders can diligently improve their character. As Kiel writes, 'Let's dig in,' to which I would add, 'Now! Before the last sinews of trust snap.'"

—**MICHAEL S. McGAVICK,** CEO, XL Group

"Trained as a PhD psychologist, Fred Kiel helped pioneer executive coaching for C-suite leaders. Decades of working closely with CEOs have enabled Kiel and his colleagues at KRW International to develop an extensive database on CEO 'character' and to identify leadership traits correlating with corporate success: integrity, responsibility, forgiveness, and compassion. *Return on Character* is a book for corporate boards seeking to identify their next 'Virtuoso CEO' and for aspiring executives hoping to take their place among the best."

—**DANIEL MENKEN,** author, *Faith, Hope and the Corporation*

"Fred Kiel provides compelling statistical evidence that the character of the CEO and the executive team materially impacts an organization's financial results and offers insightful perspectives on defining and developing character. This book is a valuable and practical resource for boards of directors, CEOs, chief human resource officers, and others who are engaged in selecting and developing senior executives, as well as those who aspire to such roles."

—**DAVE PYLIPOW,** Chief People Officer, Delhaize America

"*Return on Character* is the most comprehensive treatment of the interrelationship between leadership and ethics that I have ever read. It's not only descriptive, but also prescriptive, providing experience-driven methods for leaders to improve or reengineer their effectiveness. A must-read for any leader at any level!

—**MARK W. SHEFFERT,** Chairman and CEO,
Manchester Companies, Inc.

"*Return on Character* represents a much-needed, powerful body of research. Achieving profound self-awareness, high moral standards, and character should be the foundation of every leader's journey, regardless of title. The author's dream can and must be realized."

—**DARCY WINSLOW,** founding member and Managing Partner,
Academy for Systemic Change

Return On Character

Return On Character

The Real Reason Leaders and Their Companies **Win**

Fred Kiel

HARVARD BUSINESS REVIEW PRESS

Boston, Massachusetts

The web addresses referenced in this book were live and correct at the time of the book's publication but may be subject to change.

Library of Congress Cataloging-in-Publication Data

Kiel, Fred.
   Return on character : the real reason leaders and their companies win / Fred Kiel.
   pages cm
   ISBN 978-1-62527-130-3 (hardback)
1. Leadership. 2. Character. 3. Executive ability. 4. Management—Psychological aspects. 5. Success in business. I. Title.
HD57.7.K523 2015
658.4'092—dc23

                                                                    2014039585

I would like to dedicate this book to the thousands of randomly selected employees who generously gave of their time to respond to our surveys, knowing that they would receive nothing in return from us.

And, of course, I would like to dedicate this to the 121 CEOs who signed up for this research and also generously gave us their time and attention.

Contents

"Why was Lincoln so great that he over-shadows all other national heroes? He really was not a great general like Napoleon or Washington; he was not such a skillful statesman as Gladstone or Frederick the Great; but his supremacy expresses itself altogether in his peculiar moral power and in the greatness of his character."

—Leo Tolstoy, quoted in *The World*,
New York, February 7, 1908

Preface

Shortly after this book is published, I will celebrate my seventy-fifth birthday. For nearly forty years, I have served as an adviser and confidant to executive leaders in both large and small organizations. Most often, my clients have been chief executive officers.

Early on in this work, I was struck by how most of my clients were very principled, and yet they demonstrated so little concern for the common good. They weren't hostile to the idea, just focused only on what was good for their specific business.

I also was surprised by how little insight most of my clients had about the real levers for creating value. The executives I advised typically undervalued methods for inspiring and energizing the workforce and overvalued strategic financial and competitive moves. When tough economic times roiled the waters, their investment in talent development (including their own) was the first budget item they tossed overboard. They had little awareness that *who* they are is just as important as *what* they know how to do. The hard data resulting from our research has provided quantitative metrics that clearly prove just how limiting that lack of awareness can be, in both personal and professional outcomes.

I've written this book to offer concrete reasons for rethinking our ideas about effective leadership, and to map out the direct connection between strong character, principled behavior, and sustainable business results.

Virtuosos in every category, from music to writing to sports or medicine and law, recognize that true excellence requires, in the late leadership authority Stephen Covey's words, that we constantly "sharpen the saw."[1] Business leaders endorse this concept as well, but the current tools for improving executive performance are primarily intellectual or behavioral exercises that don't touch the core drives, principles, and personality traits of the person involved. I have based most of my career on demonstrating that delving into the core of our individual humanity is what produces transformational inner change, which in turn leads to increased virtuosity and true excellence as a leader. My professional life didn't begin this way, however. It developed through some inner-journey milestones and transformational changes of my own—changes I worked hard at achieving and that I continue to hone.

I emerged from graduate school in 1971 with a PhD in psychology and, within one year, formed my own practice. For the next fifteen years, I had one goal: career and financial success. During those years, I built two large clinical practices. I left the first one following a divorce and then built the second practice, taking it public in 1985. For a brief period, I was a CEO of a publicly held corporation. I regularly met with investors and analysts and personally experienced all the usual challenges of leading a publicly owned corporation.

People who knew me in those days would *not* have described me as a Virtuoso CEO. I was more like one of the Self-Focused CEOs in the Return on Character (ROC) study. While I never engaged in any illegal behavior, I'm sure many of my colleagues in those days felt that I was more than willing to throw them under the bus if it meant success for me. The people who worked for me undoubtedly sensed that I cared a lot more about what they could do for me than about what happened to them. I had developed some incredibly poor character habits.

I certainly wasn't taught those habits as a child. I grew up on a cattle ranch in the Midwest. At the dinner table, my father often spoke about people who demonstrated exactly the kind of self-absorbed behavior I would later fall into. "Big hat, no cattle" was his description. A peacemaker, my father would turn the other cheek before reacting with anger, and I can recall countless moments in which he demonstrated his honesty, forgiveness, and willingness to be generous and kind. My mother was highly principled, too, with strong character habits. She believed in telling the truth and was steadfast in doing so, albeit with sensitivity and kindness.

And then, there was me. By my late thirties, I had been divorced and bankrupt twice. As I reached middle age, I became increasingly aware of my moral and spiritual emptiness. Clearly, I was not living the kind of life my parents demonstrated. After some soul searching and with the excellent guidance of some talented advisers and mentors, I began to understand that I needed to change. That was the start of a difficult and ongoing process. Like anyone who attempts to alter a deeply ingrained habit, I didn't achieve immediate and complete success. But over time, and with a lot of practice (using exercises and other techniques I'll share with you in part III of this book), I found that I was able to significantly strengthen my character habits.

By early 1987, I had resigned my position as CEO and launched a new solo practice with the vision of using my energy, talents, and skills to help leaders of large business organizations "connect their heads to their hearts." My solo practice quickly grew into a small partnership and then moved on to become KRW International, a boutique consultancy with a global reach, where I still am today, and which continues its mission of helping leaders and organizations connect their actions and behavior to their values and principles. The research project that forms the foundation of this book is a direct extension of that organizational mission.

From Vision to Movement

As I approach my seventy-fifth birthday, I have a dream. I hope to inspire a movement that forever changes people's expectations of leadership and performance in organizational life, both in the for-profit world as well as in the nonprofit. I hope to inspire a movement where people demand character-driven leadership because it delivers higher value to all stakeholders—and because it's the *right* thing to do.

More specifically:

- I dream of a time when societal norms have shifted, so that leaders of organizations everywhere are *expected* to demonstrate strong character habits, not only because it is the right thing to do, but because it builds tangible value for all stakeholders.

- I dream of a time when the ROC is so widely recognized and accepted that the "invisible hand" of the free market works to create character-driven leadership cultures.

- I dream of a time when most public businesses, large nongovernmental organizations, and large government agencies are rated for the ROC their leaders produce, much as the financial health of global businesses today is rated by Moody's and Standard & Poor's.

- I dream of a time when the power of social media, the internet, and smartphone-like technology has made the character habits of management teams and leaders easily discernible and transparent.

- I dream of a time when the inappropriately opaque or hidden elements of leadership become transparent and visible—when the gap between what leaders say and what they do is closed.

- I dream of a time when investment professionals reward companies with character-driven executive teams and avoid those with Self-Focused leadership, because they understand the connection between strength of character and business success.

- And finally, I dream of a time when character development is an integral part of the essential core curricula in business schools—when *who* a leader is as a person matters just as much as *what* that person knows how to do.

Introduction

> *"A leader should stay legal, but beyond that, it's the person who is hard-nosed, doesn't succumb to soft HR practices, and ruthlessly controls costs who creates the most value!"*

> *"A good business model is what creates value, and a good business model can survive a period of poor leadership."*

> *"If a business makes a lot of money, it will attract good talent and all the culture stuff will follow."*

Being cynical is easy when it comes to the topic of character's role in business leadership. Just seeing the words *character* and *business leadership* in the same sentence brings to mind a seemingly unending list of ineffective leaders who periodically sweep through the business world, draining organizations of all real value, leaving nothing behind but angry investors and an unemployed workforce. These "greed is good" proponents can make for great headlines, but that's where their contribution to any common good ends. When it comes to running a business that achieves maximum returns for all stakeholders—investors, governing boards, employees, clients, communities, and the world they share—self-involved, bottom-line-driven leaders rarely deliver the goods.

That idea may seem obvious, but it's missing in the way we train, view, and judge business leaders. Rarely do business media cover the practices or benefits of character-driven leadership. We don't hesitate to talk about the connection between inferior leadership character and massive business meltdowns (think Enron's Kenneth Lay, Health-South's Richard Scrushy, or Tyco International's Dennis Kozlowski). But what do you know about Ken Chenault of American Express, Allianz NA's Gary Bhojwani, and Michael McGavick of the XL Group—or any other leader whose character insiders credit for the incredible *success* of the business?

Those questions represent no more than a tentative first step into the vastly unexplored topic of leadership character and its role in business results. Go deeper and the questions grow more urgent: Does a leader's character really contribute to the organization's bottom line, or are strong business results simply a reflection of a solid business model and positive macroeconomic forces? Can leaders who operate from a foundation of moral principles drive successful businesses in today's fast-moving, hyperglobal economic environment? Is inferior leadership character a problem only when the individuals exhibiting it get caught? Can we truly assess winning CEO character, and—even more critically—can we build it?

In 2006, KRW International began a multiyear research project aimed at answering these and many other questions by exploring the connections between leadership character and business results. *Return on Character: The Real Reason Leaders and Their Companies Win* is about the discoveries we gleaned from that rigorous research.

In Search of ROC

Between 2006 and 2013, KRW's research group enrolled 121 CEOs from around the United States in the ROC study. We included leaders from *Fortune* 500 and 100 companies, privately held firms, and non-profits. In the end, we had full data sets on 84 of the leaders, which included interviews with the leaders and anonymous surveys with those who work for these leaders. We obtained the stated and/or published financial results of their businesses for forty-four of these leaders. (See appendix A for a full description of how we selected CEOs for the study, the size, type, and sector they represent, and a detailed description of the data we collected.)

Drawing from our own research and that of neuroscientists, social psychologists, anthropologists, and other researchers, we created a metric for assessing the character-driven behaviors of the leaders and their executive teams and for determining their impact on the specific financial results of the businesses they lead. Here we offer an in-depth look at the close and inextricable link between CEO character and value creation we found in our research.

The leaders in our research earned character scores that created a broad curve representing leadership behavior. Each of the study participants helped trigger new understandings and insights into the nature of leadership character. Specifically, however, we home in on the differences between the ten most highly principled CEOs in our study—individuals we labeled "Virtuoso CEOs," described by their employees as demonstrating strong character habits—and the ten CEOs whose character scores were the lowest in the study. The employees of this latter group described their leaders as often warping the truth for personal gain and as mostly concerned about themselves and their own financial security. In keeping with these employee descriptions, we called this second group "Self-Focused CEOs."

Our research returned a wealth of information about CEO behavior and value creation. Two of the study's most critical findings are:

- First, there is an observable and consistent relationship between character-driven leaders and better business results. Leaders with stronger morals and principles do, in fact, deliver a Return on Character, or ROC. As figure I-1 illustrates, organizational leadership that ranks high on the ROC character-assessment scale achieves nearly *five times* the return on assets that leaders who fall at the bottom of the curve achieve.

- Second, people demonstrate character through habitual behaviors. Therefore, they can develop the habits of strong character and "unlearn" the habits of poor character. Further, by doing so, they can improve their results—in both business and personal outcomes.

FIGURE I-1

Return on assets

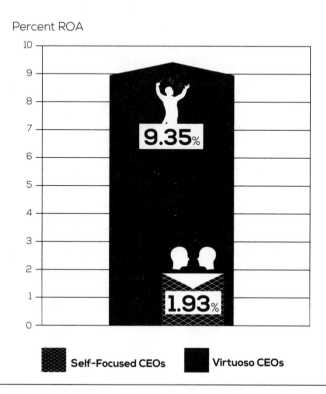

Percent ROA

- **9.35%**
- **1.93%**

Self-Focused CEOs   Virtuoso CEOs

Return on Character offers a full and detailed exploration of the ROC research findings. It describes how the CEO character is formed, and how character habits and ingrained beliefs are reflected in the way leaders select and interact with their executive teams. And the research definitively reveals the connection between ongoing, sustainable business success and the character and guiding principles that senior executives exhibit in the workplace.

We'll dig deeply into leaders' beliefs and biases—leaders of organizations as large and diverse as the Costco chain of wholesale merchandise warehouses, or as small and highly specialized as South Dakota's Larson Storm Doors. We will explore the research on these leaders' strength of character as well as their ability to form and execute a winning business model, and we'll take a close look at the way leadership character reveals itself through organizational vision and clarity of strategy. We'll examine the results achieved by Virtuoso leaders,

CEOs whose workforce ratings place them at the top of the Character Curve etched by integrity, responsibility, forgiveness, and compassion—principles that we discovered to be the Keystone Character Habits of leadership. And we'll compare their organizational results with those of the Self-Focused leaders who fall at the other end of the curve. The stories of how the low-character leaders undermine the success of even the best business plan put to rest the "greed is good" myth.

Beyond a mere profile of individual leaders and their experiences, this book also outlines a methodology—ideas, advice, and techniques for improving your own business results and those of your organization by strengthening the character habits that drive success and nurture an engaged workforce.

What You'll Find in *Return on Character*

The information in *Return on Character* is organized into three parts. In part I, "ROC and the Path toward Leadership," we examine the fundamental ideas upon which we based our research.

- In chapter 1, "Character Defined: Populating the Character Curve," we explore the basis of character and how CEOs and other leaders demonstrate it. We'll break down *all* of the elements of the ROC Value Chain to demonstrate how life experiences, beliefs, and character drive leadership decisions, from choosing and leading the executive team to executing the business model and achieving business results.

- All leaders come equipped with the same generic hardware of a working brain, but in chapter 2, "The Human Nature of Leadership: Upgrading an Outdated Model," we look beyond those physical givens to understand the ideas and practices that form the software of moral intuition, motivational drives, and personality traits that make each person unique—and determine the leadership approach of any CEO or senior executive.

- In chapter 3, "The Journey from Cradle to Corner Office: Reading the Road Map," we investigate the inner and outer journeys that form the keystone habits of leadership, and how the life experience of a CEO shapes his or her ability to develop as an integrated person who demonstrates the best of those attitudes and behaviors.

Part II, "ROC Leadership at Work," goes beyond our examination of what makes CEOs and senior executives who they are to take a closer look at what these leaders *do*.

- Chapter 4, "ROC Leadership in Action: Mastering the Essentials," details KRW's research on the day-to-day actions, decisions, and influence of Virtuoso leaders in the workplace. It takes effective execution to create value, and we explore one of the unexpected findings of ROC research: that weak-character CEOs tend also to be ineffective businesspeople. Finally, we'll dig into what the data shows about the foundation of trust that underlies effective execution and workforce engagement.

- Without a principled executive team, the CEO's influence and ability to create value is blunted. Chapter 5, "The Executive Team and ROC: Guiding the Organization to a Win," discusses the importance of the executive team to even the best CEO or executive leader. Here, we examine how the Virtuoso CEO chooses and leads an executive team that consistently promotes character principles throughout the organization, and how even a moderate-character team can drag down results and hamper innovation and collaboration.

- In chapter 6, "The ROC Ripple Effect: Bringing Every Stakeholder into the Winner's Circle," we'll look closely at leadership character as *the* relevant factor in achieving sustainable results for every stakeholder in any business. Here we explore the business results achieved by the CEOs in our study and describe the definitive links between these results and the strength of leadership character.

In part III, "The ROC Habits Workshop," we examine what people—and organizations—can do to improve their ROC by developing stronger character habits that boost the results of their own ROC effect.

- Chapter 7, "Becoming a Virtuoso Leader," explores specific ideas and concrete techniques for developing the character habits of successful leadership at any age and in any position or environment. The human brain typically reaches maturity around age thirty, but scientific evidence has shown that people can continue developing their thinking processes and shaping ideas and habits throughout their lives. This chapter shows you how to leverage those capabilities to build Virtuoso leadership.

- In chapter 8, "Developing an ROC Organization," we look at how boards of directors, CEOs, senior executives, and leaders at *any* operational level can undertake a sensible—and proven— approach to improving the overall character of their business or organization.

- In the conclusion, "Steering toward a New Direction in Leadership," I call for a movement toward character-driven leadership and explain why I'm optimistic that the time has come for a shift in the character habits that guide our businesses, government, and other critical institutions.

This book delivers the hard data my research team and I were unsure of when we first embarked on our seven-year study of CEO character and its effect on business results, but that is only part of its story. Every individual in our study had to trace the roots of ideas, attitudes, opinions, and experiences that shaped his or her approach to decision making and leadership. Those insights offer you a unique opportunity to examine the foundations of your own character, to understand hidden weaknesses, and to uncover opportunities for strengthening the character habits that can make you a true virtuoso in leadership and in life.

The work involved in exploring your own nature, identifying weaknesses in your character, and then working to overcome them can be difficult and even painful. But as with all transformative change, the outcomes can more than compensate for the work of achieving them. You may be the *only* person in your life who is unaware of the shortcomings in your character. The process and tools we outline in part III of this book (and offer online) will help you see yourself as others do—and work to improve that image, from the inside out.

ROC Is for Leaders—at *Any* Level

The implications of our findings extend well beyond the executive suite and into every aspect of business operation and performance, and beyond. We offer ideas, insights, and a new approach to leadership behavior for people working at *any* level, within organizations of any size or makeup:

- For people in *leadership* roles, this book will help you improve your effectiveness. *Who* you are as a person is just as important to your organization's success as your business and leadership skills; we outline some concrete methods for boosting your character habits *and* performance.

- *Members of the board* selecting the next CEO will find this book particularly helpful in learning how to avoid critical errors. A mistake in judgment about the character of a CEO candidate is one of the most costly errors a board can make.

- *Chief talent officers* responsible for supplying the company's leadership pipeline with high-potential future leaders can learn how to identify hidden talent in the organization—those who already possess well-developed character habits and beliefs.

- *Frontline workers* can use the insights and techniques here to assess and boost their own character and workplace performance as a first step in advancing in the organization. Or they can use the ideas and metrics to identify where their current employer falls on the Character Curve to determine whether their leadership might be driving the company toward ongoing success or dragging it down.[1]

At KRW, we have been working with organizational leadership for nearly three decades; I am convinced there are countless people in leadership roles who wish for an aspirational vision to guide their life. Many will think that the claims resulting from the ROC research are idealistic, a luxury not allowed by the harsh world that demands "maximum return to investors." To date, there has been no useful leadership model that combines a sense of duty to create value with a desire to leave the world a better place. The leaders of large and small businesses and nonprofit organizations have the potential for tremendous influence and positive impact on the world, and many wish to exert it—but they lack a playbook.

In his groundbreaking work, *Good to Great: Why Some Companies Make the Leap . . . and Others Don't*, Jim Collins describes his own version of Virtuoso leadership in what he calls the Level 5 leader, someone who "builds enduring greatness through a paradoxical blend of personal humility and professional will."[2] Collins tells us that, while he believes many individuals with the potential to be Level 5 leaders exist in our world, they're difficult to spot because their humility prevents them from taking credit for the positive results of their superb leadership. He says, "Our research exposed Level 5 as a key component inside the black box of what it takes to shift a *company* from good to great. Yet inside that black box is yet another black box—namely, the inner development of a *person* to Level 5."

Our research has gone a long way toward supplying a tool for identifying such high-value leaders and mapping this second black box—their inner development. The practices and techniques here provide the playbook. Wherever I go, I'm struck by the *hunger* people have for a meaningful shift in our national attitude toward the importance of integrity, responsibility, compassion, and forgiveness in leadership—the same hunger that brought you to this book.

Part I

ROC and the Path toward Leadership

1

Character Defined

Populating the Character Curve

Whether they express their opinion or keep it to themselves, hardly anyone is neutral on the subject of leadership character. In meetings, seminars, professional consultations, and private conversations, the topic of character can generate strong reactions. Some of this heat may be sparked by the lack of a widely shared definition of just what character means. And many people are uncomfortable talking about character at all, because they view it as something deeply personal and largely unchangeable.

According to that common view, character is something we acquired as we were growing up, a set of ideas and operating beliefs that just sort of crept up on us while we weren't looking and then calcified into a framework that would, ever after, influence our view of the world and our way of living in it. These ideas about character help place it, along with politics and religion, in the category of somewhat untouchable subjects. What good can come, after all, from talking about a personal quality that you don't really understand, can't fairly assess or categorize without bias, and, in any event, cannot adapt or influence in any meaningful way? Any talk of "morals" or "values" became suspect in the last decades of the twentieth century, as a series of religious, political, and business leaders who claimed great reverence for those ideals revealed themselves to be not even loosely bound to them. Doug Lennick and I stumbled into that minefield when we published our book, *Moral Intelligence,* in 2005.[1] In that climate, character and the morals that shaped it had become topics best left undisturbed.

In less than a decade, however, attitudes have shifted. A 2014 Google search on the phrase "morality and business" yields over thirty-one million results. From business analysts to academicians, economists, and everyday citizen investors and consumers, people worldwide are paying increasing attention to the morals demonstrated in the character of business, political, and religious leaders. But while today's business world may be much more open to a conversation about the value of character than it was ten years ago, all of the vague and unfounded ideas that circulate around the concept of character continue to cloud the discussion with misunderstanding and controversy. So my KRW research team and I prepared to enter a social minefield when we decided to study the connection between leadership character and business results—a study whose findings formed the basis for the ideas and processes of Return on Character or ROC.

As business consultants with many years' experience working with CEOs and senior executives, we were convinced that character shapes leadership decisions, tactics, and workplace behavior—all of which play a direct role in business results. To map the connections between all of those factors, we structured a research project aimed at bringing crystalline clarity to our understanding of what constitutes character, how it's formed, the role it plays in our self-concept, and how it shapes our interactions with the world. (See appendix A for a detailed description of the research design.) We may have been venturing into explosive territory, but we knew that beyond it lay the answer to the *big* question: Is the strength of a leader's character an important driver of business success?

Our first step in that journey was to arrive at a workable definition of the term *character.* That single task triggered an entire series of questions: What is character? How do we demonstrate our character through our actions, and—most particularly—how does leadership character make itself felt in the workplace? Further, just what role does character play in the CEO "value equation"? These are just some of the questions we'll be answering in this chapter, as we begin our discussion of ROC.

Coming to Terms with Character

When you think of the term *character*, what definition comes to mind? Many people immediately respond with answers such as "honesty" or "truthfulness," but human character actually encompasses much more than those fundamental elements. It's also much more than loyalty, or integrity, or spiritual beliefs, fairness, or any other single value or principle.

Of course, there are many definitions of character, but American biologist, naturalist, and author E. O. Wilson offers one in his book, *Consilience: The Unity of Knowledge*, that effectively reflects the many facets of this complex concept (emphasis mine):

> True character rises from a deeper well than religion. It is the *internalization of the moral principles of a society, augmented by those tenets personally chosen by the individual, strong enough to endure through trials of solitude and diversity.* The principles are fitted together into what we call . . . *the integrated self, wherein personal decisions feel good and true.* Character is in turn the enduring source of virtue. It stands by itself and excites admiration in others. It is not obedience to authority, and while it is often consistent with and reinforced by religious belief, it is not piety.[2]

Let's look more closely at Wilson's assertion that character is the "internalization of the moral principles of a society." He's telling us that a morally intelligent person is one who knows what behavior is expected by his or her specific culture and context as well as by human societies in general. Fortunately, we have some idea of what kinds of moral principles shape nearly *every* culture's expectations for social behavior. Various cultural anthropologists have cataloged lists of moral principles that they claim are universal for all humans, lists that typically include some forms of expression for fairness, compassion, and honesty. Anthropologist and author Donald Brown, for example, has identified nearly five hundred behaviors and characteristics that all human societies recognize and display.[3] We drew from this list when we chose the four universal moral principles of integrity, responsibility, forgiveness, and compassion—principles demonstrated in a wide range of common human behaviors and attributes, including:

- Distinguishing right from wrong (Integrity)

- Language employed to misinform or mislead (Lack of integrity)

- Redress of wrongs (Responsibility)

- Self-control (Responsibility)

- Cooperation (Forgiveness)

- Mediation of conflict (Forgiveness)

- Empathy (Compassion)

- Attachment (Compassion)

- Affection—expressed and felt (Compassion)

Steven Pinker, in *The Blank Slate: The Modern Denial of Human Nature*, lists all of Brown's universals and, about them, he says, "Thus while conflict is a human universal, so is conflict resolution. Together with all their nasty and brutish motives, all peoples display a host of kinder, gentler ones: a sense of morality, justice, and community, an ability to anticipate consequences when choosing how to act, and a love of children, spouses and friends."[4]

Further evidence of these human universal moral principles comes from a study that compared American children with those in India.[5] As my coauthor and I wrote in *Moral Intelligence*, "The differences in values were predictable: Indian children displayed more deference to elders and acceptance of tradition, while American children value personal autonomy and freedom. But their moral codes were virtually identical. Both groups of children believed that it was wrong to lie, cheat, or steal, and both thought that it was important to treat the sick or unfortunate with kindness."[6]

So while societies vary in how they honor and express these moral principles—parents in one culture may have a very different way of teaching their children about truthfulness than those in another—in some form, these principles are embedded in the cultural norms of all societies.

Wilson also makes a powerful point when he says that strong character leads to the integrated self—a joining of head and heart, where thoughts, feelings, and actions are in harmony, resulting in behavior that demonstrates the character of an individual who walks the talk of his or her belief system. Indeed, character *has* to be expressed through behavior. Integrity, responsibility, forgiveness, and compassion don't live inside us. Our behavior, especially as demonstrated through our relationships with others, is where our character comes to life. Which means that, despite the common wisdom, character *isn't* some hidden quality that no one can really know or assess. We reveal our character all the time through observable behaviors: in the way we treat other people. As we mature, these character-driven behaviors become automatic reflexes, the character habits that express our guiding principles and beliefs.

Beyond the way we internalize universal moral principles, therefore, the definition of character that informed our ROC research includes an understanding of how we demonstrate those principles in relationship to other people. Accordingly, we define character as *an individual's unique combination of internalized beliefs and moral habits that motivate and shape how that individual relates to others.*

While this definition offers some solid footing for our observations about human character, it doesn't pave over every gap in our understanding. Each of us constantly makes decisions about how to interact with other people, and each of those decisions has the potential to either harm or enhance the other person's well-being. So it would seem logical to assume that we are moral and have strength of character when our behavior enhances the well-being of others, and we are immoral and have less strength of character when our behavior harms or detracts from the well-being of others.

Of course, the real world is complex, and so is the nature of our character. Many of the choices we make, for example, may enhance the environment or outcomes of one person, while at the very same time wrecking the lives of others. Finding a balance, wherein our behaviors promote the *most* good for the *most* people, is the ongoing task of all principled people of strong character. Adam Smith, the widely quoted source of the "invisible hand," which has become shorthand for the notion that the unfettered and unregulated free market operates so that everyone benefits, was not an economist but a moral philosopher.[7] In fact, while *The Wealth of Nations* is currently widely quoted, it was Smith's other book, *The Theory of Moral Sentiments*, that was most popular in his day. Republished in 2013, the publisher has this to say: "Without Smith's essential prequel, *The Theory of Moral Sentiments*, the more famous *The Wealth of Nations* can easily be misunderstood, twisted, or dismissed . . . Smith's capitalism is far from a callous, insensitive, greed-motivated, love-of-profits-at-any-cost approach to the marketplace, when seen in the context of his *Moral Sentiments*."[8]

In general, since the days of Adam Smith, our society has recognized that honoring universal moral principles such as integrity, responsibility, forgiveness, and compassion leads to a higher standard of behavior and a safer and more secure world (which, by the way, is good for business, as the ROC research data has shown). The ROC definition of character is woven around those principles, which became the foundation for KRW's work in assessing leadership character and calculating the value it brings to business results—and to our world.

Profiling the CEO Character

With the definition of character brought into clear focus, the research team's next task was to use that definition to help create a means for assessing leadership character. Step 1 involved designing a character profile that encompassed the universal principles that supported our definition, along with the fundamental behaviors that demonstrate those principles.

In figure 1-1, you see the ROC Matrix, which illustrates the profile. This matrix includes the four universal principles of integrity, responsibility, forgiveness, and compassion, each accompanied by a list of the behaviors that express them.

Because the habitual demonstration of these universal principles supports and promotes all other behaviors and habits that express human character, we refer to these four universal principles as *Keystone Character Habits*. As the matrix indicates, the habits of integrity and responsibility are dominated by our intellect (our "head"); the other two, forgiveness and compassion, are most often expressions

FIGURE 1-1

The ROC Matrix

HE♠D	**HE♥RT**
INTEGRITY	**FORGIVENESS**
Telling the truth	Letting go of one's mistakes
Acting consistently with principles, values, and beliefs (walking the talk)	Letting go of others' mistakes
Standing up for what is right	Focusing on what's right versus what's wrong
Keeping promises	
RESPONSIBILITY	**COMPASSION**
Owning one's personal choices	Empathizing with others
Admitting mistakes and failures	Empowering others
Expressing a concern for the common good	Actively caring for others
	Committing to others' development

of our emotions, or the "heart." (We talk more about this "head and heart" connection in chapter 3.)

The behaviors associated with each Keystone Character Habit represent a person's *default* response or reflex behavior when dealing with other people. Together, the habits and their behaviors contained in the ROC Matrix form a strong framework for a principled approach to leadership. As such, they also form the basis of the ROC survey we created to assess leadership character.

Plotting the Character Curve

The KRW research team created a survey of sixty-four questions targeted at revealing how CEOs demonstrated behaviors that express the four Keystone Character Habits, along with a similar survey that explored the behavior of executive teams. (See appendix A for details on all of the research surveys.) In the surveys, we asked randomly chosen employees to use ratings ranging from "always" to "never" to tell us how often their CEOs and executive teams demonstrated such character-defining behaviors as telling the truth, owning up to their own mistakes and failures, allowing others to make and recover from their mistakes, demonstrating concern for the goals and well-being of others in the workforce, and following through on commitments.

Using the data from our surveys, we were able to calculate a character score for each CEO in our study and a separate score for his or her executive team. We determined that a CEO's character score would accurately reflect the employee ratings for the questions covering all four Keystone Character Habits. Then we plotted each score along a curve, which we labeled the Character Curve, to show how the CEOs ranked as a group.

Figure 1-2 shows the complete ROC Character Curve. Each dot on the graph represents one CEO and executive team in our study. At the top end of the curve, you see the ten individuals we identified as *Virtuoso CEOs* in our survey, as a result of the strong character habits they demonstrate in the workplace. To be considered a Virtuoso, not only must the CEO have ratings that would place him or her near the top of the Character Curve, but his or her executive team ratings had to rank equally high. One high-scoring CEO was excluded from the study because he failed to have a high-ranking executive team.

At the other end of the curve are the CEOs whose employees gave them the lowest character ratings. We chose to call the ten members of this group *Self-Focused CEOs*, since in nearly every case their employee responses described individuals of weak character who were out to help themselves, no matter what the cost to others.

In both cases, we limited our selection for the two groups to the CEOs who had given us complete financial data. All of the top-scoring CEOs provided financial data, but some of the lowest-scoring CEOs failed to do so. For that reason, we excluded seven of the lowest-scoring CEOs and replaced them with the next-highest-scoring CEOs in the Character Curve for whom we had financial data, until we arrived at a group of ten CEOs who met the criteria for the Self-Focused group.

Putting a Face on the Virtuoso and Self-Focused Character Categories

Each of the dots on the Character Curve, wherever they fall, represents an individual leader and the team he or she relies on to help execute

FIGURE 1-2

The ROC Character Curve

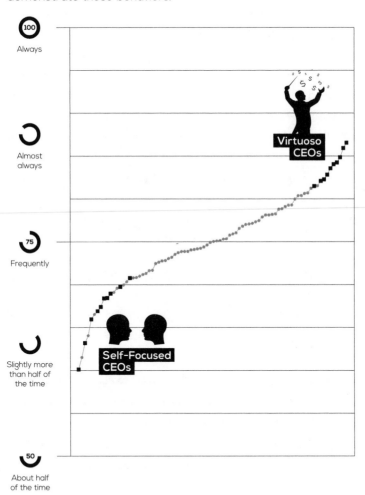

Return on
Character
score

CEO
research
subjects

The CEO and senior team
demonstrate these behaviors:

100 Always

Almost always

Virtuoso CEOs

75 Frequently

Self-Focused CEOs

Slightly more than half of the time

50 About half of the time

their organization's business plan. In our research, we focused on the groups that made up the "highs" and "lows" of the Character Curve: the Virtuoso and Self-Focused CEOs. But to understand what those categories mean in terms of character, we need to take a closer look at these groups and the people in them.

Although the term *virtuoso* typically describes a person who possesses outstanding technical ability at singing or playing a musical instrument, it applies very well to the act of leadership. Not only is leadership based on performance, but it is an art that requires disciplined practice as well as ability. The Virtuoso CEOs in our research truly are masters of the art of leadership.

Of course, every member of the Virtuoso CEO group is an individual; they all differ from each other in many ways, including age, gender, education, personal background, and the size and kind of business they lead. But all of the Virtuoso CEOs identified in our research share three common characteristics:

1. *They are skilled businesspeople.* All Virtuoso CEOs know how to create a vision, maintain a strategic focus, demand performance, and hold people accountable—and they create great value for all stakeholders.

2. *Their employees consider them to be individuals of strong character.* In each case, employee survey ratings ranked these CEOs at the top of the Character Curve by indicating that they consistently demonstrate the four Keystone Character Habits.

3. *They each have selected and lead an executive team of strong character.* No CEO was a Virtuoso if his or her executive team failed to achieve that same rank.

The Virtuoso CEOs and senior leaders in our group are also real people with their own, unique personal history. The group includes:

- *Dale Larson,* who became a CEO at age twenty-nine, when his father died of cancer and Larson found himself charged with the responsibility of running the family business. That was several decades ago, when the small company had just thirty or forty employees. Today, Larson's business employs over fifteen hundred people and dominates the storm door industry in North America with a market share of 55 percent.

- *Sally Jewell*, who in 2005 became CEO of REI, a consumer cooperative and America's largest and most successful outdoor retailer, with over 120 retail stores across the United States. Jewell had a successful career as a banker before joining the REI board in 1996. In 2000, Jewell became the company's chief operating officer (COO). She remained on the executive team for five years before taking on the role of CEO.

- *Charles Sorenson*, who began his career as a surgeon. His employer, Intermountain Healthcare, in Utah, underwent rapid growth, and in 1998 Sorenson advanced into a management role. Eighteen months before I interviewed him in 2010, he was named CEO of this large health-care delivery system. Intermountain Healthcare's growth has continued; at the time of this writing, the company owns and operates twenty-two hospitals and clinics with over thirty-three thousand employees.

As Virtuoso CEOs, Larson, Jewell, and Sorenson all represent outstanding examples of leaders whose behavior clearly expresses their commitment to the Keystone Character Habits. But what about the folks at the other end of the curve?

While the Virtuoso CEOs can accurately be characterized as putting the success and welfare of people ahead of their own concerns, the Self-Focused CEOs place their own welfare and success squarely at the top of their priorities list. Employees aren't blind to this, and they gave these CEOs and the executive teams they lead low ratings on the character survey. Employees of Self-Focused CEOs agree that these leaders tell the truth "slightly more than half the time." In other words, these CEOs and their team members *lie* to their employees almost half the time. Likewise, the Self-Focused CEOs:

- Can't be trusted to keep promises.

- Often pass off blame to others.

- Frequently punish well-intentioned people for making mistakes.

- Are especially poor at caring for people.

As we discovered in the course of our analysis, the Self-Focused CEOs create far less value for all involved: a lower return on assets for investors and less workplace satisfaction and engagement among their workforce. They appear to be most concerned about their own success and financial security.

Later in the book, we'll examine the "everyone for themselves" environment that this kind of leadership fosters, and the effect these CEOs have on their organizations' results. Among this group are these leaders (with pseudonyms, for obvious reasons):

- *Brian*, the CEO of a public high-tech manufacturing firm with thousands of employees.

- *James*, the CEO of a global nonprofit nongovernmental organization with thousands of employees operating in many countries.

- *Robert*, an entrepreneur in his mid-forties who headed up a professional services firm with offices in three US cities and around 150 employees. At the time of our interview, Robert's business was flying high, but it has since struggled and closed at least one of its branches.

In figure 1-3, you can see how the employee ratings of the Virtuoso CEOs and Self-Focused CEOs compare, in terms of their demonstration of the four Keystone Character Habits. The Self-Focused group's low scores in compassion are particularly noteworthy. The survey data shows very clearly that employees know where they stand with these CEOs—as "production units," not people.

Although in the total sample of CEOs we found a few who rated highly on one Keystone Character Habit (integrity, for example) but were rated low on one or more of the others, all Virtuoso CEOs received high ratings on all four habits.

When we asked the employees of our three Virtuoso CEOs, Larson, Jewell, and Sorenson, why they had rated their leaders so highly in these four areas of behavior, here's what some of them said:

Dale's [Larson's] integrity, his level of caring about employees and the responsibility he feels for the success of the company

FIGURE 1-3

Employee ratings of CEOs' character-based behaviors

Return on Character score

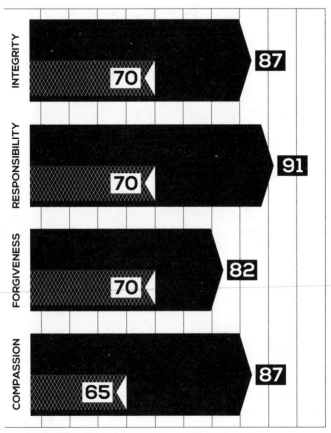

The CEO and senior team demonstrate these behaviors:

 About half of the time

 Slightly more than half of the time

 Frequently

Almost always

 Always

 Self-Focused CEOs   ▮ Virtuoso CEOs

are obvious in the way he conducts himself, whether in formal meetings or in a casual hallway conversation. For forgiveness, Dale wants people to run their own areas and he understands mistakes can happen. He allows this and allows people time to correct and recover. He does not allow ongoing errors that are detrimental to the company, which is appropriate and good.

Sally Jewell is considered extremely trustworthy and is well respected. Having worked for several major corporations before joining REI, I can honestly say I am thrilled to have her in charge and she is as good as it gets in corporate management.

[Sorenson] is very caring and open with employees and I truly believe he always wants to do the right thing for the right reason. I do not work directly with him, but he is very accessible to employees and follows through on issues and concerns. Anytime I have met with Charles, he has treated me as a valued, equal associate. There has never been a barrier between him and those under him.

When we asked the same question of employees of the three Self-Focused CEOs, Brian, James, and Robert, their responses were:

I was working on a large project which never seemed to get complete support from my CEO. [Brian] would say he supports it but his actions never seemed to match. In the end the project was canceled. Honesty would have been preferred.

There is a widespread feeling that executive management [referring to James] cares more about their own advancement and the public perception of the agency than they do about our mission. At the same time, middle-level managers and rank-and-file care about our work . . . despite the lack of soul at the top.

Right now our CEO [Robert] is having a personal relationship with someone at work. They have created a little "team" that empowers her to treat others poorly. Her success is not based on her talent, but on her relationship with him. It's disappointing to see and makes others distrust him personally and professionally.

Our research also revealed some interesting differences in the way CEOs in both categories see themselves. We asked the CEOs to rate themselves on the same set of survey questions we had given to their employees.

For the most part, it appears that the Virtuosos are relatively accurate in their self-awareness, with a few humbly underrating themselves. The majority of the Self-Focused CEOs, however, rate themselves as highly as the Virtuosos. Figure 1-4 shows, in hard numbers, how these two ratings compare.

FIGURE 1-4

Comparison of CEOs' and employees' ratings

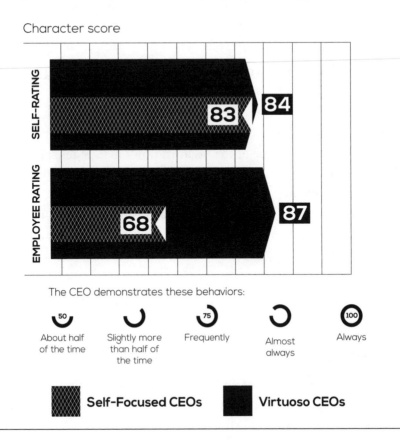

Character score

SELF-RATING

83 84

EMPLOYEE RATING

68 87

The CEO demonstrates these behaviors:

50
About half of the time

Slightly more than half of the time

75
Frequently

Almost always

100
Always

Self-Focused CEOs   Virtuoso CEOs

All other differences aside, it is obvious that these two groups of CEOs differ a good deal in how they behave at work. One group is perceived by employees to be honest, accessible, and concerned about the welfare of others. Members of the other group reveal themselves to employees as dishonest, arrogant, and more concerned about themselves than others. What is not so immediately obvious, however, is why the character of the CEO and senior leadership matters.

In a bottom-line-driven economy (which means, just about every economy in the Western world), what role does CEO character play in organizational success? Do we really care how forgiving or compassionate—or even *honest*—our business leaders are, as long as they continue to deliver the goods? To trace the connection between *who* a CEO is and *what* that CEO does, and to thereby reveal the Return on Character, our researchers had to take a closer look at just what a CEO brings to the table.

Connecting the Links in the ROC Value Chain

Just about every business has its own value chain—a series of raw materials or products or processes and other activities that combine to create the overall value of the organization's marketable product or service. That value chain plays a big role in determining the organization's business results.

All CEOs have an impact on business results by virtue of sitting in the corner office. Those CEOs—along with leaders at every level throughout the organization—also have their own type of value chain made up of:

- The various principles, beliefs, and experiences that shape their character.

- The actions that express that character.

- The individual's talent and skills in decision making, forming and leading a strong team, establishing and maintaining a culture of accountability, strategizing, and so on.

All of those elements combine to determine just what value any leader brings to the organization, and business results are a key measure of that value. The ROC Value Chain, shown in figure 1-5, illustrates how the combined effect of senior leadership character and skill sets impacts business results. (We'll take a closer look at

FIGURE 1-5

The ROC Value Chain

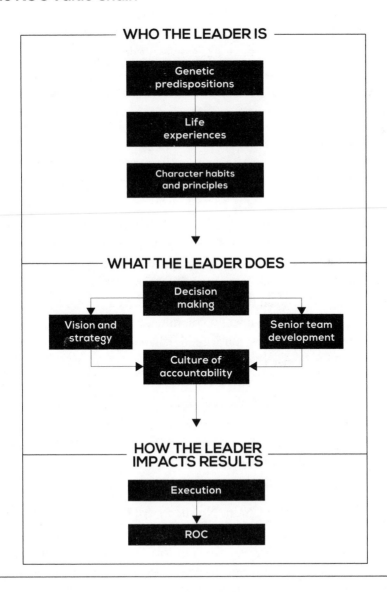

each of these elements and the research that supports them in subsequent chapters.)

The ROC Value Chain identifies the elements of a CEO's or other leader's magic formula for creating value. Let's review it step-by-step:

> *Genetic predispositions and life experiences.* While I don't endorse the "great leaders are born" concept, neither do I accept that people begin life with a blank slate. Genetic endowment sets the stage for how we will view life and approach its challenges, but then early home life and developmental experiences determine how we make decisions and deal with people. (We examine what current research tells us about the genetic foundations of leadership character in chapter 2, "The Human Nature of Leadership.")

> *Character habits and beliefs.* All of us are guided by our subconscious minds—perhaps more than we think. Character habits, acquired during our early years and modified throughout our lifetime, are a large part of our inner world, even though they operate mostly at a subconscious level. As we saw earlier, many moral actions that define and express our character are the result of automatic response patterns that bypass rational thought. These character habits often appear as our reflexive response to a given situation—the unfiltered expression of our beliefs. Character habits, in combination with a leader's beliefs— especially his or her aspirational beliefs for the organization— directly influence the individual's decision-making skills and other leadership activities. For that reason, a leader's character habits and moral beliefs matter a lot when it comes to value creation and business results. (In chapter 3, "The Journey from Cradle to Corner Office," we examine what the research has to tell us about how life experiences shape leadership character.)

> *Decision-making skills.* Leadership decisions are a key element of the ROC Value Chain. No successful CEO ever reached the corner office without learning some basic leadership and business skills along the way, such as forming a vision for the future of the business, maintaining a strategic focus, creating a culture

of accountability, and creating and leading a senior team. These skills all rest on the foundation of a leader's decision-making process, which results in both people decisions (who to have on the senior team, how to grow and develop talent, and so on) and business decisions (for example, when to make changes in the business model or how much risk to assume). While leaders make some business and people decisions intuitively rather than through conscious thought, successful leaders follow a disciplined decision-making process where intuition is combined with reflective analysis. (Chapter 4, "ROC Leadership in Action," describes what the ROC data reveals about the way character influences a leader's abilities in disciplined decision making and other Keystone Leadership Skills.)

Readiness to execute the business plan. The CEO and other senior executive leaders accomplish nothing unless the organization is well structured and the workforce is engaged, focused on the business strategy, and ready to execute the business plan. The executive team's character and leadership skills, therefore, are an extension of the CEO's influence in the ROC Value Chain. (In chapter 5, "The Executive Team and ROC," we explore what research has to tell us about the role of the executive team in more detail.)

Return on Character. The business results produced by this equation are, in fact, the organization's ROC. When the links in the ROC Value Chain are operating at an optimum level, they create great value—not only for investors, but also for customers, employees, vendors (or others external to the company who provide critical products or services), the communities in which the company operates, and, finally, the environment.

The ROC Value Chain ties together all of the elements that contribute to the business results that any leader brings to the organization. But to truly calculate and understand those returns, we need to examine more closely the individual elements of this formula—a process we'll undertake in the next few chapters.

In this chapter, we've walked through the framework of the ROC calculation. We've established just what the term *character* means and how we express our character through our behavior and relationships with others. We've also had our first look into the results of the ROC research, as we examined the Character Curve created by employee assessments of their leaders' workplace behavior—and, as we've noted, how dramatically their assessment can differ from the self-assessment of the CEOs in question.

Before we move on to our in-depth exploration of how CEO character shapes business results and how individuals and even organizations can build stronger "muscle memory" in their own character, we need to better understand how character is formed. In the next chapter, therefore, we'll take a brief tour of human nature and the way our minds work to form the morals, motivations, and personality woven throughout our character.

ROC TAKEAWAYS
Character Defined

1. **Character is an individual's unique combination of beliefs and character habits that motivate and shape how he or she relates to others.** Our character is defined by our behavior—the way we treat other people is our character in action.

2. **Character and solid leadership skills are the basis for distinguishing the Virtuoso CEOs from the Self-Focused CEOs in the ROC study.**

3. **The four Keystone Character Habits of Virtuoso leadership are integrity, responsibility, forgiveness, and compassion.**

4. **To be considered a Virtuoso CEO in the ROC research, employees must rank the CEO *and executive team* as demonstrating the Keystone Character Habits most of the time.** According to their employees, Virtuosos demonstrate these habits "almost always."

5. **Leaders identified as Self-Focused demonstrate the Keystone Character Habits only slightly more than half the time.** They score particularly low on compassion.

6. **The value a leader brings to his or her organization is determined by the individual's character (genetic predispositions, experiences, and character habits) combined with his or her business skill sets (decision making, vision, focus, accountability, executive team development).** The business results achieved through this combination represent the organization's Return on Character.

2

The Human Nature
of Leadership

Upgrading an Outdated Model

Predictions about marketplace events involve certain assumptions about human nature. Financial analysts, economists, business school professors, Wall Street bankers, and others who specialize in making such predictions want to understand how our human nature drives us as we make economic choices and business decisions. Since even the most talented analysts can't possibly have in-depth knowledge about every individual, organization, or event that will influence market trends, they rely on models to inform their understanding and construct their predictions. For a very long time, the accepted model for human nature was *Homo Economicus*— the "Economic Human," who, in classic economic theory, operates from a narrow set of self-interests aimed at accumulating the maximum amount of wealth (money or goods or other perks) with the least amount of effort.

Over the years, many experts have based their assumptions about sound business leadership on this Economic Human model. As a result, the self-interested, coldly calculated, take-no-prisoners approach to business leadership is widely considered to be "just the way it is"—a necessary evil in a world of Economic Humans where profit is king and the most cutthroat strategies win. Our research, however, found that this idea simply isn't true. The results clearly demonstrate that business leaders who fit the one-dimensional Economic Human model—CEOs whose behavior also placed them in our classification of Self-Focused leaders—are the least effective at their job. In fact, the ROC research data reveals that Self-Focused leaders fail to maximize shareholder return—the ultimate measure of value that Wall Street and most economists embrace—with Virtuoso leaders achieving as much as five times greater returns for their organizations. (We discuss the specific metrics of this finding in chapter 6.)

In order to really understand leadership character and how it shapes business results, we need to leave behind the outdated Economic Human model and embrace a new understanding—a fuller vision of human nature, how it is founded in genetics and shaped through life experiences, and how leaders express it through their decisions and behavior. This isn't just about identifying "good" or "bad" leaders or obsessively examining their mental processes. It's about understanding how to identify, choose, and become *better* leaders.

In chapter 1, we had a first look at the ROC Value Chain, which includes all the elements that contribute to the value a leader brings to the organization. The first group of these elements determine who the leader is as an individual—his or her genetic predispositions, life experiences, and the moral or character habits that result. These fundamental elements of who a leader is, in turn, determine:

- How effectively that leader forms a vision of where he or she wants the organization to go; and then,

- How that leader makes the decisions and manages the relationships necessary to get there.

In short, Character (who the leader is) + Skills (what the leader does) = Results (Return on Character).

In this chapter, we're going to examine the fundamental first element of that equation by exploring the essential human nature of those who assume leadership positions. We'll begin by debunking that centuries-old version of the "totally rational, totally self-interested" human that for so long shaped our basic ideas about business leadership, so we can fully understand how that model is inadequate for winning in today's business and economic battlegrounds. After a brief (but vital) overview of the neurological "hardware and operating systems" that come as standard equipment in most human brains, we'll take a more revealing tour through the "software" of our human nature—the motivational drives, moral intuitions, and personality traits that make us uniquely human, and unique *among* humans.

Our understanding of this much more complex and fully realized view of who our leaders are as people will position us to make much more informed observations about the character of those leaders and how it shapes the workplace experience and organizational outcomes. Even more importantly, we'll be much more capable of understanding what aspects of leadership character can—and should—be *reshaped* to improve business results.

Updating to Leadership 2.0

The Economic Human model, which tells us that people are essentially rational and self-interested, is at least two centuries old. Its application to economic and business life appears often in references to the work of Scottish philosopher Adam Smith. In *The Wealth of Nations,* first published in 1776, Smith proposed that when people single-mindedly pursue their own narrow self-interests, an "invisible hand" emerges in a free market context that serves the common good.[1] Many economists and politicians today still cling to this invisible hand, which clearly makes itself felt in some situations, such as when a brilliant entrepreneur (think Steve Jobs, Mark Zuckerberg, Elon Musk) creates a new and unique product or service that benefits millions of people. But this simplistic view of human nature and the marketplace is woefully inadequate to explain most events in today's modern, global economy.[2]

Unfortunately, we are confronted almost daily with examples of high-level leaders cast in the Economic Human model pursuing their self-interest in a way that actually *destroys* the common good. Instead of the invisible hand working to strengthen our social fabric, we more often find ourselves caught in the grip of cold, rational acquisition, as it sweeps through the economic landscape and greedily grabs up or crushes anything or anyone who gets in its way. We shouldn't be surprised that leadership formed in this old model doesn't really serve the common interests of society.

Just how low is the threshold of behavior this antiquated model sets for our leaders? Cornell University law professor Lynn Stout claims that five of the seven characteristics the American Psychiatric Association lists for diagnosing a psychopath—including deceitfulness, a disregard for social norms or safety, consistent irresponsibility, and lack of remorse—are part and parcel of the Economic Human model.[3]

The same qualities Stout highlights in that comparison match the behaviors described by many employees of the leaders who form the Self-Focused CEO group in our research. And is it any wonder? Clearly this eighteenth-century idea of basic human nature is inadequate as the bedrock for effective leadership today. With this model as the accepted standard for human nature, we should expect that some of our business (and government) leaders are going to be ineffective, unethical, or even downright corrupt.

The latest research in genetics, psychology, and the neurosciences offers us a newer and much broader perspective of human nature—a view that has the potential to revolutionize our ideas of leadership by positioning it to meet the challenges of the twenty-first century. We call this model of human nature the *Integrated Human* and use it to describe the full spectrum of physical, neurological, genetically predetermined, and acquired attributes that form our character and direct our behavior.

Just a few decades ago, when I was in graduate school, the brain sciences seemed to be stuck in old paradigms. Back then, we were taught that the brain was an instrument that reached developmental maturity in young adulthood and then began the long descent into senility and death. But much of what we knew then about the brain was wrong. Today, brain research has surged forward, thanks to the intricate brain-mapping technology of functional magnetic resonance imaging—fMRI for short. Our understanding of the brain's physiology is in constant evolution. The fields of developmental, social, cognitive, and evolutionary psychology also are moving rapidly forward, helping us to better understand how our minds—including our subconscious—actually work.[4] We also have made astonishing advances in the field of genetics. Just twenty years ago, common wisdom held that infants are born more or less as a blank slate. Today, we know that humans are born "prewired" with genetic givens that shape our development in many important ways.[5]

Together, these scientific advancements offer us the basic elements we need to compose our model of the Integrated Human. With that, we can form a more accurate and effective standard for leadership character and behavior.

In figure 2-1, you see a model of human nature and its elements based on the old Economic Human concept. In that model, our nature is guided by just two elements:

- Logical thought processes

- The drive to acquire

Operating under this model, we can expect our leaders to be coldly rational, to act on their desire to acquire without the controlling

FIGURE 2-1

The Economic Human model

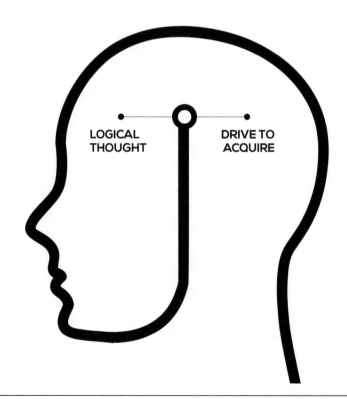

mechanisms of conscience or remorse, and to respond strictly to their own self-interests. The Economic Human model closely represents the human nature of the Self-Focused CEO.

By comparison, the Integrated Human model of human nature, in addition to the two elements of our previous model, includes:

- A conscious analytic system, known as the *slow brain* (where logic resides)

- A subconscious intuitive system, or *fast brain*

- The full range of *motivational drives* (of which the drive to acquire is only one)

- Basic ideas of moral behavior, or *moral intuitions*

- Distinguishing characteristics, or *personality traits*

Together, these elements of our nature provide all of the fundamental functions necessary for living life as a complete, Integrated Human—and they are the springboard for the development of leadership character. As our research data has shown, the ability to leverage *all* of these areas influence leadership's ability to achieve positive organizational outcomes.

The Integrated Human model of human nature celebrates the deep and meaningful connection between who we are and what we do. By applying that model to our understanding of CEO character, we are better prepared to assess and improve our own approach to leadership. Just as importantly, we can use this fuller understanding of human nature to identify and support more effective leadership in others, and to expose those leaders whose greed and pursuit of power cause so much destruction. Now, let's take a closer look into the makeup of each of the six basic elements of the Integrated Human model.

Tracing Our Basic Systems

While metaphors comparing the human brain to a computer can seem overly simplistic, the two systems share a number of similarities that can be useful for understanding the basic workings of our instincts and intellect. As such, we can think of the human brain as a magnificent piece of hardware that comes preloaded with not one but two operating systems that we use and adapt throughout our lifetimes to navigate the world: our fast brain, or subconscious intuitive brain, and our slow brain, or conscious, rational brain.[6]

The *fast brain* is where all of our subconscious intuitions, cravings, habits, and emotions reside. The fast brain's primary purpose is to provide these subconscious "spurs" to drive behavior patterns aimed at bringing us safety, security, food, and social connection. We're born with a fully operational fast brain, which begins functioning while we're still in the womb. It is always on and running, constantly scanning to collect information and continually forming conclusions about what it observes. Those conclusions often are based in intuition, emotion, or cravings. Our fast brain also spurs behavior through habits—automatic responses such as putting our foot on the brake when we see a stop sign. Those habits that determine how we relate to others, such as a reflexive response to tell the truth or own up to our mistakes, become our character habits.

The intuitions and other behavior-spurring conclusions springing from our fast brain are unsolicited and not necessarily accurate. The fast brain intuitions, for example, can trigger our gut reactions, some of which give us good advice and others that lead us terribly astray. Nor are these fast brain intuitions and conclusions consistent; they continually modify as we age.

Our *slow brain* is where we do all our conscious and analytic work. It provides us with the tools of logic and reflection. When we engage it, our slow brain operates as a reflective, analytic thinking tool; it can gather data, analyze it, apply the rules of logic, and come to new conclusions. Our slow brain can call on a number of beliefs or rules and use them to guide a decision. It also can override the intuitions of our fast brain, a process we know as *willpower.* Our slow brain can also learn to identify and ignore erroneous signals from our fast brain, which is how we demonstrate self-awareness and wisdom.

Unfortunately, our slow brain isn't always engaged. Amazingly, most researchers agree that very few of the choices we make in the course of a day—from what to order for lunch to which business alliances we form—are guided by conscious thought or our slow brain. The rest of the time, we're operating from our fast brain.[7] Our slow brain takes many long pauses, such as when we go to sleep, and spends much of the rest of the time in standby mode. In that mode, our slow brain is likely to accept any intuition, emotion, habit, or craving response our fast brain triggers, regardless of its accuracy.

Every human brain also comes equipped with a unique cognitive capacity, which is a difficult concept to define. There is little agreement in the field of cognitive science about the idea of human intelligence or what IQ tests measure. We can assume, however, that most leaders in senior positions possess sufficient cognitive capacity to do their job. In fact, you don't have to be the smartest person in the room to become a Virtuoso CEO. It's much better to be the one with the strongest character, and while our life experiences and genetic predispositions play a role in shaping our character, that character is also a product of our neurological software working in conjunction with the hardware elements we've just reviewed.

Exploring the Software at the Heart of Human Nature

We humans are born with intuitions, drives, and personality traits that determine how we interact with the world around us. These dispositions—both inherited and acquired—lie at the very core of who we are as human beings.[8]

The Integrated Human model acknowledges that most human infants also are born prewired with a set of universal principles, as noted in chapter 1, that include care, fairness, authority, loyalty, liberty, and sanctity. Jonathan Haidt, a social psychologist and researcher, refers to these six principles as *moral intuitions*, and has published many works on this subject.[9]

Haidt claims that, like the ability to learn a language, the six moral intuitions are fundamental to our nature. We are preprogrammed to be truthful, fair, and loyal—to pick up the $5 bill and hand it to the person who dropped it, to wait our turn in line, to rush to volunteer our help at the scene of a natural disaster. This aspect of our nature also predisposes us to respect authority but resist unfair domination, to feel compelled by wholeness and purity but repelled by degradation—the decay of once-living things, objects, even failing or degraded actions. Of course, we are heavily influenced by our specific cultural setting. Some people speak French and others speak Italian, but they all speak a language. Likewise, all human cultures have their own way of teaching their children to express these inborn moral intuitions. But in every culture, our morals and principles trigger our habitual behaviors toward others—habits that demonstrate our character.

The Keystone Character Habits of Virtuoso leadership—integrity, responsibility, forgiveness, and compassion—are the direct expressions of our innate moral intuitions. Not only are these intuitions part of what make us uniquely human, but the habitual demonstration of the principles they foster is essential to the kind of strong, principled character we associate with Virtuoso leadership.

Beyond our moral intuitions, we humans also are born with *motivational drives* that play their own role in shaping and expressing our human nature and character. In 2002, Harvard Business School professors Paul Lawrence and Nitin Nohria, in *Driven: How Human Nature Shapes Our Choices*, described their work aimed at identifying basic human drives.[10] Lawrence and Nohria identify four basic motivational drives common to our species: the drives to acquire, to bond, to comprehend, and to defend. This group of motivational drives forms a key element of human nature that shapes our relationships with others. The way we pursue these drives also helps determine our character as leaders.

Lawrence, in a second book, *Driven to Lead: Good, Bad, and Misguided Leadership*, applied earlier findings about basic human drives to the field of leadership.[11] In that book, Lawrence tells us that the best leaders, like the Virtuoso CEOs in our study, pursue the fulfillment of all four motivational drives equally. He calls leaders who ignore one or more of these drives "misguided," because that incomplete response to innate drives can throw a life out of balance. The drive to acquire, for example, if not tempered by the drives to bond and comprehend can lead people down a dark and very lonely path of constant acquisition with no close relationships or understanding of why they continue to feel unfulfilled. As we learn later in this book, the Self-Focused leaders in our study all demonstrated behaviors that exhibited that kind of imbalance in their approach to business *and* relationships.

Like our innate moral intuitions, our motivational drives are directly linked to our humanity. All animals share with us the drives to acquire and defend, and some animals are clearly social and form monogamous bonds. But we humans have such a singular focus on forming and maintaining social connections that the most severe form of punishment for a human is solitary confinement. Further, current research indicates that only humans possess the drive to seek understanding—to comprehend the world around us and to speculate about our destiny.

Finally, each of us is endowed at birth with a specific set of *personality traits*. In recent years, personality theorists and researchers worldwide have agreed that human beings are born with a genetically determined set point on five personality dimensions, known as "the Big Five": openness, conscientiousness, extroversion, agreeableness, and risk aversion or fear.[12]

So if these traits are passed along in our genes, why aren't they considered to be part of our neurological hardware? The answer lies in their malleability. Think of each of the Big Five personality traits as having a slider switch that moves up or down to deliver more or less of the dimension of that trait to our overall personality, as shown in figure 2-2.

While our Big Five personality traits are prewired as set points within each of us, our life experiences can "move" their settings. An individual with an agreeableness set point that tends to make him cool and aloof toward others may go through a series of life events that move him to become much warmer and friendlier. Likewise, someone born eager to take risks can dial that back and learn to be appropriately cautious or suffer a series of difficult setbacks that move her risk aversion level into full-blown fearfulness and anxiety.

Given the mobility of these set points, what role do they play in leadership character? The answer to that question is somewhat complicated. Personality in and of itself doesn't really determine our character. And it isn't necessarily an important factor in successful leadership, provided that the leader in question operates from a strong foundation of moral principles and character habits.

A leader who is excruciatingly shy may have real trouble communicating vision, passion, and strategic focus in large organizational

FIGURE 2-2

The Big Five personality traits

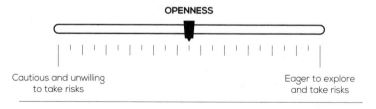

OPENNESS

Cautious and unwilling
to take risks

Eager to explore
and take risks

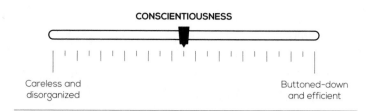

CONSCIENTIOUSNESS

Careless and
disorganized

Buttoned-down
and efficient

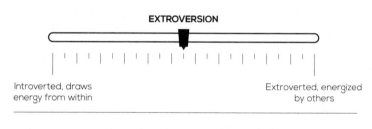

EXTROVERSION

Introverted, draws
energy from within

Extroverted, energized
by others

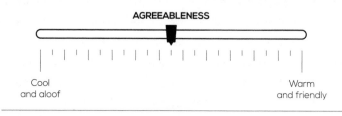

AGREEABLENESS

Cool
and aloof

Warm
and friendly

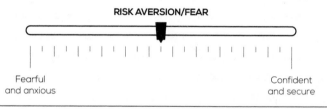

RISK AVERSION/FEAR

Fearful
and anxious

Confident
and secure

meetings. That person's extroversion setting may shift to the right over time, as the leader becomes more comfortable with his or her position and decisions. In the meantime, the leader's strong principles and character-driven leadership style are likely to win the confidence and support of the workforce, even if its members don't respond to the leader's personality. On the other hand, an extroverted leader who loves the limelight but has a relatively casual attitude regarding character habits and principles may actually find that his or her open, affable personality gets in the way of effective leadership.

In short, while personality traits shape our leadership style, they certainly don't determine either character or success. It's how we develop those traits—through life and career experiences, and through the consistent demonstration of moral principles and intuitions via character habits—that has the most compelling influence on our approach to leadership and the business results it produces.

Listening to What the Integrated Human Model Can Tell Us

So, far from being the one-dimensional caricature of human life in the Economic Human view, we are complex beings—born with inclinations to be moral; driven to acquire, bond, comprehend, and defend; and equipped with far more than a rational brain ruled solely by logic.

We have, in fact, two brains, fast and slow, to help us negotiate the trade-offs we must make to survive and thrive. We also are born with a personality, a specific set of traits, each of which develops over time in response to life experiences. Along with basic intellectual tools, these elements are fundamental to our human nature, but they also determine who we are as individuals, how we interact with others, and how we understand the world around us. Together, all of these genetic predispositions, tools, and traits combine to form a whole individual—the Integrated Human, as shown in figure 2-3.

The old view of humanity isn't absolutely wrong; sometimes people *are* completely self-focused or completely rational. But these are small pieces of the puzzle that form an incomplete model for explaining human nature and workplace behavior. In contrast, the Integrated

FIGURE 2-3

The Integrated Human

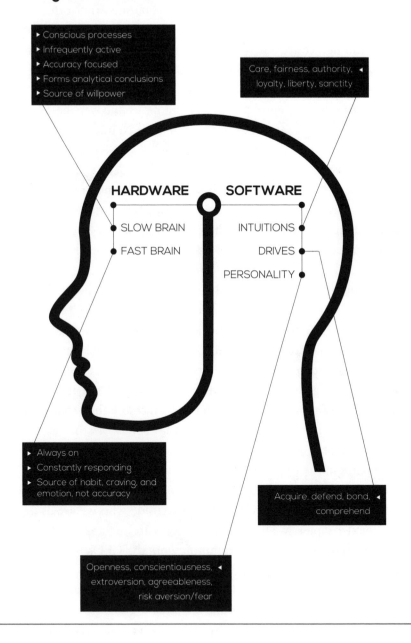

Human view helps us understand the true complexity of human nature—the neurological hardwiring, genetic predispositions, and malleable personality traits and moral inclinations that offer a much more useful understanding of how we become who we are. With that understanding, we are much better able to identify and assess the nature and character of those in positions of leadership. At the same time, this new, integrated view of human nature makes it much easier to get to the roots of our *own* approach to leadership, to uncover the sources of the strengths and weaknesses within our own character, and to know precisely where we can work to improve what we've found there.

Ongoing research is helping us more fully understand the nature of who we are as human beings and how our basic human nature supports the genetic predispositions and life experiences that determine who we are as individuals. We can use these new findings to embrace a model of human nature that describes us as capable of becoming mature, complete individuals, not just self-focused rationalists—a model that supports organizational life in all its rich complexity and celebrates the deep and meaningful connection between who we are and what we do.

In essence, our behavior is a product of our genetic makeup and basic human nature filtered and honed through the environments, experiences, and relationships that form our life journey. Together, these factors—governed by both our nature and the nurturing we receive—help shape the belief system and moral habits that form our character, and in turn, trigger the habitual behaviors that express it.

In this chapter, we've drawn together a solid concept of the role our nature plays in the first half of the ROC Value Chain: how genetic predispositions are shaped by life experiences into specific morals, beliefs, character habits, and skills that then determine who we are as people. In the next chapter, we'll explore the "nurture" factor in that part of the value chain equation, by examining *how* the CEOs in our research became who they are. By uncovering how (and if) the CEO understands his or her life story, our study revealed how these leaders' life journeys shaped their moral beliefs and worldviews, and how those factors then influenced their guiding principles and character habits as leaders. Using that understanding as our foundation, we'll be ready to move into part II, where we will begin examining the process by which some individuals develop into Virtuoso leaders—and why others fail to do so.

ROC TAKEAWAYS
The Human Nature of Leadership

1. **A leader's humanity and unique human nature form a fundamental element of that individual's ROC.** To discuss the influence on business results of any leader's personal makeup, we need a clear understanding of how our brains and natural predispositions make us human and individual.

2. **The old Economic Human view of human nature is incomplete.** Classic economic theory's view that human beings are totally rational and completely self-focused is an inadequate model for understanding effective leadership.

3. **New research enables us to form a new and complete view of human nature, the Integrated Human.** This model of human nature views people as capable of becoming mature, complete, and integrated humans, not just self-focused rationalists.

4. **Our human nature and individual character is shaped by neurological hardwiring, genetic predispositions, and life experiences in the form of these five elements:**

   - A **fast brain** that is always running and that Freud identified as the subconscious.

   - A **slow brain** that provides conscious thought processes and operates as a reflective, analytic thinking tool.

   - **Moral intuitions** for care, fairness, authority, loyalty, liberty, and sanctity that are expressed through moral principles, beliefs, and character habits.

   - **Motivational drives** to acquire, bond, comprehend, and defend, which are critical to our abilities to form relationships.

   - And the **Big Five personality traits** of openness, conscientiousness, extroversion, agreeableness, and risk aversion or fear, whose set points we recalibrate through life experience.

5. **This more complex Integrated Human model of human nature gives us a foundation for assessing leadership character,** how it affects business results, and when or where it can be reformed to improve those results.

3

The Journey from Cradle to Corner Office

Reading the Road Map

N o matter what our genetic predispositions, moral intuitions, or personality traits might be, all of us continue to build and shape our character, beliefs, and behaviors throughout our life journey. Just like all of us, the CEOs and leadership teams engaged in our study began that journey with a backpack full of the human provisions I've just named. As these future leaders grew into adulthood, however, their life experiences joined forces with those genetic givens to shape each of them into the unique individual who first stepped into a leadership role. To fully understand how the leaders in our study developed their character and the behaviors that express it, we have to consider the unique journey that each of them took from cradle to corner office.

The Return on Character (ROC) study revealed that when it comes to genetic predispositions, average is okay—you don't have to have a rock-star personality or rocket-science intellect to become a Virtuoso leader. But while just about all of the leaders in our study had an adequate supply of genetic traits, tendencies, and capacities, only a few achieved the strength of character to be considered a Virtuoso. Those individuals must have taken some turns in the road along their life journey that the Self-Focused leaders either ignored or were never given the opportunity to explore. We wanted to know more about how their journeys differed, so we could uncover any patterns in their similarities. Those patterns can shed light on how to adopt or develop the characteristics of outstanding leadership.

Everyone's life journey begins as two parallel paths, which we can think of as an inner journey and an outer journey. As shown in figure 3-1, the outer journey is one of experience, forged of critical relationships with parents, teachers, mentors, employers, colleagues, and other influential adults we encounter through educational and early work experiences. The inner journey is one of self-understanding, where, through reflection, we develop the character habits, self-awareness, worldview, and mental complexity that enable us to define ourselves *to* ourselves. Over time, as we weave our life story and connect who we are with what we do, these two converge to become a single passage that continues to unfold as we progress through the mistakes, failures, and successes that determine the course of our lives. This is the stage of our journey in which we become a complete Integrated Human.

Among the CEOs in the ROC study, those whose behavior reflected the Integrated Human model consistently created the most value for their organizations, through both increased levels of workforce engagement and stronger financial returns. In addition to their strong leadership skill sets (which we learn more about in part II), these Virtuoso leaders demonstrate strong moral and character habits and provide aspirational visions for those around them to embrace.

By contrast, while some of the Self-Focused CEOs in our study produced a positive return on assets, the majority of them failed to create significant value for their organizations, and two of them incurred major losses. To better understand the differences in the outcomes of these leaders, we can begin by looking more closely at the differences in their life journeys—differences the CEOs themselves carefully described in the course of our research.

So how did the journey to the corner office differ for the two groups of CEOs? How did their choices differ along the way? How do these leaders understand their own personal history, and how does that understanding influence the principles and morals that shape their character, and the behaviors that express that character in the workplace? In this chapter, we're going to take a closer look at what answers the ROC research revealed to these and other important questions about how we become who we are—as individuals and as leaders.

FIGURE 3-1

The life journey's two paths

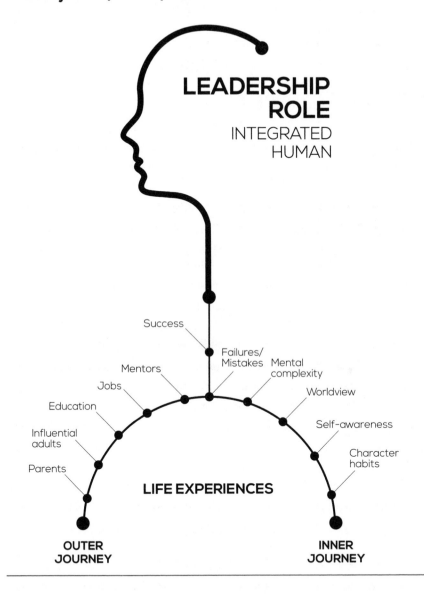

LEADERSHIP
ROLE
INTEGRATED
HUMAN

Success

Failures/
Mistakes   Mental
complexity

Mentors

Jobs   Worldview

Education

Influential   Self-awareness
adults

Character
habits

Parents

LIFE EXPERIENCES

**OUTER
JOURNEY**

**INNER
JOURNEY**

Those answers matter. No, we can't go back and rewrite our personal story to more closely follow the early path of a Virtuoso CEO. But by understanding how these individuals created and view their life story, adopted their worldview, and developed the strong character habits of successful leadership, we can uncover valuable ideas and techniques for identifying and developing the Virtuoso leaders among us—and for gaining the undeniable competitive advantage of Virtuoso leadership ourselves. Those insights are powerful tools for choosing today's leaders, training tomorrow's, and improving our own approach to leadership every day.

Telling a Coherent Life Story

Your life story is the narrative you tell yourself and others that allows you to make sense of your life experiences, from your earliest memories onward. Your life story is your answers to two key questions: Who am I, and how did I become the person I am?[1]

We all have a life story, of course, but not all of us have reviewed that story and contemplated its meaning. John Lennon once wrote that "life is what happens to you while you're busy making other plans."[2] Indeed, some of the most formative moments of our life—becoming educated, falling in love, breaking up, hammering out a career, suffering failures, achieving successes—can unfold without offering us much immediate opportunity to stop and examine the experience. It is only later, through reflection, that we can pull together and review our life story in order to make sense of our personal history. That process helps us understand the pivotal moments and decisions in our past, their patterns, and how they helped bring us to where we are in the present.

Of course, we all know that our memories can be inaccurate, and therefore the life story that we compose over the years isn't necessarily a historical account. The fuzziness of fine details doesn't really matter; most people can recall the substance of large, life-shaping experiences in their personal past. The way we *understand* our life story is the critical issue, and as part of the research project into ROC, we wanted to discover how the CEOs involved in the project understood the life story they had created.

So we asked them to talk to us about their life. The interviews involved some fifty questions, ranging from the simple, "Tell me when and where you were born," to the more probing, such as, "How were you taught to know right from wrong?" and "Tell me a story about the best thing that happened to you while growing up—and the worst." Other questions looked beyond early life to include issues involving marriage, parenting, religious practices, political preferences, and early job and career history. In a separate survey, we asked the CEOs to reveal their beliefs about personal purpose, human nature, organizational life, and the role of leadership. (Descriptions of these questionnaires appear in appendix A.)

But perhaps the most important fact revealed by these interviews was whether the leaders *knew* their life story. Could they provide a coherent narrative about their past, touching on a number of major events, both positive and negative, and including a reasonable description of the effect those events had on their personal development?

In every case, the CEOs later identified as Virtuoso leaders were able to recognize the threads that they had woven together to create their life story, and how their principles and beliefs were reflected in their actions and decisions. They also acknowledged that painful experiences occasionally tempted them to respond with fear and anger, but such a response had been a rare exception, not a go-to position in tough situations.

The leaders in our project whose employee reviews later placed them in the Self-Focused category had a very different perspective on their past. Some expressed no perspective at all, telling a life story that was disconnected and incoherent. When asked to say more about a painful or otherwise significant event they had revealed to us in their history, these CEOs were likely to say that they'd never really given the event much thought. They also showed little recognition of the connection between their historic response to events and their current response when similar events occur. With little thought about their past or how their ideas about or reactions to life had developed over the years, the Self-Focused leaders seem to have had very little opportunity to construct a meaningful platform of beliefs or principles. Whatever character habits or intuitions guided their behavior remained largely unexamined and unacknowledged by these CEOs.

For example, a Virtuoso CEO told me the following story in response to my question, "What's the worst thing that happened to you while growing up?"

Doing drugs at seventeen. LSD. I didn't do it a lot but it was very, very bad. Even ten years later, I would have a little bit of a flashback of a trippy experience and it freaked me out. That was the worst thing. I remember doing acid in my parents' house, falling down the stairs, and then leaving and going into the city and going out to clubs and meeting girls and having a great time. Then my friend told me I had really been on the floor moaning for seven hours. That really freaked me out. It was so vivid and real, I swear it had happened. Sometimes I wonder if I'll wake up on the floor of my parents' basement and find that the last forty years of my life have been a trip!

Also, being rejected. I never had a good time with girls, and being rejected was really painful. I struggled with relationships with women. That was during the disco era—I hated it. Couldn't dance. It was loud. It was emotionally trying to meet anyone in the age of disco. That would scare anyone.

I ended up working as a manual laborer for five years, which is where I cleared my head. That's when I grew up. That's also about the time I met and married my wife twenty-eight years ago. I realized then that I could get beyond those difficult years and make something of myself.

Contrast that story with this one, told to me by a Self-Focused CEO, who demonstrated an utter lack of self-reflection in answering the same question:

I had a really horrible injury from a car accident when I was a freshman in high school. My leg was broken and deformed until I had surgery in my twenties. I had been a star in athletics and suddenly I became a nobody who couldn't perform. This wasn't very much fun. I became reclusive. My high school years weren't the social success they might have been.

When I asked this CEO to tell me about the long-term influence this high school tragedy had on him, he paused, thought a bit, and then replied, "I don't know. I haven't speculated on that much. I'm still somebody who, after I'm done working, I like my private time and space."

This individual also reported that throughout his youth, he had been forced into debates with his father every night over dinner. When asked, he told us that he'd never given much thought to that experience either, or how it had shaped his approach to leadership. His greatest insight about this was, "Some people see me as a bit combative. I don't see it."

When asked, "How do you think your workforce sees you?" he paused a bit to consider the question, then replied, "I think they probably see me as somebody who is never quite satisfied, a little bit combative. Some would accuse me of preferring turmoil to change." Did he agree with that perception? "Actually, I do!" he said with some surprise. After reflecting for a moment, he added, "I guess I'd say that I adopted this as the core of my management style." Not so surprisingly, this CEO received some of the lowest scores of all the CEOs in the entire study.

These stories illustrate one of the ROC study's most interesting insights into the development of Virtuoso CEO character. Among our research participants, those CEOs with the strongest character—and strongest business results—were self-aware. They have spent time reflecting on their life journey. They have some understanding of its milestones, how they're connected, and where they continue to lead. They know where they're going, in part because they know where they've been. The *least* principled CEOs in the research, on the other hand, those whose behavior demonstrates little in the way of strong character and whose business results tend to be weak, were more likely to be running blind through their life journey.

Several of the Self-Focused CEOs haven't examined their past experiences, decisions, successes, and failures in a way that would help them construct a clear vision of how they became the person—and the leader—they are today. As a result, they lack the foundation of supportive relationships, character habits, self-awareness, and mental complexity upon which to build the kind of character-driven leadership that reliably contributes to sound decision making and strong, sustainable business results.

This finding is just one revealed by our CEO interviews. Beyond this bigger issue of identifying which leaders actually knew and understood how their past shaped them, the questions we posed in this phase of our research provided a number of interesting insights into the similarities and differences among the personal histories of the Virtuoso and Self-Focused CEOs involved in the project. Let's see what stories these leaders had to tell, and what those stories reveal to us about the road to the corner office.

Experiencing the Outer Journey

As the old saying goes, we can't choose our family. But as we construct a coherent story of our life, we do have to reflect on how early family relationships and experience shaped our ideas, attitudes, and the moral principles and character habits that underlie our approach to leadership.

Without exception, all of the CEOs in our study—both groups—had ample *job experience*. They entered the workforce as teenagers and have never left it. Likewise, there are no significant differences in *educational level* between the two groups; both are highly educated, many with MBAs or other advanced degrees. While these leaders have much in common educationally and professionally, their early life experiences and interpersonal relationships reveal vast differences in their outer journeys.

As you might imagine, it is clearly an advantage for any person to have a childhood and youth framed by loving, predictable caregivers, a supportive family, and a community of *influential adults* who serve as mentors. But that kind of outer journey isn't essential for becoming a Virtuoso leader. Of the ten Virtuosos in our study, one had a mentally ill mother and a weak father who was incapable of protecting the children from her crazy behavior. Another's mother placed him in an orphanage for several years after his father died.

Still, a supportive network of loving, stable adults does seem to offer a platform for developing strong character. The other eight Virtuosos had at least one secure, supportive caregiver, with half of them reporting that *both* of their parents provided such care.[3] Here are some representative responses we received from the Virtuoso CEOs when asked about their *parents*:

- "She was always interested in what I was doing."

- "My mom was always there when I needed her."

- "My father was very supportive of me."

- "I think he understood me. He gave me a lot of freedom."

- "We got along well—still do!"

The Self-Focused CEOs painted a much different family portrait. Two of them had two parents who offered a secure caregiving style, and only four of them had one parent who cared for them in this way. While three members of this group had warm, connected, and supportive mothers, the other seven described mothers who were edgy, avoided emotional connections, or were out-and-out narcissists. We discovered an even larger difference between the two groups regarding their relationships with their fathers. Half of the Virtuoso CEOs reported a close and connected relationship with their father, but only *one* of the Self-Focused CEOs reported the same. The remainder of the Self-Focused CEOs' fathers were remote, emotionally absent, and troubled, and two were alcoholics. Here are some of the comments about their parents that this group offered:

- "[My mother was a] very good person. Her one tragic flaw was her attraction to my father."

- "[My mother was] smart. Opinionated. Ambitious. Classy. But my older sister is really the one who took care of me."

- "She was strict and had high expectations. Our friends were a little scared to be around. I was very close to her."

- "He was an alcoholic and a mean-spirited person."

- "[Father was] remote. I look back and see that he was just a driven business guy."

As our research revealed, the influence of important relationships continues well beyond childhood and includes people outside the family circle. The CEOs in both groups recalled with fondness other adults who nurtured and mentored them throughout their early life and education. All but one of the Self-Focused CEOs had a meaningful relationship during their youth with at least one very influential and supporting adult, but only two had more than one such relationship. But again, the Virtuoso CEOs enjoyed a significant advantage in this leg of their outer journey. As figure 3-2 illustrates, they reported having about one-third more such relationships than did the Self-Focused CEOs.

After the CEOs in both groups entered their professional lives, most of them were able to connect with older, influential *mentors*. But again, the Virtuoso CEOs had the advantage of more mentoring during the early years of their careers. They formed over *twice* as many such relationships as did the Self-Focused CEOs. All but one of the Virtuoso CEOs took the opportunity to bond with one or more mentors, while only two of the Self-Focused CEOs did the same. And even then, this group reported that the quality of the mentoring they received wasn't always the best.

One of the Self-Focused CEOs told me, "I suspect the most interesting mentor I ever had was a self-made entrepreneur. He was smart and ruthless and never did anything the easy way. He routinely said the easy way would not get results. If I tried to do something that I thought was a better and easier way, he'd tell me that if I did it that way, he'd fire me."

Another Self-Focused CEO explained that the lack of mentors in her career was because she found that none of her interesting and powerful bosses had the capacity to teach. "It was almost the reverse situation: I often rose up quickly until I was helping them do their jobs."

In contrast, here is how one Virtuoso CEO recalled his early-career experience with a mentor:

> He was the sales manager of our company. I am an introvert and he went off the chart on the other side. I think I learned from him how to relate to people. They called us "the odd couple." We worked very well together. We could argue for an hour or two, but then we'd come to agreement and go have a beer. He was about seven or eight years older. He taught me a lot.

FIGURE 3-2

CEOs reporting influential relationships

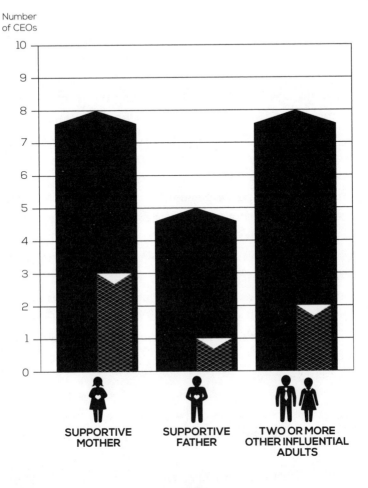

Another Virtuoso CEO learned from four mentors before he arrived in his first CEO role. He said:

The four CEOs that I worked for on my way up all mentored me. From the first gentleman, I really learned how the business worked and why the business was even around. The second was really about creativity and innovation in business. The third was more about ethics, and the fourth was really driving for results. Once again, with all four that I worked for, I really took the things I liked that they did and wanted to learn more and emulate those. For the things I didn't like, I tried to find the alter ego to their personality or how it would fit into my value system.

Both groups of CEOs in our study clearly illustrate the important role mentors play—from our youth throughout our career—in building good leadership. The data shows that leaders at every level of experience can benefit from being involved in a mentoring relationship. In fact, these types of relationships are almost universal among the most successful leaders who participated in our research. These insights may not be new but they are critical tools for executives engaged in identifying and training the next generation of leadership, as well as for those of us who are working to enter the ranks of leadership or to improve our current leadership style.

While the findings we uncovered about the outer journey from cradle to corner office tell us much about the external development of leadership character, it's the inner journey where those who become Virtuosos truly excel. So now let's take a closer look at that branch of the leader's life journey.

Marking the Milestones of the Inner Journey

While dealing with the challenges and experiences of the outer journey, each of the CEOs in our research was also undertaking an inner journey toward becoming a fully integrated adult. In this inner journey, we all develop our character in a way that harnesses our ideas and moral intuitions to our actions. We arrive at the destination of self-integration when we have connected our head to our heart.

The inner journey is one in which we develop our *self-awareness* and *character habits* in order to feel good and true about what we believe and how we treat other people. It's where we form a *worldview* that tells us what kind of place we live in, so we can engage with that world and embrace values and rules of conduct that support it. It's also where we develop the *mental complexity* necessary to understand the subtleties of decision making and behavior that power us through our mistakes and successes alike, so we can continually improve our performance *and* our understanding of our personal and professional lives. Individuals whose inner journey leads them to the destination of self-integration don't feel that something is missing in their lives, but rather feel a sense of wholeness and personal purpose.

We humans are always a work in progress, and the journey toward becoming an integrated person is as important as its destination. Sometimes that process can be painful. Despite the effort it involves, however, becoming an integrated person has great advantages for people in all walks of life—for the taxi driver and the nuclear physicist; for the checkout clerk at Costco and the senior executive at American Express; for the house-husband and the performance artist. Feeling a sense of wholeness has positive physical and mental health benefits in addition to allowing us to perform at a higher level in our chosen path.

Unfortunately, you don't have to develop an integrated self and strong character in order to become a leader. As I discovered, however, that process is almost universal among the CEOs in our study whose behavior identified them as Virtuosos—and those are the CEOs who also achieved the strongest business results. Now let's examine each step along the pathway of the inner journey, how it unfolded for the CEOs in our research, and what destination it has led them toward.

The Keystone Character Habits

In chapter 1, we learned that character is a unique combination of beliefs, principles, and habits that shape the way we relate to other people and the world around us. The four universal moral principles of integrity, forgiveness, responsibility, and compassion are an extension of moral intuitions common to all of humanity, but for an integrated person, the expression of those principles becomes a first response in any interaction—in other words, habits. Not only that, when we embrace the habits born of these principles, they begin to inform, support, and develop all other beliefs and habitual behaviors that express our character. That's why we have named integrity, compassion, forgiveness, and responsibility as Keystone Character Habits in our ROC research. And because we express our character through our behavior, here are just some of the ways we express these critically important habits:

Integrity. Acting consistently with professed principles, values, and beliefs; telling the truth; standing up for what's right; keeping promises.

Responsibility. Owning up to personal choices; admitting mistakes and failures; stepping up to serve others—that is, leaving the world a better place.

Forgiveness. Letting go of one's mistakes—and those of others; focusing on what's right versus what's wrong.

Compassion. Empathizing with others; empowering people, actively caring for others, and showing commitment to their development.

So how do we develop our habitual responses to the world? Like all habits, character habits are formed in our fast brain, or subconscious mind. In recent research on the structure of habits, Pulitzer Prize–winning reporter and author Charles Duhigg claims that a sequence of emotions, thoughts, or behaviors does not become habitual until the reward has become meaningful enough that it is eagerly anticipated.[4] Researchers call this the "craving" that triggers habit. A craving can be something physical, such as a craving for a specific food or activity. But cravings can also be psychological or even spiritual—the craving for love, belonging, status, or personal well-being. It is in our human nature to crave habits that coincide with our inborn moral intuitions of care, fairness, authority, loyalty, and so on (chapter 2 offers a more detailed explanation of moral intuitions).

These cravings can drive leaders toward self-integration by encouraging them to match their actions with the aspirations they hold for themselves. If I view myself as an honest person, I will crave the feelings that come when I live up to that standard, for example, by telling the truth. The more I crave these feelings, the more I will behave in ways to gain them, and I will strengthen my truth-telling habit. When this habit develops, it represents a wonderful integration of the head (my actions) and heart (my aspirations).

Duhigg also tells us that a *Keystone* habit is one that when present, tends to bring other desirable beliefs, emotions, and behaviors along for the ride. Again, based on our research, we have identified that the character habits of integrity, responsibility, forgiveness, and compassion function as Keystone Habits of leadership character by encouraging the development of our innate moral intuitions. So for example, a Virtuoso leader with a strong Keystone Character Habit of compassion typically also develops his or her moral intuition of fairness, which discourages favoritism. A strong responsibility character habit often inspires others and generates respect, and so on.

What sets the Virtuoso CEOs apart in our study is the *strength* of the Keystone Character Habits they demonstrate in their workplace behavior, as observed and reported by their employees. To understand how they developed such strong habits, we asked the CEOs in our study to answer questions similar to the "How were you taught to know right from wrong?" question you saw earlier in this chapter. Most of the Virtuoso CEOs reported learning their strong character habits from the important adults in their lives. Many learned them by simply adopting the character habits they observed being demonstrated by the people they admired. Some, however, were careful to sort and choose their habits.

One leader's story stood out; he was an individual who described his father as "Tough. Distant. Punishing. He was not a nice man." This CEO, in his fifties at the time of the survey, was rated very highly by his employees on all four Keystone Character Habits. When I asked him how he learned to be compassionate and forgiving when he had a father who was just the opposite, he said, "I saw how people reacted to my mother. She was very giving and people would be very warm back to her, so I suspect I began adopting her ways. I guess I learned somehow that if you are going to keep people close to you, you don't push them away."

This same individual told me that he learned to be a person of integrity by being caught—and punished for—cheating. "I remember in high school, a time when I decided that I could look over a guy's shoulder during a quiz. The teacher saw me do it, grabbed my test paper, and wrote a big zero on it. This had a life-changing impact on me. It absolutely riveted me. I flunked the first quarter, but by the end of the third quarter, I was getting 98 percent on tests."

He went on to talk about working to develop the habit of forgiveness, toward himself and others. He said that he learned "how much better I feel when I let something go and forgive. I deal with a lot of things that go wrong. I'm lucky if I'm successful 70 percent of the time, so I can't bring it home with me. I've got to let it go—both my mistakes and the mistakes others make." When I asked him about how he thought a life journey shaped character, he summed up his thoughts by saying, "At some point, people 'self-launch' and become whole."

It takes a leader who demonstrates *all* of the Keystone Character Habits, both those of the head and the heart, to really engage and motivate the people being led.[5] But here's the good news: like any habit, the Keystone Character Habits are learned responses that we demonstrate through (likewise) learned behaviors. By working to become an Integrated Human, we also are developing our innate moral intuitions into the Keystone Character Habits of Virtuoso leadership. We aren't born great leaders, after all; we *become* great leaders by training ourselves to think and act accordingly.

Breaking old habits and developing new ones is a process that involves ongoing attention and work, but it is still very doable. (We offer some practical steps for the process in chapter 7.) We're born with the raw ingredients and capabilities for making that shift. The more we think about and hone our automatic responses to the events and individuals that we encounter every day, the better able we'll be to develop the habits of strong character that will take our leadership style—and results—to the next level.

Self-Awareness and Virtuoso Leadership

The poet Robert Burns, in his 1786 poem, "To a Louse (On Seeing One on a Lady's Bonnet, at Church)," observed how wonderful it would be if only we had the gift of seeing ourselves as others see us. Burns was talking about self-awareness. But when it comes to leadership, self-awareness isn't a gift; it's necessary equipment for the job that we must acquire all on our own.

As we saw earlier, one way to measure your own self-awareness is to think about the degree to which your life story is coherent and (at least somewhat) logical. Nearly all of the Virtuoso CEOs in our research told such a life story, one that held together and made sense to them and to others. They were able to show how their early experiences relate to their later development. They acknowledged both the positive and negative aspects of their family experiences and they were able to recount how both the best and the worst times influenced their lives. The Self-Focused CEOs, on the other hand, demonstrated little of the self-awareness that comes from having reflected on life events and how they have shaped them.

We were surprised to learn, however, that Self-Focused CEOs also tend to engage in considerable self-deception. Several people have asked me, for example, "How did you manage to get CEOs who lack integrity to sign up for a research project on character?" My answer is simple. *All* of the CEOs in our study rated themselves as possessing a high level of integrity—even those whose integrity was rated extremely low by others.

We know that all human beings have a well-honed skill of denial— and often that's a positive trait. Without it, just the certain knowledge of our eventual death would throw us into deep depression and anxiety. Our facility for denial is the foundation for optimism, along with most of the aspirational beliefs described in this chapter.

However, denial also has its dangers.[6] The old saying, "the higher the monkey climbs the tree, the more others can see his behind," speaks to the keen focus we place on leadership behavior, and how clueless leaders can be as to what the view from below reveals. The Virtuoso leaders in our study seemed to understand the danger of denial and, to combat it, have honed the discipline of seeking objective feedback. Our research revealed that those leaders ask for the truth and make it safe for others to tell it, no matter how unflattering it may be. The Self-Focused CEOs in our study, on the other hand, demonstrated much less interest in gathering critical input or habitually reflecting on their potential flaws. They seemed, in fact, to have found ways to convince themselves that everyone thinks they're doing just fine.[7]

No matter how much reflection we practice, we need to get feedback from other people in order to become truly self-aware. While some organizations use employee surveys for this purpose, the effectiveness of those tools is limited if workers don't trust in their anonymity and greatly fear the repercussions of criticizing their leaders. Unfortunately, the leaders who could most benefit from the honest feedback of others often are the least likely to ask for it or to set up the conditions that make it possible.

Many of the CEOs in our research had never before received unfiltered employee feedback. When one of the Self-Focused CEOs was faced with the negative picture of his integrity painted through our survey by a random sampling of his employees, he moved quickly from surprise to denial. "Where did you get this data?" he asked. "We've been doing employee surveys for years, and my team and I always get the highest ratings on integrity. There must be something wrong with your research design!" Three months later, this "stellar" CEO and his entire management team were dismissed when his company was broken up and sold to competitors.

Gaps between the CEOs' self-ratings and those of their employees served as a reliable measure of self-awareness in our research. As shown in figure 3-3, the Virtuoso CEOs tended to slightly underrate the strength of their character habits, giving themselves marginally lower character scores than those given to them by their employees—a difference that suggests a measure of humility on the part of these leaders. The Self-Focused CEOs, on the other hand, dramatically *overrated* their demonstration of moral habits, assigning themselves much higher character scores than they were given by their employees. The vast difference between the self-ratings and employee ratings of these leaders' characters speaks to the level of self-deception at work in the group of Self-Focused CEOs in our research.

The research clearly demonstrated that the journey to becoming an integrated, whole person requires self-awareness. Fortunately, however, we can greatly enhance our self-awareness simply by obtaining the observations of those who know us well. By reviewing our life story, by reflecting on the principles and moral habits that shape our character and the behaviors that demonstrate it, and by gathering the objective feedback of those we live and work with, we can develop the self-awareness of the Integrated Human essential to the character of Virtuoso leadership—and use it to improve our results, in business and in life.

FIGURE 3-3

Ratings on strength of character habits

Character score

The CEO demonstrates these behaviors:

50 — About half of the time

Slightly more than half of the time

75 — Frequently

Almost always

100 — Always

Self-Focused CEOs   Virtuoso CEOs

The Worldview from the Vantage Point of Success

Our conscious mind lives in a private world of its own. We all create a mental model of reality, and each of us maintains a constant inner dialogue that we use to explain and understand the world around us. This mental model is our *worldview*, a cataloging system for arranging beliefs about the external world and events—beliefs we have formed from life experiences or have adopted from our culture, social group, family, and important influences such as mentors, bosses, and friends.

Your life story plays a critical role in your worldview by providing the background and explanations for how you came to have your specific set of beliefs.

We add or subtract beliefs from our worldview when we need to explain our own behavior. ROC research, as well as several other research projects, supports this conclusion: we form the majority of our conscious beliefs to explain and/or defend our actions to both ourselves and others.[8]

The Integrated Human embraces a worldview of positive beliefs about human nature, organizational life, and personal purpose. Holding that positive worldview seems to provide a definite advantage for leaders, and is clearly a factor that separates the Virtuoso CEOs from the lower-performing, Self-Focused CEOs.

To compile a clear picture of the worldview demonstrated through the behavior of the leaders in our study, we gave employees a list of eighty-five statements and asked them to rate how accurately they describe the habitually demonstrated beliefs of their CEOs. (See appendix A for a sample of these belief statements.) What beliefs seem to be consistent in the worldview of successful leaders? Employees of Virtuoso CEOs indicated that those leaders consistently demonstrate the following nine positive beliefs in their day-to-day workplace behavior:

1. Most people grow and change throughout their adult life.

2. Most people want to be honest, responsible, and kind to others.

3. Most people can be trusted until they prove otherwise.

4. Leaders find meaning through growing and stretching their natural gifts and talents.

5. Leaders are driven by the desire to leave the world a better place.

6. All businesses, no matter how large or small, share a responsibility to contribute to the common good.

7. All people deserve the same respect, regardless of the size or status of their jobs.

8. All people have core strengths and talents that should be engaged.

9. The best managers have good relationship and communication skills.

As this list demonstrates, Virtuoso leaders are rarely driven by fears and/or a negative worldview. The same can't be said for the less-principled leaders in our research. While employees report that the Self-Focused leaders sometimes demonstrate the beliefs listed above, they rated them as more often demonstrating the beliefs of a negative worldview, such as those expressed in these eleven statements:

1. Employees must not be treated too kindly by management or else they will become lazy and unproductive.

2. By generating conflict, one can usually find the truth about a situation.

3. Meeting quarterly goals is generally wiser than focusing on the long term, since there are so many unknowns.

4. When it comes down to it, most people cannot be trusted.

5. Most people have to be closely monitored to make sure they perform.

6. People have limitations and weaknesses, and it is pointless to try and change them.

7. In the final analysis, the only person you can depend on is yourself.

8. There is no one in the company who will look out for us—no one will "have our backs."

9. I am afraid of change unless I am in control.

10. I really don't know much about what drives me or gives me meaning.

11. What drives me or gives me meaning is proving to those important in my life that I have succeeded.

More surprisingly, for all the common wisdom regarding the bone-deep influence of religious and political beliefs, our research revealed that leadership beliefs on these issues really don't seem to affect the way employees assess their performance or business results, at least when the CEOs keep those beliefs to themselves.

Some of the CEOs in our research reported that they were regular churchgoers who had always voted for a Republican candidate in presidential elections, while another group said they never went to church and always voted Democratic. When we compared the business results of these two groups, reviewing levels of workforce engagement, organizational competitiveness, and business plan execution, we discovered *no* differences in any of these measures. Next we compared the character ratings of the groups and, again, found no differences. There were strong-character and weak-character individuals in both political and religious camps. So when leaders keep their personal political and religious ideas to themselves, those beliefs appear to have no measurable impact on how effectively they run their businesses.

What counts is the leader's *behavior*. ROC data reveals that leaders—whether very religious and conservative, or very secular and progressive—whose behavior expresses a character shaped by strong moral principles are effective leaders. As the research also demonstrated, leadership behavior founded on character habits and beliefs that contribute to a positive worldview is more consistently associated with positive, sustained business results than is leadership guided by a negative worldview.

Many of the common ideas about beliefs appear to be wrong, based on the results of our research. While many seem to associate a negative and pessimistic attitude regarding human nature, personal purpose, and organizational life with the savviness of success, that idea couldn't be more wrong. The Virtuoso leaders in our study clearly illustrate that the most successful leaders focus on what's *right* about the world around them.

As you work to develop your own skills as a Virtuoso CEO, you should examine your worldview to determine where it slips into the "glass half-empty" perspective rather than the "glass half-full" view of life. But at the same time, realize that a positive worldview is more than optimism. It's a faith and belief in the innate goodness of humanity—a conviction that we are all born with a shared set of moral intuitions and that we are never more human than when we develop those intuitions and demonstrate them in our connections with others.

The fear-based worldview of Self-Focused CEOs actually drives us apart, separating us from the people who can help us build stronger self-awareness; stronger moral habits; and a richer, more intricate understanding of the world we live in. In other words, our worldview plays a key role in determining how successfully we leverage the formative opportunities available all around us as we navigate the inner journey toward self-integration. To complete that journey successfully—and to be a Virtuoso CEO—you need to embrace a positive worldview.

The Virtuoso's Mental Complexity

The term *mental complexity* refers to our ability to perceive the subtle nuances that separate similar ideas, issues, and events in the world around us—the gray areas that replace the strictly black-and-white understanding of the world that most of us have when we're young. As we age, we develop higher levels of mental complexity. We learn to question common wisdom and authority and form our own attitudes and ideas. As our mental complexity grows, we also become better able to see issues from multiple perspectives and to understand that there is no single, right position on some issues, including our own. Some opposing ideas can be equally correct. When we then learn to routinely challenge our *own* ideas and beliefs, we achieve the highest levels of mental complexity. Then we are in a position to continually improve our understanding of ourselves and the world around us. And with that advancement, we can also improve our performance as individuals, as members of a community, and as leaders.

When we reach this level of mental complexity, we have developed what psychologist Robert Kegan refers to as the "self-transforming mind."[9] According to Kegan, the self-transforming mind is continually aware of not knowing everything—of understanding that every worldview is incomplete and that we can never know everything there is to know about anything. This highest level of mental complexity tends to develop as we age, but only around 7 *percent* of people achieve this level of mental complexity, including *all* of the Virtuoso CEOs who participated in the ROC study.[10]

Without question, some of the Virtuoso CEOs in our study were older and more experienced and therefore had a natural advantage in achieving a higher level of mental complexity. But all of them, regardless of age and without exception, behave in a way that indicates a keen self-awareness of their own limitations. They remain constantly open to new insights, regardless of the source.

While it is *not* absolutely necessary to have a high level of mental complexity in order to be an integrated person with a head-to-heart connection, strong character habits, and a positive worldview, it is most often true that a high level of self-integration and mental complexity go hand-in-hand. Certainly, the ROC research indicates that Virtuoso leaders are mentally complex. Their survey responses and those of their employees reveal that these CEOs see more shades of gray than black-and-white in most situations. They can mentally balance opposing ideas. They can tolerate ambiguity. They have maintained a natural curiosity about the world and events. Great leaders aren't afraid of facts; they want to understand and know as much as they can, because *that's* how they continually improve their minds, strengthen their character habits, increase their self-awareness, and deepen the mental complexity that enables them to be successful decision makers.

As you follow your inner journey to self-integration—and Virtuoso leadership—you need to constantly hone the heightened mental complexity of the self-transforming mind. Like all of the characteristics of Virtuoso leadership, attaining this level of mental complexity takes time, attention, and discipline. But the work itself is relatively simple to understand.

You can begin by abandoning any ideas about black-and-white when it comes to the world around you and its inhabitants, and cultivate your ability to detect the many shades of gray that exist within most situations. Trying to see events, ideas, and issues from the perspectives of multiple people or organizations involved in them is a great way to start. You also have to practice balancing opposing ideas in your mind. Taking both sides in a mental debate can quickly show you how easy it is to take hold of any position—and how seductive it can be to cling tightly to that view, even in the face of conflicting evidence. Instead of going heads-down and ignoring the uncomfortable truths of the world around you, learn to open your mind and feed your natural curiosity. With that, you'll have reached an essential milestone along the path to becoming a self-integrated person—and a Virtuoso leader.

Mapping the Outcome of Your Journey

Throughout this chapter, we've seen the evidence, revealed through ROC research, of the power of our life journey to shape our approach to leadership and therefore the results we achieve as leaders. While every life journey is unique, most include the same milestones: the parents, family members, teachers, mentors, and other influential adults whose behavior and guidance help direct us through the educational and work experiences that shape our outer journey; and the character habits, self-awareness, worldview, and mental complexity we develop from exposure to those people and experiences as we travel on the inner journey through adulthood. Ideally, these parallel paths converge as we develop the self-integration of a whole human being and a strong, high-achieving, principled leader.

As our research has revealed, Virtuoso CEOs have taken time to consider their life story in full, and they can draw clear and distinct lines that connect the formative people and experiences of their lives to their ongoing attitudes, behaviors, and responses to new opportunities and emerging issues. Not only do these high-functioning CEOs understand who they are and why they think and behave the way they do; they also are capable of continually testing and refining their ideas and beliefs. The mental complexity that the most successful leaders in our research achieved—as measured both by the workplace environment they create and the business results their organizations achieve—enables them to continue to excel in even the most rapidly evolving global marketplaces and economies.

In other words, the life journeys of the Virtuoso CEOs in our study offer a wonderful road map for all of us who are seeking to improve our approach to leadership and the results we achieve in every aspect of life. As we've seen, the destination of that journey is one of self-integration. By removing any gap between our character habits and beliefs and our ongoing behavior toward and interactions with others, we achieve the wholeness that is the hallmark of strong character and Virtuoso leadership. Figure 3-4 shows one way we can conceptualize the integrated self—a core of self-awareness and ideas and beliefs that shape our worldview and mark our relationships, surrounded by a level of mental complexity that continually develops as we continue our life journey and reflect on the story it tells.

FIGURE 3-4

The integrated self

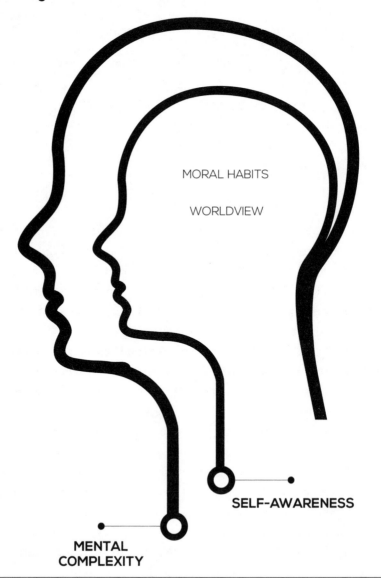

Eventually, you become capable of questioning not only the ideas of others, but even your own most cherished beliefs. As a result, your understanding of your life, your business, your marketplace, and the global economies and forces that shape them enters a state of continual growth and development. At that point, you have not only achieved self-integration; you have advanced onto the path forged by Virtuoso leaders everywhere. If you are just beginning that path, you have a full set of tools for navigating it; if you are already in a position of leadership, you're equipped for continual growth and achievement as your journey progresses.

When an integrated individual's journey lands her in the corner office, she brings along the character necessary for accomplishing great things. But strong character alone doesn't produce the outstanding results of a Virtuoso leader; there's still the rest of the ROC Value Chain to consider. No matter how principled leaders may be, they must also command the skills of leadership: making sound decisions, forming and maintaining strong relationships, building a strong team of senior leaders, and guiding them in the execution of a well-crafted business plan. Now it's time to move to the second element of the equation, to see how the leaders in the ROC research develop and leverage the skills of leadership, and what we can learn from their successes and failures. That exploration of what leaders *do* takes us to part II.

ROC TAKEAWAYS
The Journey from Cradle to Corner Office

1. **Virtuoso leaders *know* their life story.** By crafting a coherent narrative of their life, they are better able to understand the major events and influences that have shaped their personal development and use that understanding to assess and improve their response to new situations that arise.

2. **When Virtuoso leaders were children, they sought and accepted help from many supportive adults.** Self-Focused CEOs had much less support and care from family and other influential adults.

3. **In the workplace, Virtuoso leaders find and enjoy the company of one or more mentors.** The leadership-enhancing benefits of mentoring relationships extend well beyond childhood.

4. **Virtuoso CEOs develop Keystone Character Habits based on the universal moral principles of integrity, responsibility, forgiveness, and compassion.** As with any habit, they develop these through self-training and practice.

5. **Self-awareness is critical to Virtuoso leadership and requires the feedback of others.** Self-Focused leaders are more likely to resort to denial when faced with unpleasant feedback.

6. **Virtuoso CEOs embrace a worldview of positive beliefs about human nature, organizational life, and personal purpose.** Self-Focused leaders tend to be more negative and pessimistic in their worldview.

7. **Virtuoso CEOs tend to develop the highest level of mental complexity, in which they challenge their own ideas and continually adapt them to encompass new information, experiences, and meaning.**

8. **The Virtuoso CEOs all demonstrate the ideas and behaviors of self-integration.** As a result, they have achieved the strong character that, when combined with strong business skills, completes the ROC Value Chain.

Part II

ROC Leadership
at Work

4

ROC Leadership in Action

Mastering the Essentials

We have seen how life experiences both helped and hindered the leaders who participated in the ROC study as they grew into adulthood and moved into major leadership roles. The Virtuoso leaders—those who lead with great character and also create the greatest value for their organizations—found a way to make sense of their life experiences, incorporating both positive and negative events into one coherent story. At the same time, they developed strong character habits and adopted positive beliefs about human nature, organizational life, and their own sense of purpose. In short, each had become an integrated self—someone who had learned to connect his head to his heart. The leaders developed a level of mental complexity that helped them continually learn and develop their skills, ideas, and understanding of the world around them—and their role in it.

Together, these developments form the critical first element in the ROC Value Chain, shown in figure 4-1, which represents who the leader is as a person *and* a leader. Now let's turn to the other half of the ROC equation: what the Virtuoso leader does.

Anyone who has worked in a business or organization of almost any size has formed her own ideas of what it takes to be a strong leader, and what behaviors and outcomes mark the presence of not-so-strong leadership. Every one of those ideas may differ in substantial ways. But ROC research has revealed that there are skills *every* successful leader exercises in order to maintain sustained, positive business results.

FIGURE 4-1

ROC Value Chain

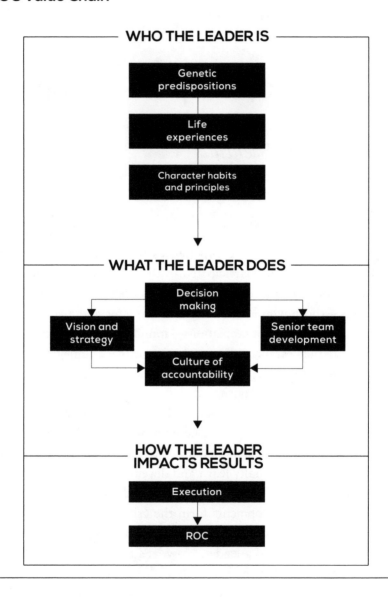

While leaders fulfill a number of critical functions in the organization, their primary role and responsibility is to make decisions.[1] Their skill as decision makers determines the fate of the organization and every person who works there or otherwise profits from it. And every senior leader must make decisions to address some of the same fundamental challenges, which include:

- Creating a vision for the business.

- Setting the organization's strategic focus and key initiatives.

- Building, maintaining, and leading a talented executive team.

- Defining and enforcing a culture of accountability.

Together, these challenges represent the essential skills that any leader must master in order to create sustainable value for his or her organization. Just as we refer to the most essential character habits of leadership as the Keystone Character Habits, we call these four essential skills—vision, strategic focus, executive team development, and accountability—the Keystone Leadership Skills. Using these skills to answer the organization's challenges in ways that create value *and* are in alignment with the strong principles of high-character leadership is what being a Virtuoso CEO is all about.

As we learn in this chapter, those identified as Virtuoso leaders in the ROC research received consistently higher ratings for their command of the Keystone Leadership Skills than did the Self-Focused CEOs, while they also achieved stronger business results for their organizations. That's ROC leadership in action.

We've seen the role of character in determining who the CEO is, and that the character factor plays a very real role in determining what that leader's organization achieves. But how does the individual demonstrate character in the execution of the essential skills of leadership? Does character play any role in the performance of these skills? By understanding what our research tells us about the answers to these questions, we're in a much better position to understand the ROC that both Virtuoso and Self-Focused CEOs produce for their organizations. And while the ROC study provides detailed information about the skills exhibited by a limited number of CEOs and their leadership teams, we can add to that information by drawing upon the findings of a wealth of other researchers, consultants, and authors.[2]

In this chapter, we're going to examine the results of our ROC research and the findings of other respected sources about the essential skills of leadership, and how CEOs from both ends of the character spectrum learn and execute those skills. We'll begin with the leadership skill that serves as the lever for all others: decision making.

Decision Making and Character-Driven Leadership

Leaders spend most of their time making decisions. Of course, they do a lot of other things as well: tending to outside stakeholders, fielding inquiries from investors or the press, attending meetings, giving speeches, thinking, reading, and so on. But the most valuable act of leadership is making disciplined decisions about the business and the people who run it. A disciplined decision-making process serves as the lever of character-driven leadership, by connecting the power of leadership character to the actions of the organization and the outcomes those actions produce.

I spoke with one of the Virtuoso CEOs identified in our research about his development as a decision maker, a man we'll call Paul (not his real name). Paul was still in his late thirties when he became the CEO of a midsized public financial services firm, which he continued to grow by more than 15 to 20 percent every year, with sustained profitability. Paul told me that he walked into that job feeling exhilarated— and at a bit of a loss as to what to *do*. "I had arrived!" he explained. "It was my first day as the chief executive officer and the first thing that struck me was, now what?" He went on to describe his first experiences as the organization's chief decision maker:

> First of all, you don't get a manual. I guess I was surprised at how much scrutiny I was under: every move, every word, everything I did. Those who were supportive used it to their advantage, and those who didn't like me looked for ways to undermine what I wanted to do. I decided that I could best deal with this

by communicating to everyone *what* we were doing and *why* we were doing it. I quickly learned that when you're in a new role, you can never overcommunicate about your plans and what you're thinking. I went into hyper-mode in communicating and did my best to stay consistent with those messages.

Paul said that even as he was making these first critical decisions about communicating vision and strategy to everyone in the organization, another realization was dawning on him: now decision making was his primary responsibility. He could no longer take difficult decisions to his CEO; he *was* the CEO.

Being in the CEO role is *mostly* about making decisions. Few organizations hire a CEO to step in and work the front line. Successful leaders—including every Virtuoso CEO who participated in our study—decide what the organization will do and then rely on others to carry out those decisions.

Bringing Discipline to the Decision-Making Process

As a species, we tend to be poor decision makers. There are many, *many* ways to make poor decisions, and just as many reasons we make them:

- The subconscious fast brain intuitively leaps to conclusions without regard for their accuracy.

- The rational slow brain is reluctant to become engaged and so allows our subconscious to unduly influence our decisions.

- We let recent experiences and emotional responses have disproportionate influence in our decision-making process.

- We unconsciously seek out data that confirms our preconceived ideas.

- We are inaccurate in our assessment of the probability of future events; we *generally* are inaccurate in these estimations.

But in spite of all the potential pitfalls we face in the decision-making process, anyone of average intelligence can learn to become a disciplined decision maker. We impose discipline on that process by using careful analysis in addition to skilled intuitions as the basis for our decisions. The best decisions are those that engage both brains, so that the quick, intuitive leaps of our fast brain are harnessed and tempered by the reflective analysis and reasoning of our slow brain. These decisions have survived the careful analysis provided by our slow brain and also "feel right" when our fast brain weighs in.

So how does the disciplined decision-making process work? In its simplest form, it goes like this:

1. In the course of making any decision, emotional markers provided by the fast brain serve up hunches (intuitions) and clues to the slow brain.

2. The slow brain begins to weigh a broad range of facts related to the decision.[3]

3. The slow brain then considers the situation from multiple perspectives and contexts to reveal more options and potential outcomes than are first apparent.

4. The slow brain then balances those options against the four motivational drives that underlie all human interaction—the drives to acquire, bond, comprehend, and defend—in order to arrive at a decision.

How do we flesh out this skeletal outline of the decision-making process? While the ROC research data didn't draw a clear picture of the specific decision-making processes any of the CEOs in our study used, numerous other studies and research projects have focused on understanding and describing such processes. We can draw from the best of these sources to form a "composite image" of disciplined decision making in action.[4] Those sources tell us that successful leaders, such as the Virtuosos in our study, use a mental checklist to ensure that they and other leaders in their organization make important decisions in a thoughtful and consistent way. Those checklists include such questions as these:

• Have we honored the process for decision making that our leadership team agreed to follow?

- Have we carefully considered how this decision supports our strategy?

- Have we compared ourselves to our strongest competitors?

- Have we compared our business practices to the highest standards in our industry?

- Have we considered all the options?

- Have we tested out this idea in any reliable way?

- Will this decision still be good in a month? A year?

- Have we looked at the impact the decision will have on *all* stakeholders?

- Have we asked, "What variables must be true for this to be the best choice?"

- Have we discussed this decision with trusted advisers?

- Is this decision supported by both our reflective analysis *and* intuition?

Of course, both successes and failures can be quite easily traced back to executive-level decision making. The same sources from which we drew our "composite image" of the successful decision-making process, however, tell us that when faced with a critical decision, flawed decision makers may:

- Make a decision and *then* seek confirming data.

- Allow short-term financial returns to outweigh long-term benefits for the business.

- Make impulsive decisions without regard to consequences.

- Place undue importance on a decision's effect on their career or compensation.

- Be unduly influenced by the last person they talked to.

- Tend to see only black-and-white choices, ignoring the gray areas.

- Rely on their gut feel rather than on careful analysis and thoughtful reflection combined with their instinctive response.

Leaders who find themselves defaulting to any of these responses in their decision-making process can improve both their leadership character *and* business results by adopting a more thoughtful, disciplined approach.

Reaping the Benefits of ROC Decision Making

Whatever your specific process may be, the very act of practicing disciplined decision making anchors you to your fundamental goals, values, and beliefs. You're no longer jumping to conclusions or rushing to judgment; you are carefully filtering your decisions through the understanding you've gained from life experiences, the guiding principles you have adopted over the years, and the long-term strategic plan you've created for your organization. That's not to say that every decision you make will be right; but it will be a reflection of your head *and* your heart. As such, it will likely be consistent with past decisions, the fundamental character habits and principles you've adopted for yourself and your organization's leadership, and the goals you've set for the future of the business. That's ROC decision making at its most valuable, as it contributes to both the self-integration of the decision maker and the best interests of the organization he or she leads.

All of these observations about decision making are consistent with a global survey the *McKinsey Quarterly* conducted about strategic decision making.[5] In the report of that survey, researchers noted that:

> Executives at companies with satisfactory outcomes rate their
> processes highly when it comes to seeking contrary evidence and
> ensuring that decision makers had all the critical information,
> giving dissenting voices the floor, reviewing the business case
> thoroughly even though senior executives were strongly in favor,
> and ensuring that truly innovative ideas reached senior managers.

In the ROC research, the important decisions that every individual identified as a Virtuoso leader made—choosing an executive team, forming a vision, strategic focus, and so on—reflected this kind of disciplined decision-making process. Their employees reported that these leaders not only are open to challenging viewpoints, but seek them out, and that all of their decisions reflect a similar set of principles and values—as do the decisions of their executive team. Here's what some of these employees had to say:

> I have worked at [this company] for two years. Early on, I saw the high standards, integrity, and values espoused and practiced from the top on down. Management walks the talk and does not spin results only to the good. This became very apparent around the time of the Enron and Global Crossing fiascos. Having an independent board of directors and an internal audit program showed the forward thinking of management well before Sarbanes-Oxley came into existence.

> [Our CEO] supports employees even though they may disagree with him. I once voiced an opinion different than the one on the table, but [our CEO] immediately voiced his understanding of my point of view. In my dealings with him, he has always been open-minded and a good listener. It makes me feel that my voice is not only heard but that I am appreciated as an employee.

In our interview, the Virtuoso CEO we've called Paul noted that he is a much better and more disciplined decision maker today than he was fifteen years ago. That's not surprising. Disciplined decision making is a skill that must be honed. In *Outliers*, writer Malcolm Gladwell claims that most skills take approximately ten thousand hours of practice before being fully developed.[6] Acquiring expertise as a decision maker, however, has challenges you don't encounter when learning to become a virtuoso violinist.

Decision makers practice their craft in constantly shifting conditions framed by unpredictable events and outcomes. For the decision maker, every practice session takes place on stage, in front of an audience that often has something riding on the performance. And too many budding decision makers try to go it alone; unlike that student violinist, they have no instructor hovering nearby to help them overcome errors and improve their performance. Without that kind of guidance, the "ten thousand hours of practice" in forming and implementing good decisions can be one long, painful, and costly exercise—for the decision maker and everyone his or her decisions affect.

It's not easy to become a virtuoso in *any* discipline, but if you want to excel as a CEO, you have to focus first on developing the skills of disciplined decision making. One of your first important decisions will be about finding and recruiting one or more skilled mentors to help you develop *all* of the critical tools of leadership. If you hope to become a Virtuoso leader, you should *immediately* search for a mentor, if you don't have one already.

Paul found such a mentor. He turned to a friend who was the CEO of a large company in his sector that was not a competitor. This friend was a seasoned leader and had been a CEO for over ten years. Both enjoyed golf and found that their time on the course was a perfect time to talk about Paul's challenges as a new CEO. Their golf game was often followed by long conversations over dinner. Paul told me, "If it were not for Jim's generous gift of his time to listen to me and challenge my thinking, I'm sure I would have made many, many more mistakes than I did." Paul learned from his mentor some of the essentials of a disciplined decision-making process.

If a very principled, high-character leader fails to become a skilled decision maker, it can blunt the individual's ability to create value. On the other hand, a leader with great decision-making skills but weak character habits is also unlikely to create much value, if for no other reason than that the workforce just won't become fully engaged in that leader's decisions, vision, or strategy. In all cases, the Self-Focused CEOs in our study had difficulty inspiring and engaging the workforce. It is as if the typical employee thinks, "If I can't believe what you say nearly half of the time, why should I get excited about your vision? You might not really mean it or stick with the decisions you've outlined for achieving it."

Decision making is the lever of leadership—the skill that serves as the connection point that links the power of leadership character to all other skills and activities of the job. But it takes more than skillful decision making to create great value for an organization. As our study revealed, leaders who create the highest value—the greatest ROC—also demonstrate a highly principled character. But poor decision making will drag down the results of even the most principled CEO.

Character and the Keystone Leadership Skills

We've seen that making sound decisions is the overriding responsibility of leadership. The most important of those decisions fall into two categories: business and people. A leader's ability to make and execute these two types of decisions will determine that individual's success as a CEO—as well as the level of success his or her leadership team and organization achieve.

The most important *business* decisions a leader makes revolve around vision and strategy, two areas defined by Keystone Leadership Skills and two factors that determine any organization's effectiveness. To lead in these areas, the CEO must:

- Determine the organization's vision for success and create a clear and compelling description of what that success will look like.

- Choose a strategic focus and communicate it to others throughout the organization and its alliances.

As we see later in this chapter, Virtuoso CEOs in our study all achieved high ratings in their ability to form and communicate vision and strategy.

But as central as they are to organizational effectiveness, vision and strategy on their own are just abstract ideas. Bringing those ideas to life requires the commitment and coordinated efforts of people throughout the organization. It also demands that everyone understands the playbook: where you're going, how you're going to get there, and what rules and boundaries frame the journey ahead. You need a strong executive team to put that playbook into action, so the CEO's *people* decisions that matter most and that call upon the remaining two Keystone Leadership Skills include:

- Forming the executive team and determining each member's role.

- Creating and maintaining a culture of accountability and drawing the boundaries of acceptable behavior.

Together, these two primary categories of CEO decisions draw upon the four Keystone Leadership Skills: vision, strategy, executive team development, and accountability. While decision making serves as the foundation for all skills and activities of leadership, I call these *Keystone Leadership Skills* because they, in essence, strengthen and hold in place every other skill or activity a leader must perform. Strong CEO performance depends on strength in these four skills combined with disciplined decision making. When leaders of strong character get these Keystone Skills right, they have positioned their organization to achieve success, both in terms of workplace environment and business results.

ROC research revealed substantial gaps between the assessments of Virtuoso CEOs and Self-Focused CEOs in terms of these Keystone Leadership Skills. But before we review the statistics on this aspect of the study, let's talk a bit about what types of activities each of these critical skills involve so that we can better understand the basis for these performance scores.

Creating a Clear Vision

Organizations typically bring in new leadership to bring new life, energy—and value—into the organization. A leader's clear vision is a powerful tool for creating significant value for any organization or individual.

When Paul arrived as the CEO of his company, he inherited a traditional organization that had done well over the years but was now at a turning point. Competitors were catching up and the organization seemed to be drifting. The firm's leadership needed to reexamine its fundamental business model. As the new CEO, Paul's first business challenge was to create a new vision for the next three to five years and translate that vision into a new business model.

He spent several weeks asking questions, collecting data, and becoming an expert about future trends in the industry. At the same time, Paul also sought to tap into the wisdom of his workforce. He reasoned that the people closest to the customers could provide an extremely valuable perspective—one unavailable to him and his team. So Paul formed a few small task forces among his managers, asking for volunteers to engage in the work of creating the new vision for his company. He made it clear that the board would be making the final decisions about the organization's vision, but that he wanted everyone's input on this critical matter.

As Paul worked his way through this disciplined analysis, he came to see major opportunities for his firm. He was able to articulate this in the form of a vision for the future that evoked in him strong positive feelings and passion whenever he talked about it. He worked closely with his board to test specific ideas, and after many discussions, the board agreed to embrace the vision and the key concepts of a new business model.

While Paul probably knew intuitively that this process would have the additional benefit of engaging his lower-level managers, he was still surprised at the great amount of positive organizational energy the process generated. People at all levels began to talk with enthusiasm and passion about the new vision.

In my experience, Paul's decision to use the creation of a new vision to ignite organizational passion and energy is a rare one. Over the years that we at KRW have served as advisers and confidants to senior leaders, we have noticed that, far from developing and exercising this very critical skill of leadership, many executives seem to lack even a basic understanding of the transformative power of organizational vision.

When we ask individual members of an executive team to describe their company's vision, most of them can come up with nothing more than a few clichéd generalizations about "growing the business." Rather than being inspirational, much of what these teams have to say about vision is boring and meaningless. John Kotter and Dan Cohen in *The Heart of Change* observed, "Far too often, guiding teams either set no clear direction or embrace visions that are not sensible. The consequences can be catastrophic for organizations and painful for employees—just ask anyone who has suffered through a useless fad forced on them from above."[7]

Writer Bill Hybels, in *Courageous Leadership*, specifically acknowledges the inspirational power of vision as "a picture of the future that produces passion." Calling the power of a vision the "energy and passion it evokes deep in one's heart," Hybels goes on to say that "vision is the very core of leadership . . . the fuel that leaders run on. It's the energy that creates action . . . the fire that ignites the passion of followers."[8]

Like other Virtuoso leaders, Paul knows how powerful and inspiring a vision can be. A year after Paul stepped into the role of CEO, his business announced its new name and logo to better convey its new vision. Paul also began to talk at every opportunity about the organization's new vision for growth and expansion in service to its customers. By creating an inspiring new guiding vision for his organization and by communicating it clearly and frequently throughout the workforce and to others outside, Paul was able to spark the passions and focus the energy of his people to drive the company forward, toward its long-range goals.

As Paul's experience illustrates, vision has a transformative power for any group or organization. But to harness that power and drive the highest ROC, the vision must be clear, compelling, and well understood by everyone who will be involved in its realization.

Establishing Strategic Focus

Natural visionaries who create and release a lot of organizational energy sometimes fail to properly guide that energy.[9] Instead of creating value for the organization, their energy is wasted. Many high-energy, achievement-oriented leaders have trouble understanding that unfocused energy is really just chaos. They mistakenly assume their organization can effectively focus on dozens of priorities at one time. Not so. Those folks are conducting an exercise in firefighting, not strategic execution. I have spoken to some senior executives who described the executive team as "running around with their hair on fire." Sadly, they say that as if it was a badge of honor, rather than evidence of a drastic error in business plan execution.

While organizational vision is a great tool for creating energy, leaders must be able to focus that energy in order to bring their strategic plan to life. This is where the second Keystone Leadership Skill, establishing and maintaining strategic focus, comes into play. This task involves creating a focused business plan with a list of key initiatives and metrics for measuring the plan's successful implementation. Finding a way to simplify the strategic plan into a few easily remembered and communicated initiatives or goals is as important to strong leadership as creating the plan in the first place. In *Playing to Win: How Strategy Really Works*, Roger Martin and A. G. Lafley offer a practical playbook for creating a vision and strategic plan for an entire enterprise or a department or business unit within a larger organization.[10]

Like many of the Virtuoso leaders identified in the ROC research, Paul reduced his strategic business plan into three memorable statements and talked about them at every opportunity. He correctly understood that a primary task for him as the CEO was to keep the vision and strategy fresh and memorable. "I visited every regional office every quarter," Paul told me. "I talked about the vision and strategic initiatives until they were committed to rote memory. When I was so tired of giving the same message over and over again, I reminded myself of how important it was that people heard it from me. It helped also to recall how my audience was always attentive and engaged."

Again, our research revealed that a leader's ability to communicate the organization's strategic focus and to engage the workforce in its pursuit is connected to that leader's credibility and character. Employees will almost always form an impression of their leadership's sincerity, motivations, and commitment to stated principles and goals. Leaders and executive teams who have established a reputation— through actions as well as words—for strong character and high principles are much more likely to engage their workforce in the often difficult pursuit of strategic initiatives and long-term goals. When employees feel confident about the character of those at the helm, they are more willing to get on board and work toward accomplishing a shared vision.

Selecting and Leading a Skilled Executive Team

A brilliant business model and strategic plan are worthless if execution is flawed. The Virtuoso leader understands that he or she doesn't often do the real work of execution. The leader's job is to *think* and *make decisions*; it's the executive team that executes the business plan. Thus, decisions about who should be on the executive team and what role the person plays is one of the most important decisions a leader makes. Those decisions represent the third Keystone Leadership Skill, and they play a deciding role in the organization's ROC.

The old saying, "One bad apple spoils the barrel," is never truer than when it applies to an executive team. All too often, I've seen newly appointed leaders make the rookie mistake of being indecisive about who to keep and who to replace on the executive team.

To achieve Virtuoso-level results, leaders need A-level executives on their team from the start. It's better to have a temporary vacancy on the team than to tolerate a player with mediocre skills or weak character habits. A lackluster senior executive team will eventually fail or, at best, achieve only modest results.

More than one freshly minted CEO has failed due to her reluctance to replace an executive team member who simply wasn't up to the new standards set for organizational leadership. Nor is it wise, or even fair, to promote someone too soon into a job he simply isn't ready for. Such a mistake can ruin the person's career and bring failure to the organization and its leader. Most A-level executives aren't interested in struggling along as part of a mediocre team. Instead, they'll get discouraged and look for other opportunities.

Selecting the executive team members is just the first task of executive team development. The CEO also has to build that group into a high-performing team. Virtuoso leaders are quick to take on that challenge in a way that results in a team of equally high skills *and* character. When assessing the performance levels of a client's executive team, KRW uses questions such as these:

1. Is everyone on the team clear about the organization's vision?

2. Do you all share a common purpose, and can everyone articulate it?

3. Does everyone clearly understand his or her role so that there's no overlap or confusion as to who does what?

4. Has the CEO made it clear which decisions he is willing to share with the team and those for which he only wants input?

5. Has the CEO established clear expectations for communication, confidentiality, and conflict resolution?

6. Is everyone clear about how the team works together—when and how often does it meet, what meetings are optional, who prepares the agenda, and so on?

In chapter 5, we take a much more detailed look at how executive teams function and how the performance of Virtuoso executive teams shape business results. But when a team can answer yes to each of the questions listed, it is ready to take on the challenges of executing the business plan. CEOs who create such teams have proven their mastery of this Keystone Skill of leadership—and they've used it to position their organization to achieve the highest ROC possible from every member of its executive group.

Enforcing a Culture of Accountability

Every business must effectively monitor and manage the risks it faces, and a culture of accountability is an organization's strongest risk-management tool. While most people are well intentioned, they also need to have clarity about expectations and boundaries. If a leader claims that "integrity is the cornerstone of our culture" but fails to spell out exactly what that means in practice, then the claim has little weight or purpose.

As leaders grow in their leadership skills and experiences, they become much better at seeing nuances—the gray areas of situations that once may have looked black-and-white. Rules are no exception. Many risks fall in the gray areas that surround rules of accountability, and that means that leaders must depend to a certain extent on the character habits of their employees to guide their behavior.

Once again, leaders set the standards for not just their own character and behavior, but for that of their employees as well. By setting and following a strict code of principled behavior among the executive team, CEOs can promote a culture that encourages leaders throughout the organization to use character standards to guide both their hiring *and* management processes.

In spite of the inevitable nuances of organization life, wherever possible, leaders must spell out expectations and boundaries in black-and-white clarity. ROC research supported the growing common wisdom, for example, that successful leaders must clearly define zero-tolerance behaviors. Costco Wholesale CEO Jim Sinegal told me, "We don't tolerate dishonesty to each other, our suppliers, or our members. One of the fastest ways to lose your job around here is to be dishonest."

Warren Buffett, in his 2010 memo to the management teams of his portfolio companies, spoke of the importance of protecting their company's reputation as he laid out his own boundaries of accountability and behavior.

> As I've said in these memos for more than twenty-five years, we can afford to lose money—even a lot of money. But we can't afford to lose reputation—even a shred of reputation. We *must* continue to measure every act against not only what is legal, but also what we would be happy to have written about on the front page of a national newspaper in an article written by an unfriendly but intelligent reporter.
>
> Sometimes your associates will say, "Everybody else is doing it." This rationale is almost always a bad one if it is the main justification for a business action. It is totally unacceptable when evaluating a moral decision. Whenever somebody offers that phrase as a rationale, in effect they are saying that they can't come up with a *good* reason. If anyone gives this explanation, tell them to try using it with a reporter or a judge and see how far it gets them . . . if a given course of action evokes such hesitation, it's too close to the line and should be abandoned. There's plenty of money to be made in the center of the court. If it's questionable whether some action is close to the line, just assume it is outside and forget it.[11]

Like Sinegal and Buffett, the Virtuoso CEOs involved in our research also maintain a no-excuses approach to enforcing a culture of accountability throughout their organization. We asked Paul for a short list of non-negotiable items for his management team and workforce. He said:

> Well, I have zero tolerance for any kind of behavior that is illegal or unethical. If a person lies or distorts the facts, I will immediately confront the person. And I expect my team to do likewise. Depending on the severity of the offense, the person may be given a second chance and not dismissed. A rule of thumb I use to decide whether or not to give a second chance is to decide how that would be viewed by the person's peers and work colleagues. If it would be perceived that I did not enforce the [organization's] values or that I gave favored treatment to the person, then I'll dismiss them. It is absolutely critical that people view the enforcement of our standards as fair and devoid of favoritism.

Unfortunately, the larger the business, the greater is the likelihood that someone will step over a boundary. When that happens, the leader must immediately take action, whether that means a reprimand or dismissal, because the integrity of the larger social order of the organization is at stake. Failure to enforce rules of accountability and boundaries sends a powerful message to the entire workforce that those rules are really just suggestions and need not be taken seriously.

Leading the Way toward Maximum ROC

As we began the ROC research project, we wondered if the strength of a leader's character would have any relationship to their business skills—even the four Keystone Skills we've just described. It seemed like a bit of a stretch. Would our research provide hard data to prove that the stronger-character CEOs would be more effective in creating an inspiring vision for the organization than the weaker-character, Self-Focused CEOs? Likewise, it seemed unlikely that the CEO's

FIGURE 4-2

CEOs' performance in Keystone Skills

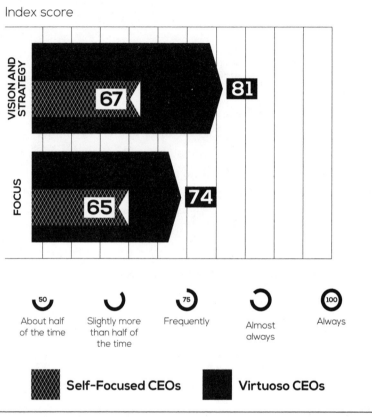

(continued)

strength of character would be highly related to that individual's skill in maintaining the strategic focus for the organization. But in this case, our intuitions were wrong. As the bar charts shown in figure 4-2 illustrate, we did find substantial differences: the Virtuoso CEOs outperformed the Self-Focused CEOs in all four of the Keystone Skills.

These differences were substantial. Employees of the Virtuoso CEOs rated their leaders' business decisions as providing more clarity of vision and strategy than did those of the Self-Focused CEOs by a spread of fourteen points for vision and nine points for focus.[12] Employee ratings

FIGURE 4-2 *(continued)*

CEOs' performance in Keystone Skills

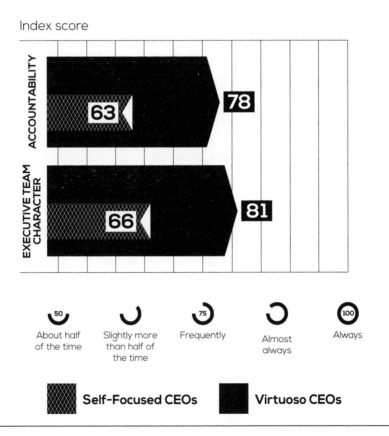

Index score

About half of the time (50)
Slightly more than half of the time
Frequently (75)
Almost always
Always (100)

Self-Focused CEOs
Virtuoso CEOs

revealed a similar difference between the two groups of CEOs in creating and maintaining a strong culture of accountability and selecting a skillful executive team of strong character.

These ratings discrepancies open a very important window into some fundamental truths about how Virtuoso and Self-Focused CEOs differ, in both their approach to leadership and the ROC or business results their approach achieves. We can think of leadership as any other acquired skill set: those who demonstrate the most mastery over the essentials are in a much better position to excel at the numerous related tasks that contribute to outstanding performance.

In this chapter, we've examined the Keystone Leadership Skills and the role they play in determining what any leader, whether Virtuoso or Self-Focused, contributes to the organization. We've used the term "keystone" to describe these essential skills—creating a clear vision, establishing strategic focus, forming and leading the executive team, and establishing boundaries and a culture of accountability—because without them, there *is* no leadership. And we've noted that disciplined decision making is the *lever* of character-driven leadership, because it connects leadership character to organizational actions and outcomes.

We've seen, however, that even though all leaders must undertake these critical leadership tasks, not all leaders perform them well. The leaders identified in the ROC research as Virtuosos consistently achieve higher ratings in their performance of these leadership essentials than do their Self-Focused peers.

In other words, leaders with strong character are more likely to be anchored in the kind of disciplined decision-making processes that result in clearer organizational vision, more focused strategies, a higher-performing executive team, and a stronger culture of accountability. Excellence in these Keystone Skills supports better overall leadership and stronger, more sustainable business results.

The keystone metaphor plays another useful role in this context by illustrating that while the CEO plays a critical central role in securing the arch of organizational leadership, that individual isn't the entire structure. The CEO relies on other key positions for support. In chapter 5, we'll take a closer look at the role of the executive team, how the character of its members is shaped by the character of the CEO they report to, and the impact of that character on workforce engagement.

If employees aren't really certain that they can believe what a leader says, how successfully will that leader's executive team be at guiding those employees in the passionate pursuit of the company's vision? How interested will those employees be in implementing the business plan and its strategies? In the next chapter, we'll find the answer to these and many other questions that clarify the link between CEO character, executive team performance, and ROC.

ROC TAKEAWAYS
Leadership in Action

1. **The leader's job is to think and make decisions.** Others within the organization carry out those decisions.

2. **Disciplined decision making is the lever of all other executive skills and actions.** Poor decision making is the one skill that can blunt even a highly principled leader's ability to create value.

3. **The most critical decisions a leader makes focus on the four Keystone Leadership Skills.**

   - Creating a clear vision.

   - Establishing the organization's strategic focus.

   - Selecting and leading a skilled executive team that demonstrates strong character.

   - Enforcing a culture of accountability.

   Excellence in the Keystone Leadership Skills supports better overall leadership and stronger, more sustainable business results.

4. **Leaders identified as Virtuosos consistently achieve higher performance ratings in these leadership essentials than do their Self-Focused peers.** Leaders with strong character are more likely to be anchored in the kind of disciplined decision-making processes that result in clearer organizational vision, more focused strategies, a higher-performing executive team, and a stronger culture of accountability.

5

The Executive
Team and ROC

Guiding the Organization to a Win

No matter how carefully researchers design a multiyear study, new insights are bound to come along and upend some stage of the process. The KRW team had just such an insight during our research into Return on Character when, after we'd already gathered character ratings on many of the first CEOs to participate in the study, we realized that we needed to gather more data about their executive teams. Specifically, we wanted to know how well the executive team executed its organization's business plan. That information would offer a deeper understanding of the true leadership skills of the executives who participated in the research, along with a broader perspective on the Return on Character their organizations achieve.

To be classified as a Virtuoso in this research, therefore, we decided that the CEO had to have a Virtuoso executive team. That meant that the employees we surveyed had to judge the executive team as strong in all four of the Keystone Character Habits of integrity, responsibility, forgiveness, and compassion.

The reasons for including this information in the study seem painfully obvious to us in hindsight. First, we should expect that an executive team will reflect the CEO's guiding principles and character habits—including the Keystone Character Habits of responsibility, compassion, forgiveness, and integrity. Because we tend to hire and collaborate best with people who fit within the framework of our approach to business, leadership, and ethics, the character profile and behavior of the executive team should offer a relatively accurate reflection of the CEO's character and principles. Second, logic dictates that the character habits of the executive team would influence organizational dynamics and workforce engagement—factors of organizational culture that play a determining role in the results that any business achieves.

Stories such as the following, told by one of the CEOs we interviewed, illustrate just how powerful those factors can be in sustaining a strong organizational culture and the principles that shape it:

> We hired a new member of the team who ended up quitting because he said the rest of us were "no fun." He had great skills and was just the person we needed to round out the executive team, but he had come from previous corporate environments where game playing and politics were how you succeeded. He found us—who were transparent and supportive of each other and a strong, cohesive team—to be mystifying and ultimately boring. He started making mischief by going to lunch with one person, pumping her for information and stories about others, and then going to lunch with others and twisting what was said and attributing it to the first person. For a while, there was tension and hurt feelings among the team, until finally they started talking directly to each other and discovering what was really going on. Then two of them sat down with him and told him to stop it. And then they proceeded to tell him how we treat each other and the unwritten cultural expectations. They told him that if he didn't stop, it was going to adversely affect his ability to succeed at the company. He was stunned. At first he mocked them, but they held firm. A few weeks later, he came to me and resigned.
>
> The most interesting part of this story is that as the leader of the team, I was unaware of the problem, since none of this happened in my presence and my long-term employees never wanted to bother me with petty politics. I only found out about it when I asked him why he was quitting and he said he didn't feel he fit in. I had to press to find out more from him, but still only really

learned the full story at a team meeting after he left, when people could speak freely. I was stunned and so proud of them, and told them so. They were pretty pleased with themselves, too, and we had a great conversation articulating the real values of the team and of our company and how those had come into full bloom when challenged.

When CEOs are clear about their expectations for strong character habits and they illustrate those habits through their own behavior, a culture of strong character and accountability can flourish throughout the organization. In this example, the culture was strong enough that its immune system kicked in and expelled the individual—who was, in effect, a virus that was infecting the system. So while the CEO's own character habits and principles are the source for the organization's overriding character and culture, it is up to the executive team to infuse the organization with those cultural attributes so that they permeate every aspect of the operation. That's an essential step in accomplishing the executive team's primary assignment, which is to create an organization that is poised to execute and achieve the vision that the CEO or other designated unit head articulate. In other words, the executive team is in charge of leading execution.

The team accomplishes this assignment by coordinating and leading the workforce in the *real* work of the organization: producing its products, delivering its services, and achieving its targeted business returns. They see to it that the widgets get made, customers are delighted, and expenses are contained. And, of course, in accomplishing its primary job of execution, the executive team must manage a number of central tasks, all of which fall within three main areas of responsibility:

- *Structure.* The executive team is responsible for determining the structure of the organization and for supporting that structure through its decisions and actions. This relatively straightforward area of responsibility involves determining the reporting order and then making sure that it works to promote the most effective operation.

- *Organizational dynamics.* The executive team also must develop and promote strong organizational dynamics by making sure that people interact productively, collaborate effectively, and contribute to a high-energy environment of innovation and accomplishment. Tasks in this category include maintaining the organization's vision at the front and center of all activities, guiding the energy that flows from that vision, and keeping the organization focused on key strategic initiatives.

- *Workforce engagement.* Finally, the executive team is responsible for ensuring that the workforce is energetically committed to achieving the organization's goals and promoting its cultural standards, which are, in turn, determined by the CEO's character habits and principles. Executive teams most directly shape workforce engagement through their interactions with employees, the level of commitment they show to helping employees improve their skills and advance their individual goals, and in the way they enforce standards of performance and conduct.[1]

All of these facts made a compelling case for adding the executive team data to the research. Unfortunately, we hadn't designed the original project to parse the character of the senior executive team or assess its effect on the organization's overall ROC.

To explore those factors, we needed a model of good organizational execution. We created the Execution Readiness model, which I describe later in this chapter, to answer that need. Because we began gathering this data mid-study, we didn't have full data sets on those CEOs and their organizations whose participation in the study had already ended. As it turned out, however, we needn't have worried. As we expanded the data covered by the research, we also expanded the total number of participants. In the end, we had more than enough full data sets to draw upon, as you will learn in chapter 6, where we lay out the full picture drawn by our findings as they relate to the character, behaviors, and business results the CEOs and executive teams in our research achieved.

In this chapter, we focus on the data related to that latter group, as we explore the responsibilities and functions of the executive team and its role in achieving the organization's Return on Character.

We'll begin with a brief overview of how CEO character influences the executive team's approach to execution and leadership. Next we'll see how employees rated the performance of the executive teams led by their own CEOs (both Virtuoso and Self-Focused), and how those ratings reflect both the teams' success in fulfilling their critical organizational role and the business results they achieve.

Leading the Executive Team

As we have seen, the executive team is responsible for executing the organization's business plan, managing its workforce, and carrying out the ongoing directives of its CEO and other senior leadership. In short, the executive team is perhaps the most important group of people in any organization.

But in order for the executive team to succeed in its role, it has to *be* a team. The members must function well together as a single unit with a common cause and shared purpose. The characteristics of a highly effective executive team have been the subject of many reputable studies.[2] Drawing upon the well-known findings of that research, we see that the most effective executive teams share these characteristics:

1. *Goals.* The team is united around a common purpose, mission, and goals.

2. *Roles.* The team members have clearly defined roles and responsibilities.

3. *Processes.* They follow a disciplined decision-making process; once they make a decision the team members close ranks and implement the decision without second-guessing.

4. *Interactions.* Team members critique and challenge each other without being offensive; they actively listen to and consider each other's opinions, feelings, and points of view, and make a special effort to help each other; they support and enable cross-functional linkages and working relationships.

While these elements describe the conditions a team must meet in order to most effectively fill its role and responsibilities, the list also offers a clear profile of the character habits and principles that shape organizational culture. To fit the model, team members must demonstrate the four Keystone Character Habits of strong leadership. They must be responsible (fulfilling their roles; working toward a common purpose), have integrity (acting on decisions without second-guessing; committing to processes), show compassion (listening, supporting, respecting points of view), and demonstrate forgiveness (critiquing without rancor or offensiveness). And while the CEO is responsible for creating the organization's culture, the executive team is responsible for acculturating the organization. The team accomplishes that by making sure the CEO's cultural standards permeate every aspect of the operation.

The effectiveness of the executive team depends on the strong character habits of each of its members. If the team has even one member who is unreliable, dishonest, defensive, or overwhelmingly self-focused, it's highly unlikely that the team will function as a high-performance unit.

The CEO is responsible for the executive team's overall performance and, as the team's leader, decides who gets on the team—and who stays on it. Many leaders think that they can compensate for a weak executive team member or two, or that the shortcomings of such a team member won't necessarily be noticeable to the workforce at large. But ROC research has shown that members of the frontline workforce rarely fail to spot the gap that opens between a Virtuoso CEO and a member of his or her team who has weak character.

One of the CEOs who participated in the research had very high character scores, but his executive team had scores so low that they knocked the CEO out of the Virtuoso category. When I interviewed this CEO, he said, "The biggest challenge for me is that it's still hard to tell people that they're not right for a certain role. I probably avoid it with some people more than I should."

This CEO knew perfectly well why his team received a poor overall character rating. He (accurately) identified that the problem rested with one individual on the team whom he was unable to confront. In their survey responses, his workers made it clear that they saw the same problems the CEO had identified with his executive team, even if they didn't understand that all of those problems traced back to a single individual. Here are some of their comments:

- "I believe [the CEO] has great integrity, but there is a gap between him and his leadership team. They seem to forget what it takes to run the day-to-day business."

- "My biggest concern is that he does not have a strong enough hold on the leadership underneath him. He is relying on his team to make correct decisions in promotability."

As these statements make clear, the CEO who enables a weak leader to stay on the executive team will carry the blame for the problems that team member creates. The entire organization will suffer for those problems.

The domino effect of bad leadership on business results is the reason that I stressed in chapter 4 that newly assigned CEOs need to move quickly to get their executive team in order. I once advised a CEO who had been concerned about his inherited team's performance for months. Nothing seemed to be getting done on time. After thoroughly assessing the team members, I was certain that one of them had lost the trust of the others. Several members of the team told me of incidents in which this individual had said one thing and then done another, or had deliberately attempted to build factions within the team.

It was clear that this executive team would never effectively come together with this untrustworthy individual in the group, so I advised the CEO to replace him. He did so, and in a very short time, the team finally had coalesced and began to perform as a high-functioning unit, but nearly a year of the organization's time had already been wasted. The CEO's slowness to solve his executive team issues was a costly error. The board had run out of patience with him and his management team, and within eight months, it had replaced nearly all of them.

Trust is obviously a core ingredient in team performance, and trust flows from the font of strong character habits. Whenever executive team members suffer from significant weakness in any of the four Keystone Character Habits, mutual trust within the team takes a body blow. Of course, misunderstandings about purpose, conflict over roles, and disagreements about how decisions are made can all erode trust, even among team members with very strong character habits. That's why CEOs need to ensure that the executive team exhibits a command of *all* of the critical elements of the highly effective executive team: goals, roles, processes, and interactions.

We've seen that the executive team has three major areas of responsibility: structuring the organization, creating strong dynamics, and engaging the workforce in the achievement of vision and goals. Now let's take a closer look at what those responsibilities entail, and how the executive teams under the leadership of the CEOs in our research project approach them.

Structuring the Organization

Like a rusted bridge support or crumbling high-rise foundation, a weak organizational structure can bring the whole operation tumbling down. For a new executive team, therefore, examining the structure of the organization should be near the top of its agenda for increasing effective execution.[3]

Of course, other issues can mask structural flaws. Uncovering those flaws can require deep probing and painfully honest assessment. If an organization experiences significant overlap in the work done by different departments or divisions, if departments function as disconnected silos operating in their own world, and if rules, policies, and procedures interfere with people's ability to get things done in a timely manner, then the organization likely has a flawed structure. For an organization to execute effectively, it must track down and eradicate the sources of such symptoms of structural weakness.

The hallmark of a well-structured organization is when it holds together as one system—that is, each part plays an important role in an interconnected whole. To assess the structural strength of the organizations in our study, our research focused on conditions such as:

- The level of empowerment people in the workforce have to make decisions that enable the organization to respond to changing conditions.

- The presence of disconnected silos.

- The strength of information sharing across departments.

What did we discover? Our research revealed that Virtuoso CEOs enjoy significantly fewer problems stemming from a dysfunctional structure than do the Self-Focused CEOs.[4] Specifically, the data shows that:

- Virtuoso CEOs and executive teams create organizational structures with fewer silos, where people are more apt to share information across departments. As one CEO among this group told us, "Silos were mainly eliminated because of the common vision and mission that drove the organization . . . The customer's success defined the organization's and the individual's success. It was this message that was the main driver to eliminate silos and encourage employees to work together."

- The people in organizations led by Virtuosos have more freedom and authority to make decisions, and are more empowered in general. As one Virtuoso leader explained, "If you have employees who are inspired by your vision and mission and you trust them to do their jobs, they will make decisions that are aligned to the vision and mission [of the organization]."

- Their organizations are simply more flexible and able to respond more quickly to changing requirements. As a Virtuoso CEO explained, "The structure and employees' understanding of the vision, mission, and strategy allowed our company to move very quickly . . . If the 'why' is clearly communicated and understood by employees, the 'how' [of accomplishing it] becomes much easier."

Beyond their lower scores in these elements of organizational structure, what did we learn about the structural issues surrounding the Self-Focused CEOs and their executive teams? Here are some comments their employees offered:

- "Managers and leaders are disconnected from frontline workers."

- "We say we want to change and to be the best, but it isn't reflected in management standards."

- "Seems like there is a lack of agreement or alignment by senior leadership and it gets taken out on the lower-level employees, so there is a limited sense of success and collaboration of cross-functional teams."

In short, ROC research indicates that leadership teams that echo the strong character habits and principled practices of a Virtuoso CEO structure their organizations to be better functioning, more resilient, and more adaptable than those led by leadership teams of less highly rated character and principles.

Creating Positive, Productive Organizational Dynamics

When I use the term *organizational dynamics*, I am referring to the myriad ways that people interact as they work together. When things go well, these interactions are positive, harmonious, and energized. When things aren't going so well, interactions within the organization and the working environment they create can be hostile, competitive, and destructive.

A flawed organizational structure can be the systemic factor that leads to dysfunctional organizational dynamics. But even an ideal structure offers no guarantee that the dynamics will be positive, harmonious, and energized. As the ROC data revealed, this is where the character habits of the executive team come into play.

When we designed this component of the research, we chose five dimensions of organizational dynamics to study. We asked the employees of the Virtuoso and the Self-Focused CEOs to indicate how often they:

1. Work in teams

2. Collaborate

3. Engage in innovation

4. Experience a high and positive organizational energy

5. Communicate effectively

Figure 5-1 shows the consistent differences in the responses we received to those questions from the employees of the Virtuoso CEOs and the Self-Focused CEOs. As the figure illustrates, the employees of the Virtuoso CEOs and their teams rated the frequency of activities that promote organizational dynamics in their organizations much higher

FIGURE 5-1

Frequency of workforce participation in activities or efforts associated with organizational dynamics

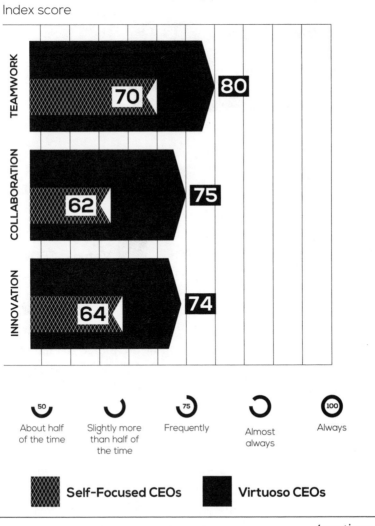

(continued)

FIGURE 5-1 *(continued)*

Frequency of workforce participation in activities or efforts associated with organizational dynamics

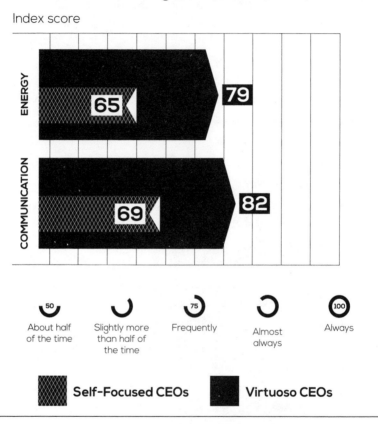

Index score

than did the employees of the Self-Focused leaders, from ten points higher on innovation to a thirteen points higher for collaboration—both significant differences that can't be attributed to chance.

As these results indicate, employees of Virtuoso leaders rated their organizations as stronger in *all* of the fundamental factors we recognize as central to business success in today's challenging global marketplace, including innovation, teamwork, and collaboration. These findings alone powerfully underscore the critical importance of organizational dynamics—and the substantial ROC edge Virtuoso leadership can offer in this area.

The employee comments we received offered even greater insights into the qualitative experience of working in an organization with positive dynamics as opposed to that of working in one run by Self-Focused leadership. When we asked the employees of Self-Focused leaders in our study to "tell us what it feels like to work in your company," here are some of their responses:

- "It feels like nothing is ever good enough, no matter what steps are taken."

- "We are constantly talked down to, blamed for the mistakes of others, and never given annual reviews. Feedback is only for mistakes, not jobs well done. Our raises are only cost of living, never anything for increased skills or as a reward for anything done for the company. When something goes wrong, middle management spends more time pointing the finger away from themselves than trying to fix the problem. Employees are severely chastised in front of other employees regularly."

- "Whenever possible, employees avoid speaking to middle management and obtain information on jobs from other employees . . . Morale is low and falling."

- "If you realize you've made a mistake, it's better to hope no one catches it than to report it. I dread each workday."

Now contrast those comments to the responses to the same question from employees who worked for the Virtuoso CEOs:

- "This is the best company in the world. It's the place I want to be all my work life. I truly feel the energy from all levels of management and coworkers . . . We are all driven to be our best and it shows. I love my job."

- "Working at this company is very intense. While this intensity at times has a negative effect, overall it is a positive. This place is certainly 'alive.'"

- "I love where I work and look forward to coming to work every day. Our work has meaning and I feel fortunate to work here with people who want to make a difference in the world!"

It seems apparent from the data that the CEOs and their executive teams have a profound influence on the quality of organizational life and, hence, on the productivity of the workforce. That energy and productivity are a direct result of the organizational dynamics fostered by the workplace character and behavior of the CEO and executive team. And as our study revealed, stronger, better character results in stronger, more productive organizational dynamics—a classic illustration of ROC in action.

Building Workforce Engagement

An organization with a clear vision, a strategic focus, and a culture of accountability will go nowhere unless the workforce is organized to work well together and is eager to perform. Every individual has a good deal of discretionary personal energy he or she can devote to his or her work life or spend in other ways. Employees who feel little connection to the organization's goals and missions, who see little correlation between their performance and their compensation, or who have been alienated from the organization's leadership through false promises, disinformation, or outright neglect are likely to be disengaged. Disengaged employees are much more likely to spend their discretionary time planning their next vacation, surfing the Internet, texting endlessly to friends, or simply daydreaming, rather than doing the work they were hired to do. On the other hand, when workers know that their success is directly tied to that of their organization or unit, and when they embrace their leadership's vision, they have a natural incentive to work diligently toward achieving the organization's goals.

So what do we know about the conditions that create an engaged workforce? Organizations that engage their workforces have four features in common:

1. They treat their employees with respect. Employees experience the culture as one that cares for them as people—where they are not treated as "human capital."

2. Employees view policies and practices regarding hiring, compensation, promotions, and recognition as fair and impartial.

3. The organizational culture provides care and support.

4. Employees have a high level of confidence in the executive team.

One could assume that the conditions that contribute or detract from workforce engagement are painfully obvious. But our research—and much casual observation—points to real disconnects in the way some companies treat their workers and the level of engagement they expect those employees to demonstrate in their performance.

To be fully engaged, for example, people need to feel that management respects them. Most people begin to feel extremely disrespected when their leaders assign them unreasonable workloads for weeks or months on end. Individuals who work for high-energy start-ups might have signed on to that kind of marathon stretch, but most workers want to feel that the organizational leadership acknowledges and supports their need for a manageable workload.

Another workforce engagement "killer" comes in the form of unfair hiring, promotion, and compensation policies. A workforce that believes that the best way to get ahead is to curry favor with one or more members of the management team has no incentive to fully embrace the company's vision and strategic goals.

Unfortunately, most of us are all too familiar with these and many other examples of the lack of workforce engagement in some organizations. As a result, the differences between the Virtuoso CEOs and leadership teams and their Self-Focused counterparts in this critical area of organizational success—displayed in figure 5-2—should come as no surprise.

Here are some of the ways employees of the Self-Focused leaders describe the level of workforce engagement that dominates their organizations:

- "The company does not stay true to its own stated goals and ethics sometimes. Certain people are favored, and once you have a bad year, it is hard to get your good name back."

- "It is difficult to feel satisfied at this job when you are just a number."

- "Recent policy changes clearly show the lack of concern for employees' personal lives. All of senior management needs to get real about the high turnover and start asking the hard questions."

FIGURE 5-2

Frequency with which the organization demonstrates qualities that support workforce engagement

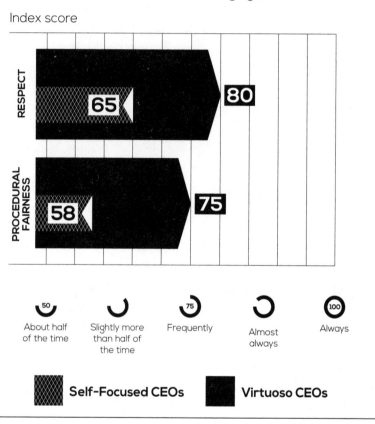

(*continued*)

Contrast those disheartening statements with these much more vibrant and positive comments from the employees of the Virtuoso CEOs and their teams:

- "The work environment is always motivating. Most of the people I work with are great to work with and are very values oriented."

- "The collective employee population seems to share a passion for this industry and the products and services we offer. The community giving and spirit of this company is also a shared passion. The company is often gathered for recognition and fun events, which generates our competitive spirit and will to win in the marketplace!

FIGURE 5-2 *(continued)*

Frequency with which the organization demonstrates qualities that support workforce engagement

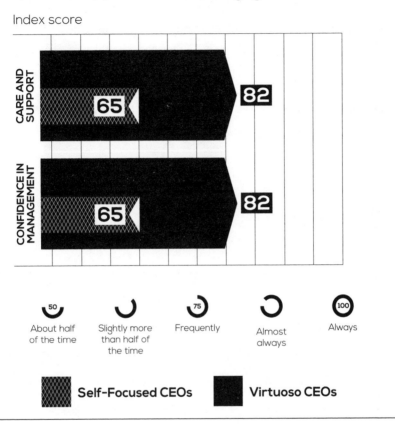

Index score

I strive to be better every day and help lead with the values, integrity, and acumen consistently demonstrated by our CEO."

- "During a time when things were really tough for our company, our CEO demonstrated confidence in his team that we could find a way out—that he believed we could do it and that he was there to lead us through it. It motivated everyone to come together and get the job done. And in two years, we hit it out of the park!"

In numerous ways, our research underscored the connection between the level of workforce engagement in an organization and the executive team's strength of character. When an executive team displays strong character habits, it naturally tends to create a positive, caring, supportive, fair, and respectful work environment—the kind of work environments most people are drawn to. We've seen that the character habits of the executive team are a direct reflection of the character of the CEO who leads them. Clearly, therefore, the organization's level of workforce engagement is directly tied to leadership character, shown in figure 5-3. Our research data revealed that the

FIGURE 5-3

Senior team character versus workforce engagement

Index score

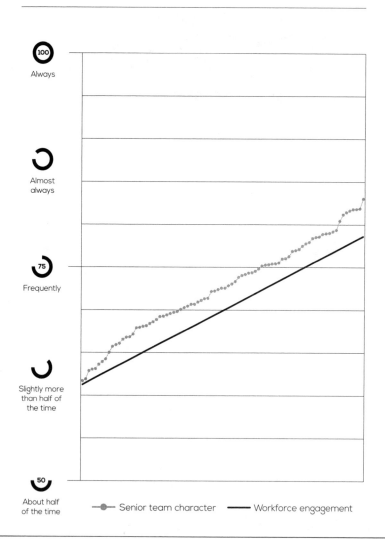

stronger the executive team's character, the more engaged the workforce will be in achieving the organization's missions, goals, and targeted business results.

Improving the ROC of Any Executive Team

ROC research leaves little doubt that the character of the CEO establishes the character of the executive team and the organizational culture that team must promote throughout the organization. As we've seen, the CEO is responsible for the executive team's membership and performance. To maintain strong leadership standards—and to achieve strong business results—the CEO must be vigilant, impartial, and quick to respond to issues stemming from his or her team's performance. Sometimes that response will require the replacement of weak team members. But other times, the CEO can lead the team to target areas of marginal weakness and then work diligently to strengthen its skills in those areas.

I've devoted all of part III to ideas and techniques for improving leadership character, the character habits leaders demonstrate through their behavior, and the ROC those leaders achieve for their organization. But here, let me remind you of the fundamental truth about character habits first discussed in chapter 3: even the Keystone Character Habits of integrity, responsibility, forgiveness, and compassion are *simply habits*. Like any habit, these keystones of strong character and Virtuoso leadership can be learned, practiced, and strengthened over time.

That means that organizations can revitalize the dismal organizational dynamics and reverse the downward trajectory of workforce engagement that results from weak-character leadership and the poor organizational structure—and business returns—it creates.

A low-scoring team can move up the Character Curve by developing behaviors that mirror the four Keystone Character Habits that our research has revealed at the heart of principled, Virtuoso leadership. Those Keystone Leadership Behaviors include:

1. Keeping promises and following through on commitments—a function of the *integrity* habit.

2. Owning up to mistakes and working to correct them—a function of the *responsibility* habit.

3. Accepting that other people will make mistakes—a function of the *forgiveness* habit.

4. Treating people as people, not numbers or commodities, by helping them develop their personal skills and accomplish their personal goals—a function of the *compassion* habit.

Of all the ways the executive team can relate to the people in the workforce, the behaviors based on these four Keystone Character Habits are the most appreciated by employees and make the most difference in their ratings of organizational dynamics, structure, and the level of workforce engagement those factors produce.

These behaviors are simple to understand, but replacing old habitual behaviors with new ones of *any* kind can be a difficult challenge. That's why the CEO and his or her entire executive team must be on board and eager to up the ante on the character they exhibit through their behavior in the workplace. As we learn in chapter 7, habits live on through the persistence of sometimes hidden forces. That's why CEOs need to put the forces of strong character and strong moral principles to work promoting the habits that drive the organizational success.

Building on the Bedrock of Character

In the first two chapters of part II, we've taken an in-depth look at the work of the CEO and the executive team. We've examined not only what behaviors characterize a Virtuoso versus a Self-Focused CEO and the executive teams they lead, but how employees rate and respond to the behavior of both types of leadership. We've also taken a close look at the specific responsibilities and most critical tasks of leadership, and how character shapes the way CEOs and the members of their teams approach that work.

Perhaps most importantly, however, we've learned that every element of the highly functioning organization rests upon the bedrock of character:

- The *character of the CEO and executive team* set the standards for the character habits, principles, expectations, and behaviors that will give form to the organization's culture.

- That organizational culture, fostered and guided by the leadership team, fuels *workforce engagement*, which establishes and feeds organizational dynamics as every member of the workforce does his or her part to help the organization succeed.

- Those *organizational dynamics* determine the level of innovation, teamwork, collaboration, adaptability, and other critical talents the organization will bring to bear in the pursuit of its mission and goals.

- The *business model* sets forth leadership's vision, strategic focus, and standards of accountability that, in turn, establish the organization's mission and goals.

When all of these elements are in place, the organization is poised for execution, ready to pursue its mission with speed, adaptability, and focus. I call this structure of highly effective execution the Execution Readiness model, shown in figure 5-4.

It's not unusual for a long-term research project to continue to grow in definition and scope as it progresses, as we noted at the beginning of this chapter. Our initial exploration into CEO character and its influence on the organization entered into much richer and more revealing territory as we expanded our work to include the influence the character of the senior executive team has on an organization. Through that new level of exploration, we were able to gain a much deeper and broader understanding of the true role of character in determining the strength and approach of organizational leadership and its effect on the workforce and ultimately on business results.

As a result, we expanded the research into the measurable ways that the character-driven influences of both the CEO and his or her executive team shape the organization's results. Those findings lead us to the understanding of Return on Character that forms the central message of this book. Next, in the final chapter of part II, we focus on the big-picture results of the ROC research. There we'll examine the hard numbers that reflect precisely what the data has revealed about the connection between leadership character and

FIGURE 5-4

The Execution Readiness model

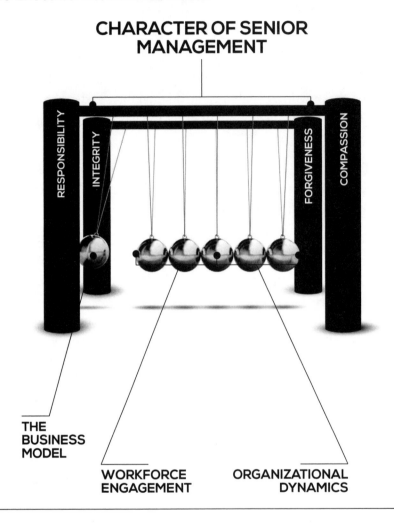

CHARACTER OF SENIOR MANAGEMENT

RESPONSIBILITY

INTEGRITY

FORGIVENESS

COMPASSION

THE BUSINESS MODEL

WORKFORCE ENGAGEMENT

ORGANIZATIONAL DYNAMICS

business results and, specifically, what those results mean for *every-one*: investors, employees, customers, economies, and the environ-ment. With that understanding, we'll all be better prepared to put the lessons of ROC to work in our own organizations and in our lives; to improve our own approach to leadership; to build stronger teams and more agile, effective organizations; and to gain the unique winning edge that only a foundation of high-character leadership can provide.

The Executive Team and ROC

1. **The CEO is responsible for creating a strong senior executive team that reflects his or her character habits and principles and promotes the organizational culture formed by those characteristics.**

2. **The work of the executive team is to create the organizational dynamics, structure, and workforce engagement that position the organization to effectively execute its business plan.**

3. **Virtuoso executive teams promote a culture and structure that foster strong organizational dynamics.** Elements of such a culture and structure include high levels of teamwork, collaboration, innovation, organizational energy, and communication.

4. **Workers become engaged when they feel like an integral part of the organization and its success.** As a result, Virtuoso executive teams lead highly engaged workforces.

5. **By improving behaviors that reflect the four Keystone Character Habits of leadership, executive team members can improve their character ratings and contribute to stronger organizational results.** The four Keystone Leadership Behaviors that executive team members can adopt in order to achieve this improvement are:

   - Keeping promises and following through on commitments (the *integrity* habit).

   - Owning up to mistakes (the *responsibility* habit).

   - Accepting that other people will make mistakes (the *forgiveness* habit).

   - Treating people as people—showing interest in them and helping them accomplish their personal goals and develop their skills (the *compassion* habit).

6. **Execution Readiness rests upon a foundation of CEO character.** Virtuoso leadership teams are much more effective at building upon a

foundation of CEO character by promoting an organizational culture that creates positive, productive organizational dynamics, which in turn builds high-energy workforce engagement and thereby drives the organization to achieve its mission and goals. The Execution Readiness model positions any business to achieve maximum returns.

6

The ROC Ripple Effect

Bringing Every Stakeholder
into the Winner's Circle

Throughout this book, you've read of character-driven leaders who have connected their head to their heart. By now I'm sure the meaning of that phrase is clear: when we approach the complex task of organizational leadership as whole human beings guided by principles and strong character habits, rather than as coldly rational machines driven solely by self-interest, our decisions and actions are motivated by a much broader understanding of value. When we care about our organization's people, culture, alliances, customers, and community as much as we care about its market share, we're less willing to disregard the common good, considering it "the cost of doing business." As the ROC study revealed, the strongest leaders understand the *true* costs of such reckless decisions.

For the past twenty-five years, I—along with my colleagues at KRW— have been energized by the single purpose of helping leaders connect their heads to their hearts. Driven by this purpose, I've devoted several years of my life and a considerable amount of my personal finances to collect and analyze hard data that might shed light on the validity of the observation that strong leaders are guided by their character habits. The central question of this research: Does leadership character have any effect on business results? More specifically, do leaders who have grown into integrated, complete people—the Integrated Human I described in chapter 2—deliver better business results than those who have failed to develop the full set of reasoning abilities, intuitions, drives, and personality traits necessary for character-driven decision making?

These questions have been decidedly difficult to answer. Researching the multiple aspects of character and the equally multifaceted processes of business leadership has been a demanding undertaking. Over 120 CEOs enrolled in KRW's research study, and we have gathered complete character data sets on 84 of them, including observations from over 8,400 randomly selected employees. In this chapter, we summarize the compelling findings we've gathered. We also introduce some of the individuals who participated in the study and learn a bit about their organizations.

While others have investigated many aspects of CEO performance, their research traditionally has overlooked the role of leadership character in organizational results. But that role has merely been hidden in plain sight. Any number of much more visible factors can be used to explain strong business results—the business model, a competitor's missteps, or uncontrolled macroeconomic forces. Prior to our research and the models it provides, there's been no way to assess character, to identify it and draw it out from the shadows of more readily defined business forces. (In appendix B, you'll find a detailed review of this subject, as well as our data on ROA and character.)

Most analysts or academics mention character as a major factor in shaping business results only after a prominent company's board has brought in a slash-and-burn CEO who promptly proceeded to destroy the organization. Then the media and markets froth with stories of how that single individual's lack of principles and character brought about the tragic downfall of a once-good company. If you're searching for examples, just think of WorldCom CEO Bernard Ebbers, who went to prison for cooking the company's books to cover up its unsustainable debt. Or Jeffrey Skilling and Kenneth Lay, who drove the nation's seventh-largest business, Enron, into bankruptcy through fraud and mismanagement. Or Robert Benmosche, who proudly defended AIG's awarding of over $450 million in executive bonuses on the heels of a controversial $173 billion government bailout—designed to save the company he (and those executives) had driven to the edge

The ROC Ripple Effect 131

of a bankruptcy, with calamitous global implications. Benmosche then went on to attribute criticisms of the bonuses to the "ignorance . . . of the public at large, the government, and other constituencies."[1]

Whenever the unscrupulousness of one of these all-too-common rogue CEOs rises to the public attention, there's no reluctance to call "bad character" the reason behind the organization's downfall. Now we can make solid progress in addressing an issue first noted in the introduction, which asked, "Why is it that we never seem to hear about how a CEO's *good* character has contributed to organizational success?" Our research results and the stories that accompany them will draw much-needed attention to that *other* side of the CEO character story.

Does CEO character significantly influence business results? The answer to this important question is a definitive yes. Through KRW's robust descriptive research study, we have found an observable, consistent relationship between a leader's character and hard business metrics provided by the organization's return on assets, or ROA.

In previous chapters, we have examined individual elements of the research and processes involved in the ROC study. Here we're going to talk about the big picture, as we see the answers our research has revealed for a cluster of questions that surround that single central issue: How *does* character influence business returns? What is the ripple effect of an organization's ROC? Does the ROC effect extend outside of improved business results, to employees, customers, communities, and beyond? To explore answers to those questions, we'll be looking beyond the hard numbers the ROC data provides to hear from the survey participants themselves—CEOs and frontline workers alike—to get their personal stories on the ROC they've observed and experienced in their own organizations. We'll also include some media and business analysts' observations of one of the companies in the ROC research—perhaps America's most well-known character-driven organization—Costco Wholesale.

Our findings are clear: leaders of strong character *do* create more value for their organization than do their low-character counterparts. They lead highly principled executive teams who in turn lead a highly engaged workforce. Their organizations excel at innovation, teamwork, and collaboration. And they achieve a higher ROA for investors.

The ripple effects of those results extend well beyond the boardroom and investors' circle to bring value to employees, customers, and the communities surrounding the organizations' operations, and even on to the environment. That's ROC in action.

The Return on Character for Investors

Our first finding gets to the heart of ROC research, as it focuses on the question of whether organizations run by CEOs of strong character achieve better ROA than do those run by leaders of weak character. To begin that exploration, we asked CEOs in the study to provide us with financial data (total assets and net operating income) for the two fiscal years before the research surveys.

Twenty-six of the CEOs didn't need to supply that data, because they led public companies with published financial statements. Of the privately held companies, some—but not all—gave us the financial data we asked for. In all, we acquired data for forty-four (or 52 percent of the total participant organizations). As we reviewed the profiles of those companies and their leaders, we discovered that they formed a sample that accurately represented the entire population of CEOs in the study. (Appendix B contains a full discussion of the sample size.) The members of this group were spread all along the Character Curve, and they represented the same mix of large, small, public, and private organizations and business sectors found among all study participants.

When we used this data to compute the average ROA (which represents net operating income as a percent of total assets) over the two-year period for which we obtained financial data, the results were startling. As figure 6-1 (also figure I-1) shows, the Virtuoso CEOs at the top end of the curve created a return on assets nearly *five times greater* than did the Self-Focused CEOs at the bottom of the curve.

Given the broad difference this data highlights, we wanted to determine whether other variables might be part of this equation. So, in addition to character, the research team compared ROA and political beliefs, size of organization, type of organization, tenure and age of the CEO, and the level of workforce engagement.

FIGURE 6-1

Return on assets

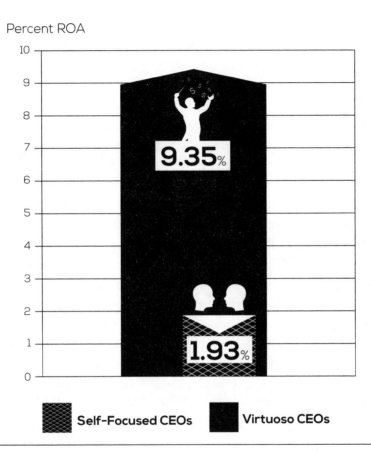

Percent ROA

9.35%

1.93%

Self-Focused CEOs   Virtuoso CEOs

We quickly determined that leadership's political beliefs don't seem to have any effect on the organization's business results. There were equal numbers of conservatives and liberals among both the high-ROA achievers and the lower ones. The tenures of the Virtuoso CEOs and the Self-Focused CEOs were nearly identical. Both groups included many long-term CEOs as well as those who had been in the role for only a year. None of these factors seem statistically linked with high or low ROA.

But two variables did stand out: workforce engagement and organization size. It should be no surprise that workforce engagement levels are higher for the companies with a high ROA—in our research, companies that also were led by CEOs with high character scores. As we saw in chapter 5, an organization's level of workforce engagement correlates closely with its CEO's character. Virtuoso leaders create positive work environments where people become highly engaged. These employees see their success linked closely to that of the organization, so they go all-in to help the company pursue its goals. Self-Focused CEOs and their teams are less successful at connecting with their workforce, and as a result, their people can be apathetic about the organization's outcomes.

The relationship between the size of an organization and ROA was a less predictable finding. The small, private companies (fewer than five hundred employees) in the ROC study didn't do as well as the medium-sized and large companies (over two thousand employees). Of course, small companies can't always afford to hire the best talent, but those in our study attracted CEOs with character scores only four points lower than the large companies, not a significant difference. So the character of the CEO does not seem to be a factor. It is more likely that the younger CEOs in the small companies were simply less skilled than the CEOs who led the large companies in the study. Also, many small companies are run by entrepreneurial founders who may be strongly driven to achieve and are willing to do so at all costs. Very few of the small companies in our study were public companies; most were either nonprofit or privately held. Larger companies also have business models that have survived the test of time and competition. As noted in our discussion about the academic research in appendix B, business results are determined by three factors and only one of them is the CEO effect.

More revealing, however, is the fact that for all size companies, the Virtuoso CEOs created a higher ROA than did the Self-Focused leaders (see table B-4 in appendix B).

After reviewing all the data, however, the results were clear. Within the study, organizations with CEOs who achieved the highest character scores also achieved the highest ROA, regardless of the size of the organization. Does this result indicate that all successful organizations are run by CEOs of high character? No. But it does establish the fact that when an organization is led by a CEO and executive team of high character, *on average* it will produce a greater ROA than organizations run by low-character leaders.

That's not to say that every leader of great character helms a high-performance organization. Macroeconomic factors and a flawed business model can sink a strong-character CEO. As I pored over this data, I was struck by how similar the game of business is to the world of American professional basketball. Most professional basketball players are very tall. There are a few exceptions, but not many. But while height is clearly a critical quality in a basketball player, it isn't the only one. There are many tall people in the world who can't play basketball. Likewise, the best business executives have strong character, but they also have to know how to run a business. Add strong character to solid business skills and you have a dream-team executive: a skilled professional leader with strong character habits. The data is clear: investors definitely have a better chance to win the game of business when a Virtuoso CEO is in charge of the organization. With global competition at an all-time high, you can't afford to go into the arena with a B-list leader. Companies who try to compete under the leadership of a skilled but Self-Focused CEO are setting themselves up to lose.

Investor return is the common measure of value creation in the corporate world. Certainly, that return is an important metric. But it isn't the only one. A business organization is a social entity, and as such, it can create or destroy value for people throughout its ecosphere. Besides investors, any number of people, organizations, and other entities feel the ripple effect of an organization's business results, including customers, employees, the communities surrounding the business, and beyond. Now let's take a look at what our study results showed about these ripple effects of ROC.

The Return on Character for Employees

What do employees want? Well, you should know. That's because in all likelihood, you *are* an employee. Even if you're the CEO of a global multibillion-dollar enterprise, you still work for someone. So ask yourself, "Do I look forward to going to work each day? Am I motivated to do my job as well as I possibly can? Am I treated with respect—as a person, not an object? Do I *matter* to the organization?" I would be surprised if anyone reading this wants to answer no to these four questions. That's because the questions revolve around the universal human desires for pride and satisfaction, and their answers lie at the heart of what drives workers—at any level—to be engaged in the success of the organization they work for.

Figure 6-2 shows how the employees of the strong-character CEOs—the Virtuosos—and those of the Self-Focused CEOs rate their sense of pride and satisfaction in the work they do and the organizations they work for.

As you can see, comparisons between the responses of these two groups show that the employees of Virtuoso CEOs reported higher levels of both workplace pride and satisfaction than did those of the Self-Focused CEOs. As we learned earlier, these two emotional responses to the workplace

FIGURE 6-2

Employees' rating of sense of pride and satisfaction

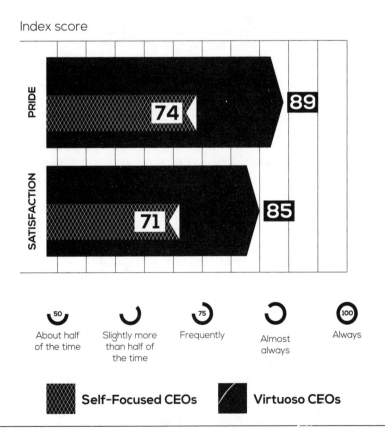

play a critical role in determining workforce engagement, which in turn plays a critical role in driving business performance and results. Now let's look deeper into these findings to form a clearer understanding of the people and organizations whose work–lives they reflect.

Better Employee Engagement, Better ROC

Bob Chapman is one of the CEOs in the ROC study who really gets it when it comes to making the connection between an engaged and well-cared-for workforce and organizational success. Chapman is the CEO of Barry-Wehmiller, a $1.5 billion global industrial equipment firm headquartered in St. Louis, Missouri, with over seven thousand employees in sixty-five locations worldwide. This privately held company states on its website, "Building GREAT people is our business," and that idea lies at the heart of the leadership model the company uses to train members of its executive team.[2]

It's difficult to state with 100 percent certainty that this people-centric model is the primary reason why Chapman's business is so successful, but it certainly *is* successful. As Chapman told a group of MBA students in one of his lectures, "Our year-over-year compounded return to investors has exceeded the performance of Warren Buffett's Berkshire Hathaway." He added, "In addition to our focus on building great people, we also have built a great business."

I first met Chapman for breakfast at a hotel restaurant near his office. Over the next two hours, he told me the story of how he came to realize that he could, and should, build a people-centric business. Chapman had flown to South Carolina as the new owner of a company his group had just taken over. He began the day by sitting down with the company's employees as they had a pre-workday cup of coffee, and he immediately was struck by how much fun they were having talking about the upcoming basketball games of March Madness.

"After the coffee time was over," Chapman told me, "I went from the experience of seeing how much fun people were having to a meeting with the customer service group, and they did not appear to be happy." Chapman had an idea: "Out of my mouth came the words, 'Good morning. We're going to play a game. You will win as the team wins.'" Chapman went on to outline a way of working that was structured along the lines of a good-natured, team-oriented competition—an approach he hoped his employees would find both challenging and fun. "They had dozens of reasons why it wouldn't work," he admitted, "but I had an answer for every one of them." Chapman had seen how animated and engaged these people could be, and he was determined to create a culture and environment that would trigger that level of workforce engagement.

"That was the turning point," he explained. "We began to discover the leadership model that we now teach. It wasn't long after that when I realized that we were really in the business of building great people."

Chapman told me that not only did he feel this was the right thing to do, but he also discovered that a happy and respected workforce is apt to be more productive. "I believe that what people want is work that is meaningful and done in the company of people we care about," he told me. "I decided that tending to people might also become a major competitive advantage."

Caring for employees and creating a work environment of respect and engagement involves more than offering fair compensation. It sometimes requires a leader to think out of the box. Chapman's company was hit hard in the 2008 financial crisis, when orders for new equipment plummeted. His company could have joined thousands of others caught in the teeth of those tough economic times and chosen the knee-jerk response of reducing costs by reducing its workforce. Instead, Chapman and his management team came up with an innovative solution that cut Barry-Wehmiller's payroll by $20 million; they simply asked their employees to volunteer for unpaid furloughs. People at higher job levels welcomed the time off. People who couldn't afford to take time off didn't need to, and everyone at the company kept their jobs. Here's the reaction of one employee:

> Bob [Chapman] encouraged the senior leadership to find another way to meet financial objectives without laying people off. This was courageous and the right thing to do if we believe in a people-centric culture. Bob's leadership was more than inspiring. It left a lifelong impact on future leaders as well as all employees.

Nearly all of the open-ended comments the employees made were overwhelmingly positive. The ROC for employees is perhaps captured best in the words of this Barry-Wehmiller employee:

> Bob [Chapman] speaks with passion and truth. He truly wants people to reach their full potential. He truly believes that business can have a huge impact on making the world a better place. Bob has inspired me to become the best father, husband, associate, and person that I can be.

Comments like these underscore the overall results of our research, which show that employees who are treated with respect, fairness, care, and support enjoy the ROC their leaders produce for the organization. And that kind of positive work environment is the reflection of the character habits of the executive team.

Chapman and his company offer compelling evidence of the benefits organizations can gain by adopting a business model based on the head-and-heart emphasis of Virtuoso leadership. At the end of our breakfast meeting, Chapman said, "Someone told me once that we have been paying people for their hands for years when they would have given us their heads and their hearts for free, if we had just known how to ask. I've learned how to ask and it's a real win-win."

The Value of a Valued Workforce

In the next section of this chapter, we're going to take a close look at a company that participated in our research and has benefited from employee engagement—bulk warehouse retailer Costco. But that company deserves mention here as well. While we've seen that compensation isn't the only way to make employees feel valued and engaged in the organization's success, Costco has become well known for both its high-quality customer service *and* the pay and benefits it offers. In short, Costco has built its substantial success on a business model that emphasizes valuing and caring for its workforce.

That care shows in the comments Costco employees shared with us during our research:

- "It is not a job or a career; it is part of who I am."

- "Every employee matters at Costco, which is proven by our great benefits offered to even part-time employees, which few companies now provide. Promoting from within over 80 percent of the time creates opportunities to strive towards."

- "Most people believe in what we are trying to do as a company. It feels like we are all working towards a common goal."

ROC research revealed the benefits of Costco's Virtuoso leadership, but the evidence has been clear to Wall Street for some time. In June 2013, in a *Bloomberg BusinessWeek* article, Brad Stone outlined Costco's approach to employee compensation and care, and credited its role in the organization's success.[3] Stone wrote at a time when the US minimum wage was at $7.25 an hour. In contrast, Costco's hourly workers received an average pay of $20.89 an hour (not including overtime), and 88 percent of the company's workers had company-sponsored health insurance. Stone also noted that at the same time, Walmart was paying its full-time employees an average of $12.67 per hour, and reported that "more than half" of its people had company-sponsored health insurance. According to Stone, Costco leadership believed that a "happier work environment will result in a more profitable company." He quoted the company's CEO, Craig Jelinek, as saying, "I just think people need to make a living wage with health benefits. It also puts more money back into the economy and creates a healthier country."[4]

Costco also believes in hiring from within. In an interview with *Motley Fool* contributor Austin Smith, Jelinek described how many of Costco's vice presidents had been with the company for many years. "Most have worked with the company in key executive positions for twenty-eight to twenty-nine years."[5] As you will learn in the next section, Costco's employee and leadership responses, as well as its business results, attest to the wisdom of the character and principles reflected in these statements, and in the company's approach to leadership.

A workforce that feels cared for is more productive than one that feels neglected, and that translates into bottom-line financial results. So why do so many CEOs and their teams fail to create a work environment that promotes this kind of workforce engagement? Unfortunately, we at KRW have seen that many senior leaders simply don't know how to go about it and are afraid to try. This lack of both skill and willingness is especially prevalent among leaders who have failed to develop into the Integrated Human model of leadership. As a result, they lack the personal resources and mental complexity necessary for the work of Virtuoso leadership.

It doesn't have to be this way. We could build in character development as part of the coursework in business schools (and as you learn in part III of this book, we can improve our own Virtuoso skills as well as those of individuals already in leadership positions). All of us can work toward making character development so essential to effective leadership that it becomes part of the essential core curricula of business schools, and serious substantial courses on self-reflection, mental complexity, and the self-transforming mind-set will be standard fare for our next great leaders.

The Return on Character for Customers

Customers also win when the organizations they deal with are led by individuals who have their heads connected to their hearts. While our ROC research was limited to the study of organizations, their CEOs, and their employees, the responses we gathered in that study strongly indicate how those who work directly with customers gauge the level of their customers' satisfaction.

The employees of Virtuoso CEOs in our research rated their organizations as much better than those of their competitors. These employees also saw their organizations as providing greater value for customers than did the employees of the Self-Focused leaders and their teams. Based on those responses, figure 6-3 shows the ROC for the customers and clients of Virtuoso-led organizations, as compared to those under the leadership of Self-Focused CEOs.

So exactly *how* do customers benefit from doing business with Virtuoso-led companies? Let's take a closer look by returning to an organization we've already recognized for its Virtuoso leadership.

FIGURE 6-3

Employees' views of customer satisfaction

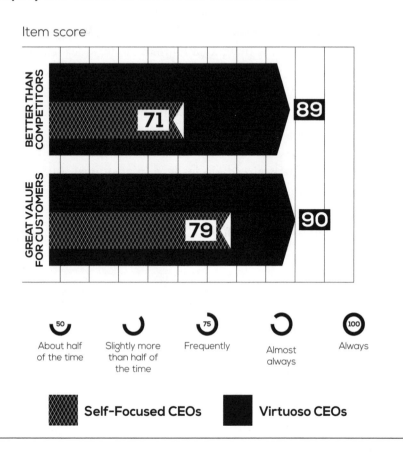

Item score

Self-Focused CEOs   *Virtuoso CEOs*

Inside Costco's Customer Service Success

Jim Sinegal, the cofounder of Costco Wholesale, who retired as CEO in 2012, built his warehouse-members model with a strong understanding of the importance of caring for customers. The benefits of that care are evident in the almost 90 percent renewal rate of Costco members year after year.[6] With nearly 50 million members at about $55 each, this renewal rate represents big money. Sinegal's core principles of leadership—and strong employee satisfaction, customer satisfaction, and business results—continue to guide the business. More than a year after Sinegal's retirement, a *Bloomberg BusinessWeek* article called Costco, "the cheapest, happiest company in the world," under the leadership of its new CEO, Craig Jelinek.[7]

The organization's reputation for integrity is a critical factor in its success. Costco is known for its promise to members, which includes the commitment to mark up the cost of items in its warehouses by no more than 15 percent.[8] This is a contract that members have come to trust. According to the American Customer Satisfaction Index, in 2013 Costco's customer satisfaction rate had gone up every year but one (2009) since 1999, and was higher than that of Sam's Club, Lowe's, Staples, and other organizations in its marketplace.[9] By contrast, in the first quarter of that year, Bloomberg reported that Walmart had placed last in the index, for the sixth year in a row.[10] Costco's picture continued to grow brighter; in the fourth quarter of 2013, its membership topped 71 million, a 4 percent increase in new membership over the previous year.[11]

Business articles touting Costco's success in courting and keeping new members abound, but ROC research and my own personal observation have revealed that there's more to Costco's winning equation than its membership contract. As one of the Costco employees who participated in our study said:

> For me, the best thing about working here is that we have a purpose, and it isn't to deliver great sales or margin to improve the share value, but to serve our members. The members pay to shop here and we have a duty to ensure that they are happy, so they stay members and attract new ones. I feel proud to work at Costco.

Another Costco employee summed up the ROC to Costco's customers:

> Costco is one of the only companies that works to improve the quality of its merchandise while *lowering* the price. We want to take care of the members and give them good reasons to come see us again.

Beyond the study, I've also made it a point to talk with Costco employees and members in locations around the United States. No one has ever told me about an unpleasant experience in a Costco warehouse. While many in the business world may balk at Costco's business model, which, as we saw earlier, includes compensation for frontline employees well above that of most of its competitors, it's hard to argue with the company's success. Between 2004 and 2013, the company's shares returned more than four times the market average, and by 2012, its revenues had advanced 50 percent, to reach nearly $100 billion.[12]

The ripple effect of ROC is illustrated in every aspect of Costco's operation: strong customer loyalty demonstrated through high renewal rates on customer membership; a satisfied, engaged workforce; and strong business results in a tough, competitive marketplace. Together, Costco's model and results offer compelling evidence of the winning that ROC character-led companies—and their customers—can enjoy.

Empowered Employees and Better Customer Relations

Low prices aren't the only key to customer satisfaction. We all know that it is easier to keep a good customer or client than it is to find a new one. Thankfully, many companies are beginning to understand that customer service is more than having a call center where success is measured by how many calls workers can field in an hour.

Kyle Markland, one of the Virtuoso CEOs in our study and the former CEO of Affinity Plus—a large midwestern credit union in which members are customers—pioneered a bold form of workforce empowerment aimed at increasing member satisfaction. He began by working with his board and team to create a new vision for the business. Where the organization's previous focus had been on achieving state dominance by becoming the biggest and most successful credit union in the state, Markland's new vision for the organization was aimed at growing by "building relationships founded on trust."

Markland and his team's first step toward achieving this vision involved changing the way the credit union's frontline employees interacted with its members. They launched this change by giving tellers the new title of "member advisers" or MAs. After a few months, Markland realized that all employees should be member advisers, so ultimately, that became the title and responsibility of everyone on the credit union's staff. In effect, the entire company shared the responsibility of caring for its customers. When the call center had more calls than it could handle, it passed the overflow on to others in the organization.

But, true change is more than label-deep. The credit union's real shift in customer care came when the executive team unleashed its member, organization, employee (MOE) decision-making strategy. MOE guided every MA to abandon procedure-based controls and instead to put the member first in all strategic and operating decisions. Affinity Plus employees were to follow this strategy even if it appeared to conflict with the financial objectives of the business. If an MA made a sound decision that benefited a member but not necessarily the credit union, that adviser would have the organization's complete backing. The threads of Virtuoso leadership are as apparent in this strategy as they are in Costco's. As Markland explained, "My theory was that if we were always benefiting the member, the financials would follow and we would ultimately be rewarded through additional member participation or referrals of family and friends."

In the e-mail he sent out notifying employees of the MOE strategy, Markland wrote:

> No employee will ever get in trouble for doing what is right
> for the member. While this may seem like a simple statement,
> it is not a hollow commitment. Every employee, every man-
> ager, every executive has to believe this and more importantly,
> demonstrate our commitment to it, every day . . . There is only
> one operating policy or guideline you ever need. Trust your
> feelings. If it feels right and makes sense, do it on behalf of
> a member. Do not consider the system capability, policy, or
> procedure—err on doing whatever is necessary for the member
> and allow your manager or supervisor to take care of the rest.
> Finally, be prepared to defend your decision! If your intention
> is to do what is right for the member, you have the support of
> management and your co-workers.

The MOE strategy changed forever how Affinity Plus made decisions and, more importantly, *who* made them. Affinity Plus empowered its MAs to provide more than the basic services of a typical bank teller. The

MAs didn't have to go to a supervisor to ask permission to cash a customer's large check. They also had the authority to waive service fees and to approve loans outside of normal underwriting guidelines. "These changes had a dramatic positive impact on employee engagement," Markland said, "as well as on accountability and results."

Markland anticipated that there would be some mistakes as the new strategy took hold—and there were. According to one of Markland's senior executives, in the beginning, employees were doing crazy things like underwriting $18 loans and even driving across state to help someone look at a used car. "But," she said, "we knew we had to encourage the spirit of this behavior without dampening it. Gradually, the range of what the MAs did to serve customers were all the things we had wanted them to do for years. Now they did it on their own." Markland added, "They took great pride in what they were doing to build relationships founded on trust *and* on the significant impact they were having on our members' lives and the communities in which we operated."

In our research study, Markland's employees frequently mentioned their empowerment as a key element of the customer satisfaction that drives their organization's success:

> Over the years here, [Markland] has consistently delivered the message that we should do our best to get to know our members, treat them as individuals, and be creative. He encourages honesty, responsibility, empowerment, and compassion with our fellow coworkers as well as with our members. We are regular people doing extraordinary things.

> Kyle's [Markland's] vision, guiding principles, and business plan clearly demonstrate his qualities of integrity and responsibility and compassion. He knows people will make mistakes, but as long as they have our members' best interests at heart, these mistakes are forgivable.

> I will never forget that at one seminar he told us that if we made a bad decision on a loan, as long as it was what was best for the member, he would personally 'have our back.' I have thought of

that many times and it is a huge confidence, and empowerment booster.

Kyle [Markland] is a wonderful person to work for. He always takes responsibility for the company and wants to ensure we are doing what is best for people. He has compassion for ALL people, including his employees. He wants to make a difference in the lives of people, and that is what Affinity Plus is doing: changing the world one person at a time.

The customers or members of Affinity Plus were definitely the winners from this trust-based empowerment strategy. After its implementation, membership satisfaction soared. As Markland had predicted, happy customers soon began to enlist family members and friends, and personal referrals soon accounted for over 80 percent of all new customers. The organization's growth surged as well. "We were growing at two to four times the industry average," Markland reported.

The credit union's financial results were equally robust. When the downturn came in 2007–2008, Affinity Plus maintained its solid footing. The quality of its loans, from consumer loans to home mortgages, was very high. After all, each of them was provided in the context of an established relationship between a customer and his or her MA. If a loan or new product wasn't right for a member, "we just wouldn't do it, no matter how good that might have been on the short-term for the organization," Markland said. "If it was right for the member, then we would move a mountain to get it done."

No business organization operates in a vacuum. As much as the concept of customer service has eroded over the past few decades, even virtual online companies still have a connection to people. Affinity Plus proved that it was possible to build trusting relationships with customers online. As Markland said, "The main ingredients of a relationship are there: trust, care, compassion, empathy; they just look different."

Why do so many companies treat their customers as objects and provide them with poor service or products? Creating alienated, dissatisfied, even angry customers can't be good for the bottom line, yet it's a persistent behavior in so many organizations. Both the ROC research and personal observations have convinced me that this short-sighted, Economic Human model of behavior starts at the top of the org chart, with the executive leadership. I've seen too many large organizations where the CEO and executive team live in their own bubble of bottom-line leadership based on cost cutting through a constant reduction in the quality of both their offerings and customer care. These leaders and their organizations fail to treat most people outside the bubble—including customers and the majority of employees—as real people. That's not a sustainable business model.

Virtuoso CEOs and their executive team members tend to be more immediately engaged with both their customers and their employees. As their results (and the results of our research) have shown, organizations that operate on a foundation of integrity, responsibility, forgiveness, and compassion position themselves to build trust-based relationships that increase customer satisfaction *and* organizational returns. Those are the Keystone Character Habits of Virtuoso leadership, and the universal principles that form its foundation.

The Return on Character for Communities and the Environment

An organization's reach can extend well beyond its physical walls and marketplace. Walmart, just one of the thousands of large companies with global reach, influences the lives of as many as *200 million or 300 million people* in an endless variety of ways. Here are just some:

- The decisions made by the Walmart CEO directly impact the lives of the company's 2-million-plus employees around the world.[13]

- When these figures include the families of the employees, the impact of Walmart's leadership decisions could extend to 6 million people or more.

- Add to that total the innumerable vendors and supply-chain players and their employees and the number logically could grow by another 10 million or 15 million.

- Then there are the hundreds of millions of customers who also feel the impact of the company's executive decisions.

- When an organization achieves that kind of size and reach, the decisions it makes about the products it will stock, where they are made, what they are made of, how and where they are sold, how long they last, and how easily they are recycled or disposed of indirectly impact a portion of the world's population that may be too big and diffuse to calculate.

These facts haven't escaped the attention of Walmart—or the marketplace. Walmart is increasingly aware of both the responsibility and the costs that accompany its position as "the world's largest retailer." It has discovered, for example, that focusing on sustainability, from reduced packaging to the conservative use of electricity, has the positive business result of reducing expenses, even as it casts a positive light on its profile as a world citizen.

Some other companies, however, make sustainability the core of their business strategy. Patagonia is one such company, and its former CEO, Casey Sheahan, was a participant in the ROC study.[14] During a lengthy interview, Sheahan shared with me some of the passions that drove him as the organization's leader:

> I think our culture has strengthened and improved and has been rededicated to the mission because of the continuing issues in global climate change. We have a favorite phrase: "There's no business to be done on a dead planet." The culture has really rallied around the urgency of the current environmental crisis. If we prove that an environmental company can be profitable and throw off profits to help with this, it feels good. It's exciting to come into work every day.

Likewise, Sally Jewell, the former CEO of another outdoor gear giant, Recreational Equipment Inc. (REI), was proud of her purpose-driven company, as well as its business results. When we met in her office in 2007, she told me:

> I think there is a pride here that we are working for a higher purpose. And we have grown our company. We're a co-op, so no one

has a gun to our head about growth, but even so, we add six or seven new stores per year. And we've grown about 15 percent in the number of stores and about 8 to 10 percent in comp stores. This is extraordinary.

It was easy to find numerous examples of CEOs in our study who have a sense of responsibility about the common good. All we had to do was go to the upper end of the Character Curve and take a look at the Virtuosos. The highest-scoring belief statement for the Virtuoso CEOs (as rated by their employees) is:

Senior management demonstrates a concern for the common good of the communities in which the company operates.

The average score for this item for all of the Virtuoso CEOs was eighty-nine on a scale from zero to one hundred, where one hundred signifies "always." This is in contrast to a score of sixty-six for the Self-Focused CEOs.

We also asked employees to rate how much they believed their company was "leaving the world a better place" and was also "managed well and financially stable." Figure 6-4 shows how the two groups of CEOs were rated by their employees.

As we learned during the course of our research, Virtuoso CEOs just naturally express a concern for the common good. They understand that most people are inspired by a noble purpose, and they seem to be driven to show each day that their company is adding to the common good rather than destroying it. When organizations place the common good solidly within their strategies and goals, the benefits for their communities and the environment at large can be real and impressive.

REI, for example, puts stewardship at the core of its purpose, and its annual reports include a stewardship report that details the company's efforts at creating an environmentally responsible and sustainable organization through community, sustainable operations, product stewardship, and workplace.[15] Patagonia also issues annual reports on its efforts in environmental and social responsibility, efforts that include environmental grants and internships, responsible supply-chain sourcing, and the use of low-environmental-footprint fibers and materials.[16]

FIGURE 6-4

Employees' rating of their companies

Item score

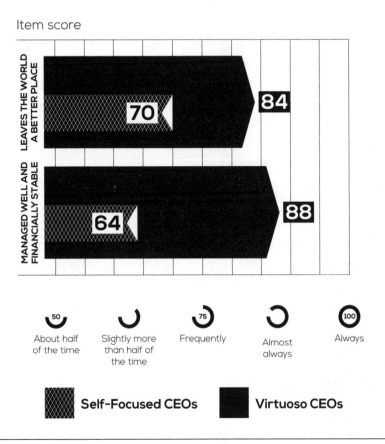

LEAVES THE WORLD A BETTER PLACE: 70, 84

MANAGED WELL AND FINANCIALLY STABLE: 64, 88

50 — About half of the time

Slightly more than half of the time

75 — Frequently

Almost always

100 — Always

▨ Self-Focused CEOs   ■ Virtuoso CEOs

This evidence runs in direct conflict with the viewpoint we so often hear, that "doing good" and "doing well" are incompatible as organizational goals. My conversations with Bob Chapman, Jim Sinegal, Kyle Markland, Casey Sheahan, Sally Jewell, and dozens of other CEOs not mentioned here, combined with the results of the ROC data, demonstrate beyond a reasonable doubt that far from being incompatible, "doing well" and "doing good" are most often two sides of the same coin: the creation of positive value.

All of this is the real and measurable ROC—one that benefits all of us, every day. These are returns whose benefits may be even more valuable tomorrow than they are today.

The Panoramic View of ROC

The ROC Matrix illustrates the four universal principles that form the Keystone Character Habits that guide Virtuoso leadership (see figure 6-5; also figure 1-1). Two of those habits, integrity and responsibility, are associated with the intellectual aspect of leadership, the head. The other two, compassion and forgiveness, rest in the heart of Virtuoso leadership. When we began this study, we wondered which of these two spheres of leadership character is more important when it comes to engaging the workforce and executing the business plan. Our findings have been counterintuitive.

Why? Because we assumed that integrity was the most important character habit and that it could stand alone. We believed, for example, that an executive team of strong integrity could get by with being just okay in showing responsibility, forgiveness, and compassion. And we figured the data would support the commonly accepted view that forgiveness and compassion might be nice to have in a leader, but certainly aren't relevant to the hard-nosed pursuit of ROA. As you've seen, those assumptions were wrong.

FIGURE 6-5

The ROC Matrix

HE♠D	HE♥RT
INTEGRITY	**FORGIVENESS**
Telling the truth	Letting go of one's mistakes
Acting consistently with principles, values, and beliefs (walking the talk)	Letting go of others' mistakes
Standing up for what is right	Focusing on what's right versus what's wrong
Keeping promises	
RESPONSIBILITY	**COMPASSION**
Owning one's personal choices	Empathizing with others
Admitting mistakes and failures	Empowering others
Expressing a concern for the common good	Actively caring for others
	Committing to others' development

The factors that build organizational dynamics (collaboration, innovation, adaptability, teamwork, communication) are inextricably linked to those that create workforce engagement (respect, fairness, care and support, confidence in management). Most of the latter are directly related to the character habits of the heart. Virtuoso leadership—and the results it obtains—are strongest when the executive team draws on all four principles represented in the ROC Matrix, and their decisions, actions, and Keystone Character Habits are guided by both head *and* heart.

In this chapter, we've explored the broad reach of the ROC ripple effect to see how the ROC can extend beyond any individual CEO, employee, organization, and marketplace to impact entire communities—even the world. But what can we do with this information? We're all the product of our genetics and our past; human nature, education, mentors, career events, and other life experiences shape our approach to leadership and our understanding of its role. But like all of life around us, we humans carry the potential for continual growth and development. Our ideas about leadership don't have to be like ants caught in amber, frozen in time and forever locked in the past. We can use the findings from the ROC study and other information offered here to develop new ideas, new processes, *new character habits* that can take our leadership skills to the top of the Character Curve. As a result, we can achieve more satisfaction in our own work and we can create a more satisfying, engaging, and productive environment for everyone who works for and with us. And we will achieve a positive bottom line. All of this is the true measure of ROC, one we can all enjoy.

In part III, we're going to put the ideas of ROC to work so that you can achieve the improved personal and professional results you've been reading about. From deciding what areas of personal change you want to tackle, finding the character goals that most inspire you, and adopting the practices that will help make those goals a reality, to selling, launching, and implementing organization-wide changes in leadership approach, you will move from the sidelines of old-school leadership and into the winner's circle of ROC.

ROC TAKEAWAYS

The ROC Ripple Effect

1. **Character matters.** ROC research data has shown that organizations run by Virtuoso CEOs and executive teams enjoy a unique competitive advantage.

2. **The ROC effect on the bottom line is real and substantial.** Beyond a reasonable doubt, the data shows that *Virtuoso CEOs deliver nearly five times the return on assets compared to Self-Focused CEOs.*

3. **Virtuoso CEOs and their teams build highly engaged workforces delivering better value to customers.**

4. **Organizations with Virtuoso leadership have stronger customer relations and report greater customer satisfaction.**

5. **The Keystone Character Habits of Virtuoso leadership lead to more responsible organizational decisions and better organizational citizenship.** ROC research demonstrates that organizational decisions and leadership behaviors can have a meaningful effect on communities and environments.

6. **Together, these influences create the ROC ripple effect that can extend benefits well beyond organizational walls and operational boundaries.**

Part III

The ROC Habits
Workshop

7

Becoming a Virtuoso Leader

The first comment I get from many people when they hear the results of KRW's research into leadership character is: "Well, that's all great, but once you're an adult, your character is set—it can't be changed." My response is a quiet but firm, "Yes, it can." I'm firm in that conviction because I've seen many adults successfully take on the challenge of improving their character. Not only that, I've seen how much happier, more satisfying, and successful their lives have become as a result.

In chapter 2, we talked about the way a person's character forms and, in every subsequent chapter, how behavior expresses that character. The way people treat others is one of the most direct reflections of character, and that behavior is based on the long-standing patterns of character habits. As I've noted, this is the best piece of news you'll read in the whole book. Why? Because people can shape and change habits, and character habits are no exception to that truth.

In this chapter, we're going to go beyond reassurances that you *can* change your character, as we walk through a logical and very doable process for accomplishing that change in six steps (see figure 7-1). You can't skip any of the steps. You need to work through each in order, accomplishing one before you move to the next. To help you in the process of personal change, each step is accompanied by its own flow chart, which you can use to make sure you've covered all the bases in that step before moving on to the next. I've also explained this process with a story of character growth that I hope will, because of its unique circumstances and events, serve as a clear and compelling guide through the universal human experience of personal change.[1]

FIGURE 7-1

Six steps in the process of personal change

While figures and flow charts fail to communicate all of the confusion, angst, joy, and exhilaration involved in the deeply personal nature of character change, the six-step process of personal change is really a very orderly exercise. You can think of the process as a *whole person* workout that involves logic and intuition, thinking, and feeling. Some have referred to personal change as a spiritual experience, and it may have some of that same feeling for you. Maybe it will feel like a daily exercise program that quickly becomes as natural to you as breathing. Or it may feel like one of the most important and transformative experiences you've ever undertaken.

In any event, personal change is, by definition, *personal*. Changing the habits that shape your character is an act that penetrates to the very core of who you are as a person. Such change isn't quick or easy, but it's well worth the time and attention you'll invest in it. Developing the character of strong, principled leadership helps you in every aspect of your life: decision making, relationships, goal setting, conflict resolution, life and career satisfaction, and so much more. Of course, it also involves hard work. But when have you ever gained anything that meaningful in your life *without* having to work for it?

Many leaders would like to avoid this sort of process and dismiss it as too deeply psychological or esoteric, like some New Age fad. (If you have a history of emotional or mental illness, I recommend that you consult with a mental health professional before you engage in the exercise described in this chapter.) But the six steps of personal change are grounded in the plain, hard evidence of neuroscience, and supported by respectable research into how personal change actually occurs. KRW didn't invent this process. But based on my education and training as a psychologist and my years of experience in helping individuals and organizations achieve meaningful change, I believe it represents a simple, practical model of the very widely shared experience of human growth and change. I'm confident that by the time you've reached the end of this chapter, you'll agree.

Step 1: Acknowledge Invitations to Change

Mark was stunned. Just one short hour ago, he had been feeling great. He had actually been looking forward to this one-on-one with his boss and CEO. That's because Mark knew he was in the running for a promotion to become the president of the company's largest business unit—a promotion everyone recognized as a signal that this person was a serious candidate to become the company's next CEO.

Now, just an hour later, that dream was over. Mark had felt a little twinge in his gut as his boss, Michael, started out the meeting a little awkwardly. But the real body blow came when Michael said, "I know you're hoping to hear that I'm promoting you to be the president of our best business unit, but I've decided to place Carol there instead." Mark couldn't remember much of what Michael said after he spoke those words. But he knew that sometime during the course of the meeting, Michael had said that he didn't think Mark's peers would be willing to work with him as their boss. Now Mark was back in his office, alone, confused, hurt, and angry—and trying desperately to understand exactly what had just happened.

Mark didn't know it at the time, but he had just been given an invitation—a push into the first step of the process of personal change. If someone told Mark at that moment that this was a gift, he wouldn't have believed it.

But being confronted with an undeniable truth about the way others perceive our behavior and character *is* a gift. The gift can be a challenge we don't immediately know how to handle. When faced with the knowledge that our usual way of managing our life or relationships or career doesn't work, we may find that we have no backup plan. But any invitation to change is also an opportunity to grow into a more mature and integrated person.

In one way or another, many leaders have found themselves the unhappy recipient of this same kind of invitational *gift*. That's because life is a series of change experiences. We saw in earlier chapters how both the inner and outer journeys to becoming a fully integrated self is quite often a challenging and bumpy road. Many obstacles we'll encounter on that road are really just the need (or opportunity) for change in disguise. And that disguise rarely comes in the form of a gentle detour into a roadside oasis. More often, we experience the invitation to change as an abrupt shift in a new direction or a bruising tumble into a gaping pothole.

We've seen this process play out spectacularly on the public stage, as well. For example, Tim Armstrong, the CEO of Patch (a subsidiary of AOL), had his own invitation to change immortalized on YouTube. Armstrong was in a packed conference room for an all-hands meeting with hundreds of Patch employees in physical or virtual attendance. Armstrong had made it clear in advance that during this meeting, he'd discuss confidential and possibly controversial plans for the company, but midway through his introductory remarks, he noticed that a member of his team, Abel Lenz, the creative director, was filming the meeting with his smartphone. With no hesitation or forethought, Armstrong pointed at Lenz and blurted out in anger, "Abel, put that camera down right now. Abel, you're fired!"

Of course, the whole incident went viral on YouTube in a matter of minutes. Two days later, Armstrong issued an apology but didn't rehire Lenz. One could guess that Armstrong's apology didn't matter much to anyone, especially since it was embedded with a list of excuses.[2] While we have no idea what kind of personal angst Armstrong went through after this incident, most of us could imagine asking ourselves, "*Why* did I do that? *Why* didn't I calmly ask Abel to turn off his camera and then go on with my meeting? I could have pulled him into my office afterward and handled this thing in private, firing him, yes, but without such a humiliating scene." But that's the thing about invitations to change; we can rarely address them through hindsight. Faced with our limitations, confronted with the fact that our way of knowing and dealing with the world no longer works, we can't stand still or turn back. Instead, we *have* to find another way forward.

Most of us have had a similar experience in our lives. Your own invitation to change may have come in any of a number of forms. For example:

- Painful feedback from coworkers or your boss—or both.

- A flood of uncontrollable emotion, such as anxiety, anger, or sadness, which you then seem compelled to express to everyone around you.

- A vague but persistent feeling that your life has no meaning or purpose.

- A new goal or path that will require you to develop new depths in your character or to adopt new habits or behaviors.

Of course, not all invitations to change are painful. You might launch into a personal change process out of a keen desire to improve your life, to achieve more meaning, or to create a legacy. Through a process of self-examination, you may become inspired by a new aspirational goal for your life. Or you may have reached a point where a change you've previously thought impossible becomes essential—as when a pregnant woman makes an unwavering commitment to stop smoking, even though her attempts to do so in the past have been unsuccessful.

No matter what their source, all invitations to change share one thing in common: they make you aware that your current understanding of the world is inadequate, that you have encountered the limits of your level of personal integration. Your existing worldview, your level of mental complexity, or your ability to act in a way that reflects your core values and principles is no longer working, and you have to find a new way forward.

When you understand that and are ready to embark on the journey of personal change, you've already completed Step 1 of that process—a step mapped out in figure 7-2.

Whatever triggered your initial invitation to change, remember that the process is an unavoidable part of the human experience, as well as an essential step in honing Virtuoso character. We may be able to go along for lengthy periods of time in relative peace and contentment. But life never stops. Even when our life seems static and unchanging, it isn't. We grow older; technology advances; institutions rise and fall; world events set off ripples that are continually heading our way. The successful negotiation of life requires personal change, and certainly the demands of strong leadership intensify that need. Sometimes those changes will unfold gradually, but more often they come in unplanned leaps and lurches. Our job is to stay on our feet and continue moving forward.

FIGURE 7-2

STEP 1: Acknowledge invitations to change

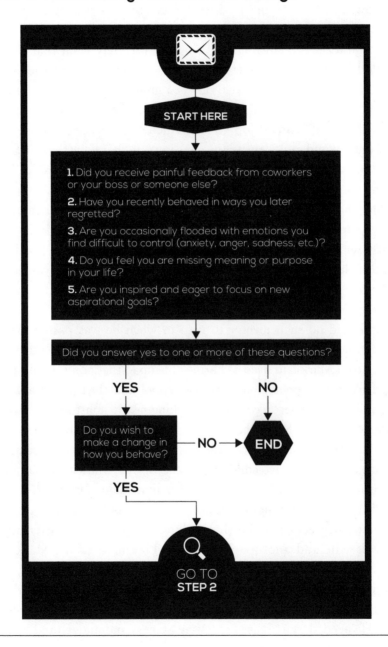

START HERE

1. Did you receive painful feedback from coworkers or your boss or someone else?

2. Have you recently behaved in ways you later regretted?

3. Are you occasionally flooded with emotions you find difficult to control (anxiety, anger, sadness, etc.)?

4. Do you feel you are missing meaning or purpose in your life?

5. Are you inspired and eager to focus on new aspirational goals?

Did you answer yes to one or more of these questions?

YES   NO

Do you wish to make a change in how you behave?   — NO →   END

YES

GO TO **STEP 2**

Step 2: Discover What You Want to Change

Acknowledging that you need to change something deeply personal about yourself in order to eliminate a character flaw or pursue some new aspiration is one thing. Figuring out precisely what that change should be is another thing entirely. For example, "I want to get a better performance review next time" is a goal worth pursuing, but it's *not* an adequate description of what you need to change in order to reach that goal. To develop your character as a leader, you need to fully understand and identify the gaps in your character that currently stand between you and the achievement of Virtuoso leadership. Identifying your character goals requires deep self-examination.

You won't always know immediately what aspects of your character you need or want to change. Even if you believe that you know very clearly what type of changes you want to make, it's still a good idea to enlist the help of a mentor, consultant, or friend to help you as you undertake an in-depth examination of your character and where to focus its development.

Mark had no such mentor to turn to when he was passed over to become the next president of a global business unit—he'd never felt he needed one. Mark had lived a charmed life up to that point. He'd earned an MBA from a prestigious business school and then joined a global consulting firm. After five years of working nearly nonstop and earning more frequent flyer points than he could use, he left that job to go to work for his current employer. Along the way, he also fell in love, married, and became the father of two children. In other words, Mark's life was good.

But now Mark was experiencing his first major failure. His sleep was disturbed, and things in his past he hadn't thought about for years began to surface, both in his sleep-killing dreams and in conversations with his wife and another close friend. Like most of us, Mark was born with the software and hardware necessary to form the Integrated Self model we saw in chapter 3. Now, however, he was faced with the necessity of examining and reflecting on both his outer and inner journeys. He needed to increase his self-awareness and understand how he arrived in the current situation.

After a couple of weeks spent in anxiety and confusion, Mark was ready to go deep into that examination process. He asked to talk to Michael, so he could hear (and this time listen to) the reasons behind Michael's decision. After several minutes of polite talk, Michael explained again that he was afraid that some key members of the team would balk at reporting to Mark. "If I gave you that job," Michael said, "I was afraid I'd lose some of the best talent in this company."

Mark knew that sometimes he had been pretty harsh and maybe a bit overdirect with some of his peers, but he also saw them as extremely competitive and maybe even secretly envious of his obvious successes. It had never occurred to him, however, that some of them would leave the company before they'd accept him as their boss. Fortunately, Michael was willing to invest in Mark's development; he agreed to bring in a consultant to help him build his leadership capacity and capability.

For most of us, the process of self-examination benefits from the input of multiple sources. By talking with our boss, coworkers, friends, spouses, and other significant adults in our life, we can gather real data to work with in determining what areas of our leadership character need development. From casual conversations between peers to a consultant's in-depth confidential interviews, we can put together an assessment of who we are as a person (the strength of our character habits and the worldview expressed by our behavior) as well as what our leadership behavior says about our character (how disciplined we are in decision making and how strong we are in basic leadership skills).[3] We need that kind of hard data in order to eliminate our blind spots so that we can truly see and understand how other people experience our leadership and perceive our character on a daily basis.

In Mark's case, he was taken aback by the data his leadership consultant gathered. He'd always believed that his direct reports never complained because they were happy with his leadership. But he learned that most of them were intimidated by him and often were afraid to tell him anything other than what he wanted to hear. Mark began to understand why his peers didn't care for him. He heard many of them describe him as a person who had few loyalties. One said, "Mark would throw me under the bus in a heartbeat if he thought it would serve his cause to get ahead."

Mark was in a position shared by many who are early in the process of character development. The goal of this step in that process is to understand what specific aspects of our character we need to change, and then to make the determination to move forward. We can choose a number of strategies to accomplish this step (see figure 7-3):

- Examine the values, habits, and other lessons about behavior, relationships, power, and leadership that we learned early in life, but that may no longer serve us well.

- Review our life story and integrate even its painful moments to create a clear and coherent whole.

- Use a journal to record our responses to daily events.

- Use mindfulness training, meditation, or other daily practice to learn more about our core self, so we can access the knowledge and understanding it holds for us.

- Identify situations that trigger the emotions or behaviors that we want to adapt.

Don't be put off by the idea of examining your character and uncovering its flaws and gaps. While that process may be somewhat uncomfortable—even painful—it won't harm you. Some level of discomfort is almost a necessity for gaining authentic insights into self-defeating or useless patterns in our behavior. We continue to develop our understanding of ourselves and our character throughout our lives. Over time, not only does the process lose its sting, but the increased level of self-understanding it brings us can actually make us more confident, more comfortable in our own skin.

Now let's take a closer look at how you can implement some of the options this step offers.

Getting to the Root of Your Character

As we learned in part I, our character is the expression of our moral intuitions, motivations, habits, emotions, logic, beliefs, and cognitive capacity at work. In chapter 3, we saw that one of the first milestones

FIGURE 7-3

STEP 2: Discover what you want to change

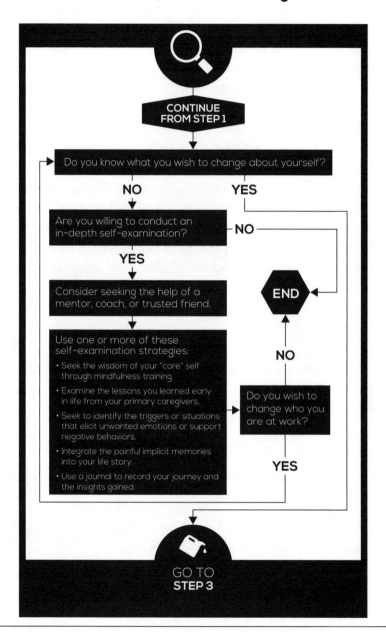

in the development of our character as a leader is compiling and considering a coherent story of our life. The influence of early caregivers forms a critical element of that story. The more you can learn through examining the patterns of behavior and the character habits your caregivers taught you, the better able you'll be to form a useful profile of your character. Exploring such fundamental influences can help you identify areas of your character that get in the way of forming solid relationships, finding your professional direction, or advancing your understanding of yourself and the world around you. In short, you have to "know yourself to grow yourself."

There has been a good deal of research on how to understand one's early experiences with parents and caregivers. As Dan Siegel, clinical professor of psychiatry at the UCLA School of Medicine, writes in *Mindsight: The New Science of Personal Transformation*, "Childhood relationships shape the patterns of our internal world, especially our windows of tolerance and our capacity to reflect on our own internal world."[4] The following questions, adapted from Siegel's work, are designed to help you examine this part of your personal history:[5]

1. What was your childhood like?

2. How would you describe your relationship with each of your parents?

3. Were you close to other people as a child?

4. Which of those people were you the closest to—and why?

5. What words best describe your early relationship with your mother? Your father? Other caregiver(s)?

6. What memories do you have about the words you just used to describe your caregivers?

7. What was it like when you were separated, threatened, upset, or fearful as a child?

8. Did you experience loss as a child? If so, what was that like for you and your family?

9. How did your relationships change over time?

10. Why do you think your caregivers behaved as they did?

11. When you think back on all these questions, how do you think your earliest experiences have impacted your development as an adult?

To gain the most from this examination of your personal history, you should write out your answers to these questions and/or talk them through with another person you deeply trust.[6] Look for insights about how habits and beliefs you acquired early in your life are playing out in your current world.

Through this process, Mark remembered that his father loved to boast about how he outsmarted the people he worked with. Mark also recalled a painful high school experience in which one of his closest friends had encouraged him to run for class president, then had won the election himself, entering just four days before the class voted. Mark recalled vowing to himself that he would never again be so trusting of "friends." He also decided that his father's mode of constantly looking for ways to outsmart his peers was a good strategy. Mark adopted this strategy and it had worked marvelously well—until that day in Michael's office.

Uncovering the sources of your character and moral habits is, in many ways, an essential element of compiling a coherent life story. By piecing together a clear picture of how you formed your understanding of the world, you can identify the source of the negative ideas, emotions, or responses that may be promoting those aspects of your character that you need to address. As you work to uncover the roots of your character, remember that your goal is not to get lost in old pain or to justify lapses in your character habits. Your goal is to uncover the source of your character gaps or flaws, so you can begin the process of overcoming them.

Identifying Situations or Triggers Embedded in Your Hardware

Have you ever met a stranger who you immediately liked or disliked, even before you had any information about them to warrant your response? That reaction can be triggered by something as simple as the person having the same hair color as your ex-husband or the regional accent of a boss who hassled you earlier in your career. To develop the character of a Virtuoso leader, you have to be able to identify the people, situations, or events that trigger such subconscious negative reactions, so you can control and even eliminate that knee-jerk response going forward.

Our brains tend to remember everything, but as you learned in chapter 2, our fast brain and slow brain encode memories in two ways. Our slow brain does so consciously; we know what is happening to us when it happens, and we're aware of the act of storing something in our memory bank. But our fast brain stores data at an unconscious level, without any awareness on our part. Sometimes our unconscious reactions are helpful. Often, however, they trigger responses that are inappropriate, unproductive, and damaging to our interactions and outcomes.

Fortunately, with careful observation, you can become alert to the kind of situations or events that trigger the subconscious responses you want to eliminate or change. Once you're aware of them, you can begin to exercise conscious control over them. Learning to identify these triggers and manage your response to them is a critical step in adopting new habits and behaviors that can reshape your character in powerful ways.

You can begin this examination of previously unexplored, automatic responses by talking with a trusted friend or mentor. With enough discussion, you can begin to uncover the emotions or situations that serve as your negative triggers. But beyond those discussions, you also can learn to watch for the triggers and trip wires in your character so that you can begin the process of disconnecting them. The following three techniques can help you in this exercise:

1. *Carefully observe your first response.* A relatively easy way to quickly read the strength of your character habits is to observe your first impulse or response when interacting with another person. If your first response is to be truthful, own up to your own mistakes, and take responsibility for your personal choices, or to be forgiving and concerned about the other person, you probably have strong character habits. However, if you find that your typical first response is to benefit or protect yourself no matter how your actions affect others, you likely have some work to do.

2. *Use a journal to record your journey.* Simply writing down in a private journal the events and insights that unfold as you work to understand and strengthen your character is surprisingly valuable. Even if just an itemized list of observations, conflicts, hunches, unanswered questions, stumbles, and wins, try to keep a daily record of your personal journey of self-examination.

3. *Practice mindfulness training.* Mindfulness training—learning to be aware of your thoughts, feelings, and actions without judging them—is among several tried-and-true methods for examining your life. Many business schools offer mindfulness training as part of the personal toolkit for aspiring MBAs. Mindfulness training may be simple relaxation training— learning how to start at the bottom of your feet and step- by-step move up your body, *mindfully* focusing on relaxing each muscle group until you reach the crown of your head. Then, perhaps, repeating it again. Or it may be traditional meditation—emptying your mind over and over again as you relax in a sitting position with your eyes closed. Focusing on breathing is a strategy many people use when meditating. Many people find that time alone walking or running is a form of med- itation and leads to mindfulness. Of course, many forms of religious prayer, chanting, and engaging in group liturgical exer- cises lead to mindfulness. People often come out of mindfulness sessions with an increased awareness of what they want out of life or at least some clarity about a specific issue or need.[7]

The process of identifying what you want (and need) to change— getting to the roots of your character habits and understanding the subconscious triggers that have helped shape them—can take days or even weeks. Clarity like that doesn't come quickly. But, remember that building the characteristics of Virtuoso leadership is a journey, not an event. By gaining clarity about the person you want to become and the leadership character you want to demonstrate, you're forming the character goal that will drive every other step of the process ahead. As the flow chart for Step 2 indicates, when you know that you want to change the behaviors that express your character, and you know which of those behaviors you want to change, you're ready to move to the next step in the process of personal change.

Step 3: Find the Fuel for Change

Changing your character is hard work. It takes a lot of energy and personal resolve. Willpower alone can't do it. Researchers have discovered that willpower is a very limited resource—a finding that has long been apparent to just about anyone who's ever struggled to lose weight.[8] Luckily, there is a different and more predictable reservoir of energy you can tap when you want to make such deeply personal changes as those we're talking about in this chapter. It involves the discovery of deep meaning: finding fuel for change or a character goal that inspires you.

For example, after a friend of mine learned that people didn't always believe what he said, he resolved to strengthen his character habit of integrity. He found the energy to pursue that character goal by reminding himself that he wanted his children and grandchildren to remember him as "a man of his word." This goal was very important for him, a character goal that infused him with energy every time he thought about it.

If you already have formed that kind of powerful, inspiring character goal, you have completed Step 3 of the personal change process. If you haven't found a character goal strong enough to fuel the hard work ahead, you can use the flow chart shown in figure 7-4 to help you through Step 3 of the personal change process.

As the flow chart illustrates, the first phase of this step involves writing a personal vision statement—a description of the character you want to achieve, the person you want to be, the leader you want to become. By the time we approach the role of leadership, we've had some experience in writing out the goals and mission of our organization or business unit in a way that will inspire everyone to achieve them. Now, it's time for you to put that skill to work in outlining a visionary goal for your character development. This is a highly personal process, and while you may enlist the help of a friend, mentor, colleague, or consultant in the process, yours is really the only view that matters in creating this vision.

FIGURE 7-4

STEP 3: Find the fuel for change

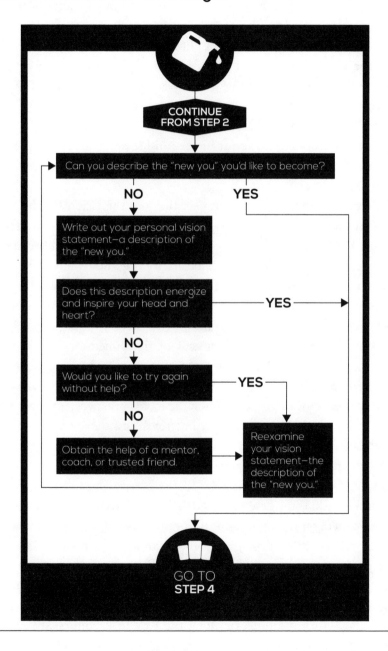

At this stage, Mark's consultant pushed him to describe the new version of himself that he wanted to become. Now was the time for Mark to let himself dream—to envision the type of leader he would like to be and to describe how he would experience life if he successfully made the transition in character necessary to accomplish that goal. "I want people I work with to be inspired both by who I am and by what I know how to do as a business person," Mark wrote. "I no longer need to be the smartest guy in the room, but I do want to be one who others respect and want to work with." As he began to talk and write about his vision for personal change, Mark became energized and enthusiastic, and he could feel that he was on the right path.

There is no good substitute for writing out the vision for the "new you." You may have a perfectly clear mental vision of your character goal and you may have fully described to a trusted friend or mentor the type of personal change you'll be attempting. But you need to write it down in order to fully own that change and become committed to achieving it. Consider it a character contract you've made with yourself.

To help organize your thoughts in this step, you might return to previous chapters to remind yourself of the dimensions of the integrated self, the Keystone Character Habits of Virtuoso leadership, and the behaviors and characteristics that demonstrate those habits. Your goal isn't to simply copy down the ideas, practices, and character traits you've been reading about, but revisiting those ideas can help you identify the elements of your own ideal self.

As you're writing your personal vision statement, keep reading it (even out loud) to yourself and/or to the person you've asked to help you in this task. If the description energizes and inspires you, then—like Mark—you're on the right path. If not, keep tweaking your statement, just as you would keep shaping your organization's mission statement until you hit the right note of purpose, aspiration, and targeted outcome.

Be aware that you may never arrive at a *final* vision statement. Instead, shoot for something better by continuing to internalize all of the ideas you form and learn along the way to becoming the person you want to be—your version of your ideal self. You want your vision to expand and shift as you think more deeply about your character and the ways that you want to develop it.

That's what Mark did. In various conversations with his consultant, his close friend, his wife, and with Michael, he described many versions of himself. Here are the themes that ran throughout all of these versions:

- Mark wanted to become a person who was admired for telling the truth and keeping promises—a person of integrity.

- He wanted to become more accepting of mistakes, both his own and those of others—a person of forgiveness.

- He wanted to inspire people through his commitment to help others achieve their personal development goals, and through his desire to leave the world a better place—a person of compassion.

- He wanted to improve his decision-making skills and become a more skillful team leader—a person of responsibility.

- And he still wanted to be a CEO someday.

Your list may share none of these specific elements, but it should describe the same kind of fully integrated person, one whose head and heart are connected in the pursuit of strong leadership character. Even as you put your vision in writing, remember that you can (and should) update and revise it at any time, as you discover new facets and depths to the type of character you want to develop and the type of person you want to become. When you feel excited, inspired, and maybe even a little bit anxious as you read your character statement, you've accomplished the tasks of Step 3 and are ready to move to the next step in the personal change process.

Step 4: Identify the Keystone Change

In the past, you may have made a New Year's resolution that inspired you—a goal that made you feel wonderful every time you imagined achieving it. Unfortunately, most such resolutions remain unrealized. Why? Because too often, we don't form a clear vision for executing the goals we've set. Bringing that vision into focus is the next step in your process of personal change and character development. That step involves identifying the *Keystone Change* that will contribute the most to your character as a Virtuoso leader.

We've talked a lot about *keystones* in this book: Keystone Leadership Skills, Keystone Character Habits, and so on, because they offer such a big power boost to the process of leadership character development by promoting and supporting the development of other equally essential skills and habits. You can bring that same boost to your process of personal change by identifying the Keystone Change that, when you achieve it, will incorporate many other positive behavior and character adjustments.

There may be dozens of changes you might make on the way to achieving your vision of character-driven leadership. But to help identify your Keystone Change, compare your character goals to the Keystone Character Habits and the behaviors that demonstrate them, as outlined in the ROC Matrix. For example, let's say that your goal is to become better at successfully infusing your organization with a high level of positive energy. As you look at the ROC Matrix, you will find that there are many ways you could adapt your character to tackle that goal:

- You might work to become more open to change, ask for help from others and be more welcoming of their ideas—to build your *compassion* as a leader.

- You might need to be more aware of your defensive motivations, so you can catch yourself when you reflexively reject the new ideas of others—to build your leadership *integrity*.

- You might need to break the fast brain habit of pessimism or to develop your ability to think abstractly about products or processes in a way that helps you imagine a broader range of possibilities—to become a more *responsible* leader.

- You might need to learn to let go of your mistakes and those of others, and to remain focused on the positive understanding the organization gains from them—to become a leader with the ability to *forgive*.

In examining this list, you might decide that most of the options for change you've noted deal with conquering your fear of failure. So you might decide that the most important change you can make is to become more comfortable with mistakes—yours and others—so that you're able to view them as learning experiences rather than shameful failures. Your Keystone Change then is to accept mistakes as a fact of life and to learn to live with and grow from them, rather than punishing yourself and others for merely being human. By becoming a leader capable of forgiveness, you will also become more compassionate, more responsible, and demonstrate more integrity as you encourage those around you to innovate and collaborate without fear of recrimination for the inevitable mistakes along the way.

When you're exploring areas for character development, don't limit your options. But no matter how long your list might be, your task in this step of the process is to define the one big thing—the Keystone Change in behavior that would contribute the most to achieving your vision of Virtuoso leadership.

As you can see in the flow chart for Step 4 shown in figure 7-5, if you struggle to identify your Keystone Change, you can always enlist the aid of your trusted advisers—a mentor, friend, or consultant who can talk with you through the process. If you have a few close coworkers who you truly believe are pulling for you to succeed, you can ask for their advice as to which of your change goals seems most compelling and essential.

But, remember that you can do some of this investigative work on your own. Take the list of potential behavior changes you've created here and then test them against the characteristics you outlined in your personal vision statement in Step 3. Which change would have the broadest impact on your ability to achieve your personal vision? That change is, most likely, the Keystone Change you should be targeting on your journey to develop the character of Virtuoso leadership.

Mark had trouble with this step. He began by mining the lists he'd put together, but was still uncertain he had identified his Keystone Change. Initially, he was resistant to discussing the issue with others at work. He did, however, and after a conversation with one of his direct reports and a peer, he realized that both of them were echoing his own tentative ideas about his most essential area for change. After testing the idea with Michael and his consultant, the identity of his

FIGURE 7-5

STEP 4: Identify the Keystone Change

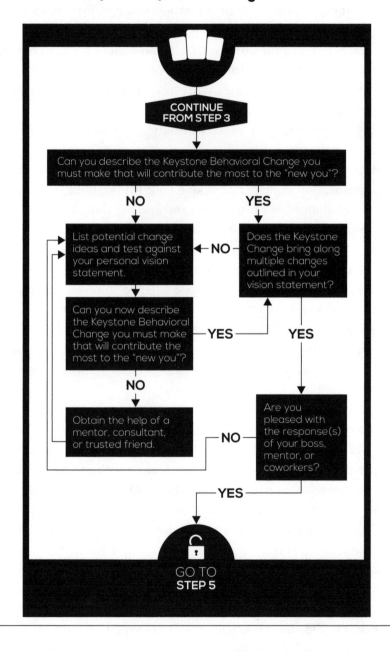

Keystone Change became clear; everyone wanted him first and foremost to "own up to his own mistakes."

When you, like Mark, have reached this stage in the personal change process, you are facing what may be the hardest step of all: discovering how you might unintentionally sabotage your own good intentions for change and then disarming that response.

Step 5: Disarm Your Security System

Your brain views change, by its very definition, as a threat. That's because the brain thrives on routine. Once your brain establishes a pattern, it's going to work hard to maintain it. Changing patterns as deep as those that shape your character can trigger surprising levels of discomfort and anxiety.

To successfully navigate the sometimes difficult journey of character development, you have to muster all your energy to identify and disarm your brain's instinctive resistance to change. That disarmament requires that you face the assumptions that trigger your unwanted responses and behaviors *and* the true outcomes they produce for you. Then you can create a workable action plan to short-circuit those responses and replace them with new assumptions and more productive behavior. Your enthusiasm and excitement about achieving a new pattern of leadership behavior and character can cancel out the majority of the anxiety and discomfort such change can trigger.

Using Your Keystone Change as a Starting Point

As I said, this step is one of the most difficult to make in the personal change process, and it involves multiple phases. Using your Keystone Change as a starting point, you complete this step by walking through these individual tasks and checkpoints (we'll use Mark's Keystone Change of "owning up to my mistakes" as an example in this list):

1. Describe in writing what you typically do *instead* of the behavior represented in your Keystone Change. ("When I make a mistake, I immediately try to assign blame to others.")

2. Describe what you imagine would happen if you did the *opposite* of that typical behavior, in order to reveal hidden commitments that are driving it. ("If I did the *opposite*, I would admit the mistake. But I have always wanted to look strong as a leader, and if I admit to my mistakes, I am demonstrating weakness.")

3. Now describe what would happen if you failed to keep those hidden commitments. ("If I admit to mistakes, people will think I'm stupid and weak. They won't listen to me or follow my directions or support me in my ideas. I'll lose respect and credibility.")

4. Determine whether those outcomes truly feel valid; if they are, you must continue to keep your hidden commitments. ("Do I really earn respect by blaming others?") If your answer is:

   a. Yes, you need to return to Step 2 in the personal change process and discover what you *truly* want to change.

   b. No, then move to the next task in this step.

5. Write an action plan that includes the new commitments and assumptions described in your vision statement and Keystone Change. ("I demonstrate strength by owning up to my own mistakes. I encourage others to acknowledge their own mistakes, too, rather than being afraid of my reaction to their errors.")

6. Share your action plan with your trusted adviser, mentor, or coworker.

The flow chart in figure 7-6 maps out all of the elements of this critical step.

Through this step in the process, Mark uncovered his hidden, long-term commitment to infallibility—to always graduate at the top of the class, to always win, to never make mistakes. After a number of sessions in which Mark and his consultant talked at length about his hidden commitment to making excuses so as to appear flawless, Mark began to see the fallacy in this worldview—and in his view of himself.

This sounds like a relatively simple conclusion to arrive at, but *many* of us have trouble accepting the fact that we make mistakes, that others expect us to make mistakes, and that we damage the perception

FIGURE 7-6

STEP 5: Disarm your security system

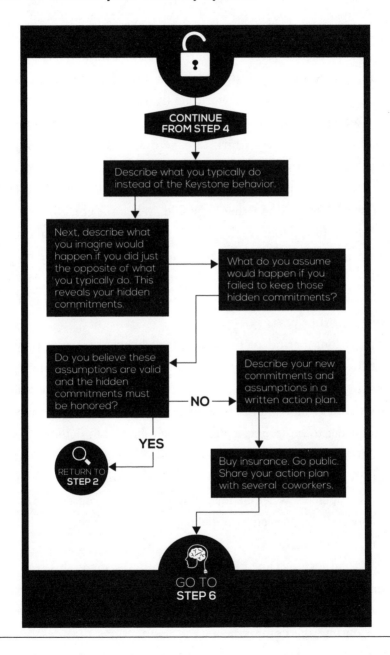

of others (and our own self-image) more by trying to deflect blame or deny our mistakes, rather than accepting them as a learning experience and moving on. It can take a lot of self-discovery and reasoning to arrive at such a simple conclusion.

In Mark's case, it took some hard truths and undeniable evidence before he was able to see the weaknesses in his long-held assumptions about himself and the world he lives in. The consultant asked him, "When one of your best direct reports makes a mistake, do you think less of him?" Mark said he didn't. The consultant then asked, "If that same direct report made excuses and tried to cover up his mistake or pass blame on to circumstances, would you think less of him?" Mark knew that he would. When the consultant asked, "Do you think anyone really *believes* the stories you make up to justify your actions?" Mark had to admit that it was unlikely that they always believed him. Then the consultant asked the *real* question Mark had to consider: "Does this seem like it might be lack of integrity on your part?"

After a long period of thought, Mark knew there was only one answer to that question. And the answer revealed some other important truths. By making excuses, Mark was triggering precisely the reaction he wanted to avoid from his peers and coworkers. Now he understood that, in order to be seen as a strong leader, he had to demonstrate the strengths of integrity, responsibility, forgiveness, and compassion that identify Virtuoso leadership. Otherwise, he realized, no one would see him as competent. When he made excuses, he was presenting himself to others as a frightened, unreliable guy who would rather lie than admit uncomfortable truths.

Mark had just disarmed his brain's security system—his resistance to change. When you have achieved this phase of Step 5, you are ready to move on to its finale: creating a written action plan. Your plan should outline the commitments and assumptions that describe the *new* Keystone Behavior that will help you implement your personal vision of leadership character.[9]

Creating Your Action Plan

At this stage in your personal change process, you have begun the serious work of forming new moral habits and character patterns. Create a specific action plan that lays out what you will do in place of the old pattern you previously have been using to support your hidden commitments and assumptions. In Mark's case, he knew he was more apt to be successful if he enlisted the help of the people who had contributed to his assessment or met with him to discuss the characteristics of his leadership that most needed revision. As part of his action plan, he told those people he wanted to become more comfortable accepting responsibility for his decisions, and asked them to remind him (in private) when they saw him reverting to his old pattern.

When you know what change you want and need to make in order to develop the leadership habits and character you have targeted, *you must create a manageable action plan for achieving that change.* In creating that plan, you can look for ideas by reviewing the milestones that mark your journey of personal change.

In Mark's case, for example:

1. His journey was set in motion when he failed to receive a promotion.

2. That failure ultimately led him to focus his attention on strengthening his character habits. Mark didn't have a skill deficit; he had a character habit deficit of failing to own up to his mistakes.

3. In order to change that habit and own up to his mistakes, he had to stop lying—he had to make telling the truth his first response.

4. In order to own up to his mistakes, he also had to be forgiving of himself, so he needed to begin practicing forgiveness by letting go of his mistakes.

5. By owning up to his own mistakes, he would communicate to others in a very powerful way that he cared for them as people.

He was telling them that he's no better than they—that he shares a common humanity with them.

By choosing the single Keystone Change of "owning up to my own mistakes" and by disarming his reflexive defensiveness in response to his own errors, Mark was strengthening all four moral habits at once.

Your action plan must be specific to your Keystone Change, patterns, and capabilities. Let's say, for example, that you have decided to replace your typical pattern of reflexively rejecting the ideas of others out of a defensive need to be "the decider"—to improve your own integrity as a fair and reasonable person. Your action plan might include these items:

1. When others share ideas with me, I will *always* respond first by saying something like: "Well, let me think about that," or "Let's talk about how that might work."

2. For every reason I come up with for why an idea won't work, I will try to come up with a reason that supports the idea.

3. Before I make a commitment or decision, I will consider the specific reasons driving my decision.

4. I will practice owning my defensive motivations, by occasionally saying to the person or group that has generated the suggestion, "I don't want to make a snap decision about this that might lead me to reject a good idea simply because it's not mine. Walk me through your reasoning."

5. If I *do* decide to reject the idea, I will do so only after nailing down at least two solid reasons (that have nothing to do with my ego). Those reasons will need to be more credible and weightier than those for accepting the idea.

6. When I've made the decision to follow a suggestion, we will move forward as a team and accept the outcome as a positive experience that has either advanced us toward our goals or helped us learn from our mistakes.

This list may have no relationship at all to your action plan, but it illustrates the purpose of this final phase of Step 5. Your goal is to create an action plan that will contribute to your self-integration and strong character as a Virtuoso leader.

Step 6: Rewire Your Brain

Our character is made up of patterns of thought, emotion, intuitions, and behavior that we develop over the course of our life. Those patterns influence the way our brain processes and responds to information, so developing new dimensions to our character requires forming new neural pathways. Luckily, our brains are quite capable of accomplishing this very predictable process. It always works as long as you follow the rules the brain insists you use.[10] That's what Step 6 is all about.

Where you focus your attention is where the neurons flow. You create neural pathways by focusing your attention consistently and repeatedly on some thought or task. The mindfulness training we discussed earlier, in Step 2, is a useful technique for learning how to better focus your attention. Another technique, which is the heart of this final step in the character-development process, is to practice new patterns of thinking throughout the day. Together, these actions help rewire your brain, creating new neural pathways that result in the new thoughts, responses, and behaviors you have targeted as goals in your character development.

This is where the energy and enthusiasm from your vision of your new character as a Virtuoso leader plays its most important role. That energy can help keep your attention focused on practicing your new patterns of behavior. Maintaining this practice requires the work of both your head ("I know I should do this because . . .") and your heart ("I want to do this so I will feel more comfortable when . . ."). As you practice, you can continually check in with others and use ongoing self-assessment to track your progress. That's an important part of Step 6; to maintain your motivation, you need to periodically acknowledge and celebrate your ongoing progress. The flow chart in figure 7-7 maps out each of the elements of Step 6.

As you can see in the flow chart, there are many tools or reminder mechanisms you can set up to focus your attention on your new pattern. You can schedule a regular, daily, ten-minute time-out to assess your success so far that day in aligning your character aspirations and

FIGURE 7-7

STEP 6: Rewire your brain

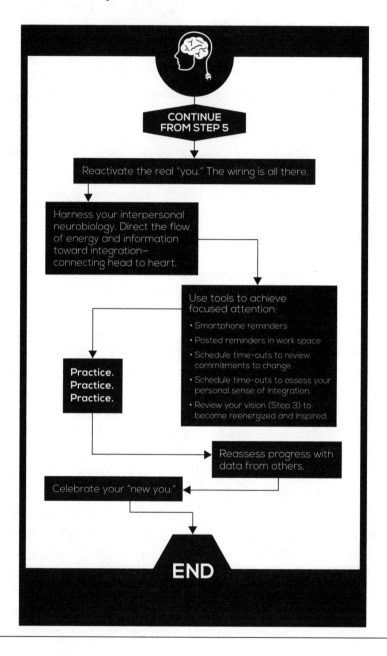

CONTINUE FROM STEP 5

Reactivate the real "you." The wiring is all there.

Harness your interpersonal neurobiology. Direct the flow of energy and information toward integration— connecting head to heart.

Use tools to achieve focused attention:
- Smartphone reminders
- Posted reminders in work space
- Schedule time-outs to review commitments to change.
- Schedule time-outs to assess your personal sense of integration.
- Review your vision (Step 3) to become reenergized and inspired.

Practice. Practice. Practice.

Reassess progress with data from others.

Celebrate your "new you."

END

actions to become more integrated as a person. You can use some of that time to reenergize yourself by looking at your vision statement—the inspiring picture of you as a Virtuoso leader. You can post personal reminders in your workspace or on your iPad or smartphone. You can schedule regular times with a friend, mentor, or other adviser to review your progress. You can also set up times to check in with your peers and direct reports to seek their feedback.

As time goes on and your new pattern feels secure, there will come a moment when you'll wish to celebrate the new you. This may be simply acknowledging to yourself how much you've changed or it may be something you talk about with your close friends or a mentor.

And what about Mark's passage through Step 6? He chose to celebrate his sense of having successfully changed by stopping by Michael's office late one Friday afternoon to thank him for setting him on the path to character development. Mark stepped in and said, "I'm sure you recall our session nearly a year ago when you told me you were putting Carol into the president's role. Well, I just wanted to stop by to tell you that I totally agree with your decision. She's done a great job. But I also wanted to thank you for having the courage to make that decision. While I was disappointed at first, that experience set the stage for me to make some important changes. I've made great use of the consultant you provided and I've learned a good deal during this past year—first and foremost is my recognition that I can actually make a mistake or two and still add value to the enterprise! Again, I want to say thanks." Mark also received some unsolicited praise from Michael, who told him that Mark's peers had also noticed a significant shift in how he related to his teammates.

Celebrating our progress is an important part of the process of character growth and development—or any type of personal change. We begin that process with acknowledgment as we confront the character gaps and flaws that stand between us and the person we want to become. But we also have to acknowledge our successes as we grow beyond those obstacles. By celebrating those successes, we're also honoring the importance of the progress we've made.

That progress matters. As we've seen, the effects of our leadership character and decisions can extend beyond our own personal satisfaction and professional growth to shape lives, outcomes, and environments across the nation or around the world. If we only recognize the negative effects that result when we've fallen short of our leadership goals, we risk losing the big-picture vision that keeps driving us onward. We have to own our mistakes, confront our lapses in character, and continually work to improve our approach to leadership. But to do that, we need to remember to keep our focus on where we want our journey of character development to take us, rather than getting lost in every misstep along the way.

As we've seen, we never *truly* stop growing as leaders, human beings, and citizens of the world, which means we never reach the limits of the ROC our Virtuoso leadership can achieve. To power the kind of ongoing character growth that brings the strongest results, we need to celebrate our accomplishments as Virtuoso leaders—and the ROC such leadership brings us all.

Taking Virtuoso Leadership to the Next Level

While we humans have been growing and extending our skill sets throughout the history of our species, we've only recently begun to understand our brain's powerful potential for change. As we've seen in this chapter, that potential extends to the very core of who we are as individuals, as leaders, and as members of the global community. The tools and techniques we've learned about here are our guide to that core-level growth, an invaluable map for the journey of leadership character development.

Not all great leaders are simply born that way or carried to the frontlines of decision making through the hidden, inherent gifts of wisdom, fairness, and strategic savvy. Instead, *anyone* who is willing to undertake the careful practice and sometimes demanding work of character development can grow into the kind of Virtuoso leader described by the participants in our research project—and sought by investors, shareholders, customers, and economies everywhere.

We've also seen, however, that few leaders operate in isolation. Whether Virtuoso or Self-Focused, just about every leader relies on his or her senior executive team to help guide the organization and set the tone for its culture, principles, and value. The skill with which a leader puts together and maintains that team is a direct reflection of that individual's overall commitment to the organization's sustainable success. Which means that, in order to truly demonstrate Virtuoso leadership, the leader must promote and develop Virtuoso character throughout the executive team—and the organization.

That kind of organizationwide character development is the subject of the next chapter. There we'll outline a number of ideas and tactics for extending the personal character-development skills we've learned here to help promote the Virtuoso character of the senior executive team, managers, and others throughout the organization.

The goal of the six steps for character growth is to achieve a higher level of self-integration. As we are about to learn, if we want to realize the true potential of ROC, we have to incorporate this process as an indispensable ingredient in every element of our leadership development program. By giving those we work with tools for developing their own Virtuoso character, we help build the strength of our own ROC leadership model and, at the same time, promote the kind of innovative, collaborative, and agile performance that drives any organization toward sustainable success.

ROC TAKEAWAYS
Becoming a Virtuoso Leader

1. **You *can* reshape your character.** You can strengthen your character habits and, by so doing, improve your leadership skills *and* results.

2. **Character development and all effective personal change involve these six steps:**

   Step 1: Acknowledge an "invitation to change."

   Step 2: Discover what you want to change.

   Step 3: Find the fuel for change.

   Step 4: Identify the Keystone Change necessary to accomplish that goal.

Step 5: Disarm your security system.

Step 6: Rewire your brain.

3. **Virtuoso leadership never stops growing.** As you continue to develop your experience and understanding as a leader, you can expect to find new and meaningful ways to develop your leadership character.

8

Developing an ROC Organization

What happens when a young, energetic Virtuoso CEO takes over a dysfunctional organization and shapes it into a profitable and successful business? In the previous chapter, we saw how people can take themselves through the process of character development and personal change. But—in spite of a US Supreme Court ruling that says corporations are people—organizations don't change themselves. *Leaders* change organizations. And it takes a Virtuoso leader to change an organization in the most positive way.

Virtuoso leadership isn't a solo act. Not only do CEOs rely on their entire organization to promote and reflect the values, principles, and culture of Virtuoso leadership, they also need the entire organization to participate in the process of adopting those standards. The entire organization—the CEO, the board of directors, the executive team, *and* the workforce—drives the most effective organizational change.

Growing your own character isn't an easy job, as you learned in chapter 7, and neither is developing the character of your organization. But it can be done. This chapter offers you a road map for that process. You will see similarities between this process and the one for individual character development, so the ideas you encounter here will be familiar. That means I will dispense with a lot of the step-by-step instruction and flow charts. But, as before, I will illustrate the techniques outlined in this chapter with a case study—a fictional example based on a true story. The name and the setting are changed, of course, to protect the privacy of the individual in the story.

The process of organizational change involves multiple phases, which include:

- Identifying the need for changing the organization's current culture, vision, and performance—organizational triage.

- Creating an executive team that shares the CEO's new vision.

- Crafting that vision's message and communicating it to the rest of the organization.

- Identifying and eliminating obstacles that stand in the way of executing changes necessary to implement the vision.

- Empowering the workforce in organization-wide reform.

- Finding the most effective ways to work with the board of directors throughout the process.

We'll translate the ideas, tactics, and techniques of personal character development to the task of an organization-wide shift toward stronger leadership character and more principled decision making and behavior. As you read through the description of this process and the case study, you'll discover that creating an organization of strong character and unshakable principles isn't just a lofty goal or a good idea. It's the good business of ROC.

Launching Organizational Triage

Heather had only been in her new job as the CEO of a midsize enterprise software firm for a month when she called in a consultant. She already looked stressed and tired and was eager to talk. The story she had to tell wasn't all that unusual.

The board of Heather's company had fired its previous CEO and launched an immediate search for a replacement. Heather, a senior vice president, had been in the company for only a little over a year, but she applied for the job—and got it. That had been just a few weeks ago, and during that time, Heather had come face-to-face with a parade of problems that she now was going to have to address.

As is so often the case in this kind of fast transfer of corporate leadership, Heather had taken the helm of a badly leaking ship. The previous CEO had used the company primarily as his personal fiefdom—making decisions in isolation, sending out decrees for changes aimed at making his own position more profitable or pleasant, with little understanding or interest in how his new initiatives would actually work for the organization or its clients. He had even relocated the company's headquarters from a midsized, energetic city to a suburban backwater, not because it was a good business decision, but to bring his office closer to his new home.

While Heather knew the company was in trouble, she had no idea how serious the problems actually were until she had several sessions with both the chief financial officer and the chief legal officer. The former CEO had devoted a lot of time and energy to covering up the company's problems, revealing only good news to its board of directors. Now, as Heather uncovered all of that hidden information, it seemed to her that everything in the organization was broken.

Morale was at a low point. After a layoff initiated by her predecessor, the family-oriented climate many of the long-term employees remembered had decayed into a culture of fear. Many business practices the former CEO put in place either made little sense or bordered on being illegal, and the new policies frequently required employees to do things they felt were not right. For example, the company had pushed its invoicing ahead of schedule to meet its short-term financial goals, regardless of the impact such stunts had on key customers.

The most challenging problem was that the company's core product had become obsolete, and competitors were picking off its longtime loyal customers one by one. The previous CEO had made a strategic acquisition two years before, gaining access to a new technology platform, but it was still stuck in development. Some of that delay was due to cost-cutting measures and a 10 percent workforce reduction the previous CEO had put in place to make the company's short-term financial performance look better than it actually was. Unfortunately, this layoff included several technical experts who were among the few people who understood the legacy product. To make the company's position even worse, many talented people had fled the organization to get away from the CEO. By the time Heather stepped in, the company's employee turnover rate was over 70 percent.

To put a bow on the whole ugly package, the executive team Heather inherited was mediocre at best. Her new direct reports had all been her peers before she got the job, but she didn't really know most of them well, because the company had always operated in silos. Nevertheless, it was clear to Heather that at least two of them were in over their heads and needed to be replaced.

Heather had just completed what I often refer to as "organizational triage"—that period when a new leader walks into a troubled organization and must set to work immediately to uncover all of its warts, bruises, gaping wounds, and—with luck—those few bright, healthy spots that offer hope for a new beginning.

As in the "invitation to change" we learned about in chapter 7, this first step in the process of organizational change can be, and usually is, difficult for everyone involved. But until you understand the full scope and symptoms of the organizational illness you're facing, you can't come up with a workable treatment plan. When an organization is bleeding—workforce, clients, profits—you have to move quickly to identify and treat its most dangerous and potentially fatal problems.

The framework for Heather's investigation was similar to just about any organization-wide macro review, which must assess:

- Current financial status
- Policies and practices
- Current staffing and expertise levels
- Workforce morale
- Core product or service
- New developments in the pipeline
- Executive leadership

As a new CEO moves through this assessment, he or she is, at the same time, determining what people, processes, and personal tools of leadership will be necessary to address the problems the process uncovers. Those personal tools are especially critical when the organization is facing a change of character and culture, rather than just a tweak to a manufacturing process or reporting structure. So let's see what tools Heather brought with her to the corner office, and how she applied them to the task ahead.

Creating an Executive Team with a Shared Sense of Vision and Urgency

As you know, the Virtuoso leader is an individual with strong character habits, including the four Keystone Character Habits of integrity, responsibility, forgiveness, and compassion. Beyond that fundamental character framework, however, the Virtuoso CEO also:

- Is a skilled and disciplined decision maker.

- Creates a compelling and inspiring vision.

- Provides strategic focus.

- Creates a culture of accountability.

- Selects and leads a high-performance executive team.

Heather had strong character habits. Her first impulse at work was to tell the truth and stand up for what's right, and her coworkers knew her as someone who kept her promises. She found it easy to own up to her mistakes and always took responsibility for her decisions. But in addition, Heather treated others as real people. She was quick to show support and care for her coworkers and treated people at all levels with the same respect and attention. In other words, while Heather hadn't mastered all the skills of Virtuoso leadership, she did come into the role of CEO armed with a Virtuoso's character. The principles and behaviors that accompanied her character formed Heather's toolkit for revitalizing her struggling organization. Now she needed to make sure her executive team was working with the same set of skills.

Because this was Heather's first time as a CEO, she had known she was going to need solid advice and skilled help to pull the organization out of its downward spiral and onto an upward trajectory. First,

Heather turned to a former boss as a mentor, an experienced and successful CEO who was very pleased she asked for his advice and counsel. She also brought in a leadership and organizational change consultant who could help her focus on the most important tasks at hand. And the most urgent of those tasks involved honing her executive team.

Leading and guiding an organization through a change process, especially when the future is uncertain, requires Virtuoso leadership from both the CEO and the executive team. People at all levels in such organizations may be fearful and mistrusting. They may have been through more than one cycle of promising leadership, only to be disappointed and betrayed. An executive team with weak character habits is unlikely to have much success in its efforts to reengage a disillusioned and fearful workforce.

A primary task for any new CEO is to build and hone an executive team that shares the leader's values and vision and is capable of communicating both to the organization at large. For a CEO who's come in to rescue a company in trouble, the executive team also must share a keen sense of urgency about ushering in organizational change.

In *The Heart of Change*, John Kotter and Dan Cohen say that the first step in bringing about organizational change is to "increase urgency."[1] They note that each stage of the change process comes with its own pitfalls, but nearly half of all change efforts fail right from the beginning, due to a missing sense of urgency among management. When is the urgency rate high enough? Kotter and Cohen claim that if *only 75 percent of management* is genuinely convinced of the need for change, the effort will fail. In other words, you need to have your entire executive team onboard, as well as most of your frontline managers and other leaders in the workforce, to effect meaningful organizational change.

For most new CEOs, the first few months are a honeymoon period. The board is invested in proving that it has made a good decision and it expects the CEO to make some changes, even if he or she causes some disruption and confusion. To take advantage of this grace period, Heather's mentor and consultant encouraged her to move quickly to form her new executive team. She asked the two weak members of her team to leave the company and hired new executives from the outside to take their place.

That process had offered Heather the interesting challenge of hiring the best talent to join a failing company. She had been completely candid in final interviews, fully disclosing to each of the candidates of her choice the seriousness of the company's situation. But she also had described the exciting opportunity they would have to be part of a team that could really make a lasting difference. Heather had carefully assessed the personal characters of the candidates before inviting them to join her team. She didn't want the values and morals she was determined to instill within the organization to be lacking in any of its leaders.

Heather continued to move quickly as she guided her new team. The second new hire had been onboard less than a week when Heather took all six of her direct reports to a three-day offsite meeting where she made certain each of them shared her sense of urgency and fully embraced the team's goal of turning around this struggling company. She also led the team through a series of tasks common to most teams launching the process of organization-wide change, which included:

- *Restructuring the organization*—doing away with organizational silos and creating an interdependent team in which everyone shares a common purpose and goals.

- *Structuring the executive team*—guiding the team as it defined each of its respective roles, and determining how often the team will meet, how it will work together, and the basic rules of confidentiality it will follow; in Heather's case, this task included eliminating the role of chief operating officer, so that she could be more directly in touch with each part of the organization.

- *Establishing a decision-making process*—outlining a disciplined process that combines both analysis and intuition, and creating a shared understanding about how the CEO and executive team will participate in that process; in Heather's case, she stated her intention to fulfill her role as the final decision maker and her expectations for the team's support of her decisions, even if some individuals didn't fully agree with them.

Heather ended the meeting by telling the team that she was working with the board to craft a new vision for the company. She made it clear that she wanted good input from the team members, and they discussed some of their ideas before the meeting adjourned. Then, after setting a delivery date for the vision statement, Heather closed the meeting.

Heather now had in place a solid executive team, and the team had a clear structure for its work. With that foundation, she was ready to move to the next step in her organization's cultural evolution.

Crafting and Communicating the Vision

No organization—even one that *isn't* caught in the struggle to survive—can successfully find a new direction forward if it doesn't have a crystal-clear vision of where it wants to go. As we saw in the previous chapter, creating your personal vision of the leader you want to become is a sometimes difficult process with huge implications. The process is no less difficult or its outcomes less critical when creating a new vision for an organization.

Heather had already had some brief discussions with the board chair about the importance of crafting a new organizational vision, and she was fully expecting to engage in some helpful and robust planning with perhaps two or three of the board members. Now she was disappointed to learn that the board didn't really want to spend much time talking about the vision. As the board chair eventually admitted, with real frustration in his voice, "Look, Heather, we just want you to turn around this damned thing so we can sell it! That's the vision!"

Unfortunately, this is a response that many new CEOs hear when they've been brought in to lead a company in trouble. In many cases, the board members have become disengaged from the idea of success and are now simply focused on survival, no matter what form that may take. In other cases, the board itself has played a role in creating the problems the company has experienced, and so it has neither the will nor expertise to participate in finding solutions, let alone to help craft an entirely new vision for the organization. This is when the character and leadership skills of the CEO truly must move to the forefront, as the new leader works to get the board of directors aligned and solidly grounded in the new character goals and direction he or she hopes to promote throughout the organization. (We talk more about the board's role in change later in this chapter.)

In Heather's case, her board of directors had essentially forgotten anything it had ever known about the nature, function, and goals of a true organizational vision. The previous CEO had a vision for the business, of course, and he had talked about it quite a lot in board meetings. As the board members recalled, that vision was to reach specific goals for revenue growth and earnings before interest, taxes, depreciation, and amortization (EBITDA)—a goal that offered nothing in the way of inspiration or direction for the workforce.

Heather worked hard at communicating how *she* envisioned the company's future, a vision that described not just the company's market presence, but its operations as well. She created two documents: "The Future of Our Customer Experience" and "The Future of Our Organization," both of which laid out specific policies, practices, goals, and boundaries that defined the organization as Heather and her team envisioned it. Together, these vision statements stood as two firm pillars of the character-driven business model Heather intended to create and follow—sources that anyone in the company could turn to when in doubt about the company's focus.

Heather and her team used these two documents as the content for a host of strategic communication channels. Heather held numerous town hall meetings. She met with department heads, with individual departments, and with customers. She and her team carried the same message to all parts of the company and to all regional offices, and included a lengthy Q&A session in each meeting, so they could gauge how effectively they were communicating the organization's new vision. Heather spoke about the vision so often that she wondered sometimes if she still made sense, but she saw how inspiring it always seemed to be to her audience. This gave her the energy to communicate, communicate, and communicate some more.

This kind of multichannel and multiphase rollout is an essential tool for introducing an organization to an entirely new vision—and culture. As the CEO or as a member of the leadership team, your goal must be to permeate every facet of the organization with the values, principles, and character habits that your vision embodies.

Kotter and Cohen say that "Good communication is not just data transfer. You need to show people something that addresses their anxieties, that accepts their anger, that is credible in a very gut-level sense, and that evokes faith in the vision."[2] Their recommendations certainly describe the approach Heather and her team employed for communicating their new vision to the organization. Now the team's task became more targeted, as they moved to identify and eradicate the company's built-in (and often hidden) barriers to change.

Finding and Removing Obstacles to Effective Execution

Heather's first six months as a CEO passed so quickly that she hardly had time to catch her breath. She had made great progress in those months. She had formed a new executive team, bringing in some great new talent from the outside and making two internal promotions. She reorganized the structure so that it reflected more clearly the way the work needed to get done. And she and her executive team had energized and inspired the workforce with her vision for the future. Nevertheless, the executive team was still too often caught up in firefighting. A week rarely passed without a crisis, either with a product problem or with a major customer issue.

Heather asked both her mentor and her consultant for help: "I need a way of assessing the organization to discover the biggest obstacles we're facing in execution—what they are and where they reside in the organization." By revealing the obstacles to effective execution, Heather would essentially be uncovering her organization's hidden obstacles to change. Once revealed, those obstacles would become targets for the incremental changes necessary to realize the organization's overall vision.

After talking this through with her advisers, Heather decided to use the diagnostic tool KRW's research team created to measure the organizational effectiveness of the CEOs in our research project. This tool is based on the Execution Readiness model shown in figure 5-4 in chapter 5.[3]

I won't go through an exhaustive description of the layers of organizational readiness in this model, because we walked through those elements and their role in the organization's ability to execute its business plan earlier. The diagnostic instrument based on this model assesses these elements by asking participants to rate, on a scale of 0 to 9, the accuracy of over a hundred statements about their organization. Examples of these statements include:

- "Our CEO talks about the vision for our organization's future growth and success."

- "Management throughout the organization is focused on short-term goals rather than a long-term vision."

- "I am given the freedom and authority to make necessary decisions and take action. I feel empowered."

- "Our company's priorities are constantly changing."

- "In my department, we spend our time moving from crisis to crisis and 'putting out fires' rather than focusing on our long-range goals."

- "Departments in this organization function as silos—they operate within their own world, often unaware of their effect on and connection to other departments."

- "People in my area have unreasonable workloads."

- "There is favoritism in this organization."

- "People on my team trust each other."

Whether you use this diagnostic tool or another process to gather input from your workforce, that information is a critical tool for highlighting both assets and barriers to the effective execution of the business plan. When the organization is managing each of the Execution Readiness elements successfully, you can predict with some certainty that it will be effective in executing its business plan. Where the assessment uncovers problems in any element of Execution Readiness, it provides leadership with a blueprint for essential organizational change.

That change may involve anything from removing barriers to collaboration to making the reporting structure or pay scale more equitable or building more accountability into reporting processes. Whatever they involve, all of these individual, targeted changes are critical elements in the overall process of driving deep and meaningful change in any organization.

Heather embraced this model and its diagnostic tool. She realized, though, that she would have to convince employees that the assessment really was aimed at gathering their input regarding the organization's strengths and weaknesses, rather than just a means for identifying (and getting rid of) problem employees. Before launching the survey, Heather gave a number of webinar sessions and talks to the workforce to fully describe the process, the organization's reasons for conducting it, and the need for employees to be totally candid in their responses. Beyond assuring the workforce that its responses would be completely anonymous, Heather also promised that the executive team would share the results of the survey with the entire company. She went on to stress that she would be mobilizing a volunteer advisory committee to problem-solve once the data had been collected.

The workforce response to the survey process was very gratifying. Ninety-two percent of the workforce responded. Better yet, the results weren't sugarcoated. Real issues and conflicts between different areas of the company stood out in the workforce's assessment of the organization and its operations. Heather was excited to have this in-depth diagnostic; it allowed her to know where she and her team should put their effort. And it helped her identify her priorities for changing the organization.

Empowering Others in Organization-wide Change

When executive leaders have identified specific areas of the organization that are standing in the way of its progress, their next step has to be quick and certain, as they move to address those problems. As with the assessment process itself, most organizations find that they benefit from involving the entire organization in change. Empowering the workforce in such change is yet another hallmark—and strength—of

Virtuoso leadership. It raises the standard for workforce engagement even further, by giving everyone a stake and a hand in creating the company's success.

Heather was fully committed to empowering her workforce in the change process that she and her executive team were driving. After she and the team reviewed the results of the organizational Execution Readiness survey, she launched another series of town hall meetings at all of the company locations, in which she shared the data they had gathered. While none of the results were surprising to most people, those open discussions underlined Heather's commitment to transparency.

True to her word, Heather followed up the meetings by calling for volunteers to form a cross-functional, companywide advisory team. She and the executive team chose nine members from a much larger group of volunteers. The executive team and this new advisory team met offsite for a two-day planning session during which they created a short list of change initiatives that could be quickly implemented. Other volunteers were called on to serve on a separate challenge team for each initiative.

Any organization can benefit from this strategy, which is aimed at short-term wins. Without question, saving a struggling organization demands a big-picture, long-term approach, as does building organizational character and culture. But for broad organizational change to be effective, it has to produce at least some noticeable and immediate improvements.

Most organizations don't veer off into trouble quickly, nor do most struggling organizations find a rapid and smooth path back to stability. If a company has been floundering for months or even years under poor leadership, it can develop a bad case of cynicism. Often, everyone involved in the organization, from the workforce to the board of directors and even clients and vendors, has become skeptical of things ever improving. Short-term successes and improvements break the hold of that cynicism and help speed the organization on toward its larger goals. Things like eliminating silos to improve cross-departmental communication and collaboration, or restructuring to eliminate individuals or departments that have been widely acknowledged sources of dissatisfaction or favoritism can bring a much-needed blast of fresh air to the organization—and pave the way for more changes ahead.

Heather took her consultant's advice to heart on this matter and began including examples of her organization's short-term gains as part of her on-going communication about the company's new vision. She managed to create a virtuous circle: the more she showcased the positive changes, the more her challenge teams, the advisory team, and executive team wanted to create noticeable improvements.

Eighteen months later, the success of Heather's strategy—and her team's efforts to reshape the organization's character, culture, and approach to business—was apparent throughout the company and its operations. With a new leadership team and character, the company had been successful in rehiring several of the technical experts it had lost, and the new technology platform was working well after a successful launch. Customer satisfaction and loyalty were at an all-time high, and the company's employee attrition rate was down. Heather had aligned the company around a common vision and organized it to perform with a fully engaged and energized workforce. As a result, the organization had changed dramatically from a failing business to a growing and highly profitable industry competitor.

The board of directors was very pleased with the results Heather and her team had achieved. In the process of achieving those results, however, Heather had learned some valuable lessons about just what level of support she could expect from the board. Her experience was much like that of many CEOs who are fighting to save an organization in trouble. In many cases, those boards expect new leaders to accomplish systemic organizational change and then to let the boards know when they've achieved it. As for actively being engaged in supporting that change, unfortunately, many boards don't see that as part of their mission or agenda. For that reason, learning to work with the board and elicit as much support from it as possible is another critical task for the CEO attempting to drive organizational change.

Managing Expectations for the Board's Role in Organizational Change

In effect, the CEO and executive team are part of an organization's larger ecosystem. Every CEO reports to some sort of governing body.

Bill Bojan, CEO and founder of Integrated Governance Solutions, an organization devoted to improved business leadership and governance, has created a useful way of looking at organizational life from a total systems viewpoint.[4] He told me, "In a healthy governance ecosystem, there is an integrated balance between the board, the executive team, and the monitoring functions (compliance, risk management, ethics, sustainability). An imbalance in any one area can undermine the integrative health and vibrancy and direction of the entire system/institution."

In Heather's company, the board had only one mission: to make money. It had bought the firm from the founder and planned to keep it for three years and then sell it. Unfortunately, the first CEO it hired had made that impossible. By the time it brought in Heather, the company was probably worth *less* than the board had paid for it. Given that the standard mission in the private equity world is to buy undervalued companies, reshape them into more profitable businesses, and sell them, the board's impatience was understandable. On the other hand, it *was* in its best interests to help Heather succeed.

While the board didn't interfere with Heather's plan, however, it certainly didn't add anything of value to her leadership. She had hoped a small committee of board members would help her craft the vision. It had turned her down. She also had hoped for the board's enthusiastic support for her efforts to diagnose and remove the organizational barriers to execution that had formed over the years. That didn't materialize either. When she met with the board chair at his regular quarterly visit and enthusiastically reviewed with him the Execution Readiness report, he'd shown no interest at all. "Heather, it's fine that you did this, if that's what you think you need," he'd told her. "But don't show it to the rest of the board. You know we don't put much stock in this sort of touchy-feely thing." Instead of serving as an engine of support for Heather, her board was acting more like an impatient spectator, waiting for her to find her own way into the winner's circle.

Boards that choose to wait on the sidelines are missing a great opportunity to contribute to the value their CEOs can create. Boards also can destroy value by interfering and stripping the CEO of power. One of the Virtuoso CEOs in my study faced just such a dysfunctional board. While he had worked with this board for years and was never very pleased with its performance, he was shocked when the board struck down his plan for restructuring the organization and forming a different executive team. This board misunderstood its role. If the CEO's plans for reorganizing caused him to fail to meet the performance goals he and the board had agreed upon, then the board should act and hold him accountable for his performance failure. But in this case, the board tried to do the job of the CEO. By stripping the CEO of the power to create his own team and organization, this board irreparably damaged his ability to lead the organization. Ultimately, this Virtuoso left the company, to the great loss of all of the organization's stakeholders.

As Heather's experience illustrates, Virtuoso leaders can take an organization through deep and systemic organizational change, even without the support of a fully functioning board of directors. But that process puts extra demands on the CEO, and it denies senior leadership and the organization at large the energy and enthusiasm that an engaged board can contribute to such a critical and complex undertaking.

When a board functions well and holds its CEO accountable to agreed-upon performance standards, it's really just fulfilling its own obligation for oversight. Jack Lederer, a longtime expert in board functioning, told me, "Boards are key to keeping CEOs and their teams focused on what matters: vision, strategy, financial performance and people performance."[5] As such, the board of directors plays an integral role in organizational change. Whether that role creates positive or negative results is determined by how well the board members understand the process and dynamics of organizational change—and their responsibility in achieving it.

Strengthening Every Link in the Value Chain

Remember the ROC Value Chain I introduced in chapter 1? Let's take one final look at figure 1-5, as a reminder of the responsibilities every CEO carries for achieving the ultimate goal of his or her organization—the business results. In this chapter, we've seen how strong, character-driven leadership plays a role in envisioning and implementing organizational change. But in *every* chapter, we've seen that the character of Virtuoso leadership—as demonstrated by the CEO to the executive team, to the board of directors, and even the workforce at large—plays a central role in shaping organizational outcomes.

John Kotter whose approach to change leadership we've referenced multiple times in this chapter, is a foremost authority on transformation efforts in organizational life. The change processes outlined in part III share many of the elements of Kotter's eight-stage process of change, which includes establishing a sense of urgency, forming a powerful guiding coalition, creating a vision, and so on.[6] In spite of the close parallels between our concepts of organizational change, however, there is one area in which Kotter and I differ. Where Kotter's eight stages focus exclusively on what the leader does, he ignores *who* the leader is—the critical first element in the ROC Value Chain and the central focus of this book.

Much of the current leadership literature appears to be based on one or both of two assumptions: that the average leader is a person who already has adequate character habits, *or* that the leader's character habits really don't matter as long as he or she isn't breaking any laws. Both our research and my professional experience have taught me just how deeply flawed these assumptions are when it comes to predicting success in implementing organizational change or in achieving strong business results. I have seen that CEOs with weak character habits encounter difficulty beginning with the first step toward that change. How does a CEO establish a sense of urgency if the organization believes only about half of everything that CEO is telling it? How likely is it that a CEO who demonstrates weak character is going to be able to muster the trust and teamwork necessary to form a guiding coalition? How capable is a Self-Focused CEO of creating a vision that can inspire the entire workforce or of developing strategies for achieving that vision?

As the ROC Value Chain illustrates, effective leadership requires both business skills and strong character habits. And just as we have seen in the process of successfully leading organizational change, the results leaders achieve are a product of *who* they are as well as what they do. That's where the unique competitive advantage of Virtuoso leadership can make itself most apparent.

We've seen that organizational change involves some of the most fundamental and formidable challenges of leadership, from identifying and accepting the need for change, through crafting a new vision and creating the team necessary to drive it, to engaging everyone in the workforce in the process of targeting and achieving each element of the change process, and managing the board's expectations of that process. Through every step of this journey, the short-term successes and long-term outcomes are shaped by the strong character of the CEO and executive team leading the way.

More importantly, we've learned throughout the course of this book that character matters, that our character is a product of our genetic heritage and life experiences, that we express character through our habitual behaviors, and that like all habits, *we can change our character habits*. We've seen that by changing our leadership character, we can begin the process of improving the character and culture of the organizations we work for. When we effect that kind of deep and meaningful change, we can change the lives of everyone our organization touches—our workforce, our clients, our communities, and our world.

When the people who work with and for us are confident in both the skills *and* character of those who lead them, they also can feel confident that the energy and focus they bring to their own role in building organizational success will be acknowledged and rewarded. Whether launching an organization-wide change initiative, entering into a new marketplace, or taking command of familiar territory, an organization grounded on the rock-steady foundation of Virtuoso character is positioned to win. That's both the promise and reward of ROC leadership—benefits we all can enjoy.

ROC TAKEAWAYS
Developing an ROC Organization

1. **Organizations don't change themselves.** *Leaders* change organizations.

2. **Virtuoso leadership isn't a solo act.** It requires the participation and cooperation of the entire organization.

3. **One of the CEO's primary tasks is creating an executive team that shares the leader's organizational vision.** The team also has to share the CEO's sense of urgency in accomplishing the changes necessary to bring that vision to life.

4. **The CEO and leadership team must implement a multifaceted effort to communicate their vision for organizational change.** That effort must permeate every area of the organization.

5. **Effectively leading an organization is a combination of *who* the CEO is and what the CEO *does*.** Effective leadership takes both business skills and strong character habits.

6. **The board can play an important role in organizational change.** It can add value by supporting and guiding the CEO or it can become an obstacle the CEO must work around.

7. **Short-term successes can help fuel even a cynical workforce** to keep working toward long-term change.

8. **Organizational change involves a sense of urgency, an inspiring vision, and a Virtuoso team that empowers and guides the whole organization to participate in diagnosing and removing barriers to effective execution.**

Conclusion

Steering toward a New Direction in Leadership

When KRW's research team began to analyze the data we collected from over eighty-four hundred randomly selected employees about the eighty-four CEOs who participated in the ROC study, we were continually surprised as the findings took shape. I had expected to discover a relationship between hard business results and character, but I also was prepared for that relationship to be relatively weak. Instead, we found that when a business is led by a Virtuoso CEO and senior executive team, we can predict with some accuracy that the business will achieve a greater positive ROA than businesses led by Self-Focused CEOs and teams. The ROC study, in other words, revealed that Return on Character is both real and significant.

There's nothing ambiguous about our research findings. Nor are they insignificant. By demonstrating a credible link between truthful, compassionate, responsible, forgiving, and fully integrated leadership and positive business results, the ROC research may be able to provide a foundation for better business education, training, and practice. I've written this book to begin laying that foundation. And that work continues through you. I hope the ideas, stories, and techniques in this book have convinced you that *you can* make a difference in shaping the nature of business leadership and the common wisdom that describes it. *You* can become a Virtuoso leader. *Your organization* can reflect the culture and character of Virtuoso leadership and, as a consequence, achieve better and more sustainable business results. There are serious reasons to believe that the transition to character-based leadership not only is possible, but has already begun. Now let me leave you with the hope that you can help drive that transition—and in the process, change the world.

Looking for World-Class Leaders

No one would argue against the idea that our world is in tough shape. If there were only 1 or 2 billion of us on this planet, things would probably not be so bad. But there are more than 7 billion people on earth, and all of them are competing for water, food, fuel, and some level of social and economic security. We all know the list of problems facing us today—terrorism; climate change; overpopulation; resource depletion; water pollution; nuclear weapons; human rights violations; unrest in Asia, the Middle East, and Africa; and economic tensions between many of the world economies, to name just a few.[1]

But those problems aren't the whole equation. On the positive side of the ledger, there is hope. According to Kishore Mahbubani, former Singaporean ambassador to the United Nations and current dean of the Lee Kuan Yew School of Public Policy at the National University of Singapore, a review of the last thirty years shows that some of the world's most serious problems have improved more in recent history than in the previous three hundred years. Mahbubani writes:

> Global poverty is disappearing. The global middle class is booming. Interstate wars have become a sunset industry. Never has so large a percentage of the world's population been as well-educated and well-traveled as it is today. We are becoming more integrated and interconnected.[2]

Mahbubani also points out that a century or two ago, each nation-state was like its own boat on the global sea, and the primary task for each nation's leaders was to guide their own boat. Today, he goes on to note, each nation-state is more like a cabin on a cruise ship. Leaders can determine what goes on in their own cabin, but all share the fate of the mother ship—and unfortunately, *there is no captain or crew in the ship's wheelhouse.* Why? Because few leaders seem to understand the shared nature of their voyage—that their own safe passage is, in a large part, dependent upon the safe passage of everyone around them. We need leaders who are capable of being in the wheelhouse. We can no longer allow the fear-based, self-interested, Self-Focused leaders like those at the bottom of the ROC Character Curve to be the norm. We need Virtuoso leaders to take over and provide thoughtful, skilled leadership for these challenging times. That kind of shift will be monumental, but it won't happen all at once. Like any significant change in social norms, a new expectation and attitude about strong leadership must begin in the hearts and minds of each of us, as individuals. As we replace each of our old ideas with a new understanding, society shifts slightly toward cultural norms that reflect the change, just as each grain of sand in an hourglass marks the passing of one moment into another. Even though those incremental movements can be hard to notice individually, together they can form the kind of seismic transition that changes everything.

If you're skeptical about the chances for this kind of evolution, consider some of the social changes we've witnessed since the mid-twentieth century. In the 1960s, smoking was a common and accepted practice. You could smoke a cigarette in an airplane, in the back row of movie theaters, in restaurants and workplaces, even in hospital rooms—basically, the smoking section was whatever space a smoker was currently occupying. Fifty years later, in many areas of the United States, the only places where you can legally smoke are in your own home or car (and as I write this, seven states in the United States have a ban on smoking in automobiles when children are present). Smoking, once a widespread social norm, has become taboo, with many smokers hiding their habit from friends, coworkers, employers, and even family members.

Next, consider the shift in attitude toward sexual orientation. In the first decade of the twenty-first century, it was still illegal for any member of the US military to admit that he or she was gay. No state allowed same-sex marriage, and in general, the American public could accurately be described as largely homophobic. Skip ahead just a few years to 2014 and we find that the US military has abandoned its much-ridiculed "don't ask, don't tell" policy to accept openly gay members into its forces; the Boy Scouts of America has announced that it will accept homosexual boys into its ranks (it still banned gay Scout leaders, but most believe that ban will soon die as well); and the movement toward legalizing same-sex marriage is sweeping across the United States. Our culture reached a tipping point, resulting in a national shift toward the acceptance of gay life and marriage.

So game-changing shifts in public attitudes and social norms can— and do—happen. I believe that even as I write these words, we're experiencing the first individual elements of such a shift in the expectations we have for leaders in the business and nonprofit communities. I call this movement "the greening of the corporate soul," because it seems to be much like the process we see when the dead leaves of the past season's vegetation fall away and are replaced by the vibrant, green shoots of a new season—and a new life.[3] Wherever I speak, I find an audience that is more than ready for this new flush of leadership understanding to flourish. People are hungry for information that allows them to believe that we can and, in fact, *must* demand more from our leaders. I recently had a one-on-one meeting with the managing director of a large New York–based private equity firm. He looked and talked like the stereotypical private equity investment banker—a believer only in financial outcomes—until I began to speak about the connection between character and business results that ROC research has revealed. At that point, he smiled, his face softened, and he leaned forward with great interest. As our talk progressed, it became clear to me that this business leader wanted to believe that what he knew in his heart about the positive benefits of character-based leadership was also something he could embrace intellectually, based on hard data.

That's the data we've been discussing throughout this book, research-based evidence that demonstrates that good leadership— Virtuoso leadership aimed at promoting the common good, not just individual, winner-take-all acquisition—can be good business. We've come to accept the sad notion that when it comes to profit, anything goes, and "anything" can include abandoning our compassion for others, lying, ruling rather than leading, and bleeding out every last drop of the world's social or environmental stability in the name of increased market share or bottom-line ROA. Now we have undeniable evidence that businesses, governments, and economies can best benefit their bottom lines by claiming the ROC produced by principled, character-driven leadership.

Like that investment banker I met with in New York, people are hungry to have a model of leadership that they can believe in, one they can aspire to, one that is founded on and nourished by a shared humanity. We humans find it deeply satisfying to live in a way that is aligned with our innate moral intuitions. That kind of self-integration nourishes our mind, body, and spirit, and it forms the beating heart of the social movement I see happening today. As society sheds the old, tired ideas that have historically shaped our slash-and-burn approach to business, new ideas emerge to take their place. The withered concept of "might makes right" falls away as a new ethos of fairness and equality takes root and grows. The "do as I tell you" message of lone-wolf leadership fades into memory, as new voices remind us that we're all in this together.

Both our research and my personal experiences lead me to believe that the corporate soul of America *is* growing greener and healthier. But I have another reason for that belief, based on data just as carefully gathered and analyzed as my own research findings.

A Word to Millennials . . .

As we've seen throughout this book, many leaders from the boomer (born between 1946 and 1964) and Gen X generations (1965–1980) embrace the values and principles of Virtuoso leadership and are helping to train the next generation of leaders and organizations in them. But I have special hope for the next generation—the millennials, the generation born after 1981—because of what we know about who they are and how they think. So for just a moment, all of you other readers listen in while I have a word with the younger members of the audience.

You millennials represent nearly 60 percent of the total global population and are on the cusp of supplying leaders to every corner of the world's stage. Researchers have studied your generation in the United States quite carefully, and in 2014, the Pew Research Center issued a report about what they've learned.[4] Among those findings:

- Nearly half of you are nonwhite.

- As a group, you are socially liberal but fiscally conservative.

- While half of your generation claims to be politically independent, you vote heavily Democratic and embrace a belief in an activist government.

- You support same-sex marriage and marijuana legalization.

- You are "detached from institutions, but networked with friends." At the time of Pew's research, 81 percent of you were on Facebook, where your median friend count was 250.

- You are the first generation of "digital natives."

- You are less trusting of others by far compared to the older generations. Just 19 percent of you say "most people can be trusted," while 40 percent of the boomers embrace that view.

- You are more heavily in debt but better educated; you are the best educated cohort of young adults in American history.

- You are amazingly optimistic in spite of having been battered by the recent recession and the cost of a higher education. Nearly 50 percent of you say the "country's best years are ahead."

The oldest of you are only about thirty-four as I write these words, but by 2030 your generation will occupy most of the significant leadership roles in the world: governmental, educational, judicial, religious, and business. Yes, just ten to fifteen years after this book's publication, your optimistic generation will own the C-suite, where the CEO and the senior teams reside.

A majority of you believe that our nation—and our planet's—best years lie ahead. The very strength of that belief gives me hope that your generation just may be right. But our best years are yet to come only if you millennials demand a higher standard for leaders. That's the standard I've tried to set forth in *Return on Character.*

Your generation can make it the norm for leaders to embrace the beliefs demonstrated by the Virtuoso CEOs. The Virtuoso CEOs' worldview shares much with your own. These leaders tend to focus on what's right with the world around them, and they tend to believe that we are never more human than when we are connected with others. Of course, the Virtuosos also seem to demonstrate a firm belief in the innate goodness of humanity, which may seem to be in conflict with your basic lack of trust in the world around you. But these leaders want to leave the world a better place, and that shared goal is perhaps the strongest link that connects you millennials with the principles of Virtuoso leadership.

As you grow and develop in your understanding of the world around you and the people who inhabit it, we can expect your trust and faith in humanity to grow as well. Then, your generation truly will be in a position to make Virtuoso leadership the norm in business, government, economics, education, and other global institutions in which you currently have so little interest. In short, I see the movement toward Virtuoso leadership slowly growing, and I believe that it will be *your* generation that makes that movement the new national—and global—norm.

... And for Leaders and Readers of All Generations, a Call to Join the Movement

I'm confident that thousands of you readers—of every generation— want to change the world. Like me, you're sick and tired of the self-focused behavior of so many leaders around the world and the unmitigated disasters that fear-based form of misguided leadership keeps dragging us into. Instead of working to build a better, more sustainable model for business, for social structures, for economies, for living on a thriving and healthy planet, the decisions of Self-Focused leaders seem to be rooted in mindless, shallow self-interests that in the end benefit no one, including those leaders and the institutions they run.

You have the power to change that. You can create a new standard of leadership for all the world's major institutions. Societal change begins inside the hearts and minds of people—human beings like you and me. That's where all change happens. Those of us who have created the current leadership norm or who have allowed its problems to fester and grow have to accept the reality of its failure. As has been the case for societies throughout the history of humanity, we have sailed along in blissful ignorance or flat-out denial of the enormity of the challenges we've created. Luckily, we now have the information we need in order to shift toward a new model. We also have the networking technologies necessary to support the kind of global collaboration that can implement such a shift. Today, more than ever, we understand that we are all global citizens—occupants of numerous cabins linked together by the common fate of one enormous ship, the planet Earth. We need leaders of integrity, responsibility, forgiveness, and compassion to take over the wheelhouse. We need you!

You know who you are, whatever your age. You're eager to take charge of the future and make a difference. You are concerned for the common good. Just like people everywhere and throughout the ages, you want to have a good life and to leave a bright future for your children and grandchildren. Toward that end, I hope you will rethink, abandon, and call out the withered and outdated ideas of Self-Focused leadership and hone your own skills of virtuosity. With that, you'll be ready to jump aboard and help steer our economic ship safely through the many obstacles we face and on to explore new waters of better leadership, better business outcomes, and a better world.

How will we know when we've crossed over into an era where higher expectations of character and principled leadership have replaced the current norms? When you see these signs, you'll know that we have truly arrived:

- Business graduate schools embrace the new science of human nature and the Virtuoso leadership model; when *who* the MBA student *is* gets as much attention as *what* the student is trained to do.

- Leadership education based on the new model begins in middle school and continues through secondary and university education.

- The use of financial metrics fades as the only standard for judging leadership effectiveness.

- Journalists routinely showcase leaders who demonstrate the new norm as well as those who fall short, but in either case, make explicit comparisons to the new standard.

- Boards of directors select Virtuoso chief executives and adopt the new model as the standard against which to evaluate CEO performance.

- Boards use a large database to benchmark their senior leaders' performance against those companies of similar size and sector.

- Global consulting firms and talent management professionals adopt the new standard.

- Individuals use the new model for personal professional development.

- Additional evidence-based leadership studies duplicate our findings and further confirm the connection between strong character habits and leadership effectiveness.

All of us who currently hold major leadership roles are especially well positioned to make a difference in the way that role is understood and experienced. In our quiet moments, I suspect that many of us have noticed an uneasiness about how the current economic focus on creating value *only* for the investor is often at the expense of other stakeholders. Now we have data that shows how unreliable and unsustainable that metric of business success really is.

Even more importantly, with the ideas, techniques, and advice you've gained from this book, you now have specific tools and processes for adopting a more integrated and satisfying approach to leadership— one that creates more value for you, your employees, shareholders, clients, customers, and community. I'm not just telling you that you *can* make a difference; I've passed on to you some of the best tools available for accomplishing that goal.

No single person or generation can bring about this kind of global change. As any Virtuoso leader would say, we're all in this together. I encourage everyone, of every age, to join in today's growing movement toward Virtuoso leadership. As for me, I'm on board the cruise ship and ready to help support any strong, new Virtuoso leaders who step up to take command. But please get on with it. The tides are swelling and we need all hands on deck.

Appendix A

The Research Design

How We Selected the CEOs for the Study

From the beginning, KRW approached the ROC study as *descriptive* research. We wished to apply some rigor to the subject of how CEOs actually behave in the workplace and the impact their behavior appears to have on the workforce and profitability.

CEOs were invited to participate in this research mostly by word of mouth. A CEO client of KRW, Mike McGavick (currently the CEO of XL Group), introduced me to Jim Sinegal at Costco. He agreed to participate in our first pilot project. Sinegal in turn introduced me to Steve Rogel at Weyerhaeuser, and so on. I also met CEOs in social contexts, on airplanes, and in other serendipitous ways.

The CEOs in this study are from nearly all regions in the United States, and two are from Canada. We briefly enrolled a few CEOs from Europe, but decided to postpone research beyond North America because of resource constraints. The data from those European participants, therefore, is not included in our study.

Once a CEO received his or her research report (which summarized the anonymous survey data), we asked him or her to provide us with an e-mail introduction to two or three other CEOs who might be interested in participating. E-mail introductions led to a request for a ten-minute introductory call from me. At the end of the call, I asked the CEO if he or she would like to receive a formal invitation to participate in the research along with a copy of our first book. Nearly every CEO I talked to asked to receive the invitation. Each CEO was required to sign a statement requesting to be included in the study.

One hundred and twenty-one CEOs signed up over the seven years. Of those, we were able to obtain complete character data sets on eighty-four. A number of reasons caused a few to drop out of the research. For some, circumstances changed suddenly, such as a major business event or a change in job status. However, the most frequent reason for failure to complete the study was a company policy of not allowing employees to be surveyed by outside organizations.

The feature of our research program that seemed to appeal most to the CEOs who participated is that we said we planned to publish the results and attempt to influence how business schools teach leadership. We believe that most business school programs gloss over the subject of character. Our CEOs all quickly agreed with this assessment and were eager to participate.

CEO Gender and Race

The overall age and gender distribution of our sample fairly closely reflect the demographics of CEOs in North America. Most of the CEOs in the study are men, and a majority of them are over age fifty (84 percent). We have seven women CEOs in the sample, or about 9 percent. This compares to the twenty-four women CEOs in the *Fortune* 500, who make up just 5 percent of that list. We have only two persons of color in our study (2 percent), compared to 5 percent nonwhite CEOs on the entire *Fortune* 500 list.

We recognize the need to extend this research to diverse ethnic and racial groups. For now, we are reporting our research on the current reality: most CEOs in North America today are white, male, and over fifty.

Business Sizes, Types, and Sectors

Size

Size by number of employees	Number	Percent
<500	42	50%
500–2,000	24	28%

Size by number of employees	Number	Percent
2,000–10,000	8	10%
>10,000	10	12%

Twenty-two percent of the CEOs in our sample ran large companies (which we defined for the purposes of this study as having more than two thousand employees). Ten of the companies were very large, with more than ten thousand employees.

Seventy-eight percent of the CEOs in our study ran companies with fewer than two thousand employees, and 50 percent of the CEOs ran small companies with fewer than five hundred employees.

While many Americans assume that most businesses are large, the fact is that 99 percent of the businesses in North America are small, with fewer than five hundred employees, according to the US Government Census Bureau, https://www.census.gov/econ/smallbus.html#EmpSize.

Type

Type	Number	Percent
Public	26	31%
Private	44	52%
Nonprofit/Government agency	14	17%

Most of the nonprofits are large organizations. Six are large health-care systems. Two others are large social service organizations.

According to the *Wall Street Journal*, the number of publicly traded firms in the United States at the end of 2013 was 5,008.[1] US Census data indicates that this is less than one-tenth of 1 percent of the total business firms in America. While the number of public firms in this research study is only twenty-six, it represents 31 percent of the total sample—a significantly higher percentage than that occupied by the total number of publicly traded business firms in America.

The next phase of the ROC research will primarily concentrate on enlisting publicly owned firms.

Sector

The following table shows the percent of companies by business sector for the total sample of eighty-four CEOs:

Business sector	Number	Percent
Computer/technology	7	8
Entertainment/media	7	8
Financial services	14	17
Food and beverage	7	8
Government agency	2	3
Health care	7	8
Manufacturing	5	6
Professional services	11	13
Retail	12	14
Social services	2	3
Transportation	2	3
Other	8	9
Total:	**84**	**100%**

CEO Data Gathered in the Study

Each CEO in the ROC research study provided data by participating in the following tasks:

1. A two-hour interview about his or her personal history

2. Sentence completion task describing his or her core convictions and beliefs

3. Self-assessment of the strength of his or her character habits

4. Self-assessment of the degree to which he or she embraced a specific set of beliefs about fears, human nature, the world, organizational life, the role of the CEO, personal purpose, and family life

5. His or her voting record in US presidential elections

The following sections describe each of these elements in detail.

Interview Questions

1. What words or phrases best describe your current corporate culture?

2. Would you have described your culture any differently two to five years ago? Five to ten years ago? If so, why?

3. Has the culture helped your firm's performance over the past few years? How has it helped or hurt the firm's performance?

4. When and where were you born? (age, birth location, and Zodiac sign)

5. Where did you attend school and what degree(s) did you earn?

6. What was your birth order?

7. How many siblings do you have? What are they doing today?

8. Did you serve in the military?

9. Describe your family life as it was when you were growing up.

10. Describe your father as he was when you were growing up. (How did he relate to you?)

11. Describe your mother as she was when you were growing up. (How did she relate to you?)

12. Who was the primary caregiver in your home?

13. Were your parents' roles well defined? If so, what were they?

14. How were you disciplined as a child?

15. Were you spanked?

16. What kind of books did you read growing up? What do you read today?

17. Were you a member of the Boy or Girl Scouts?

18. Did you have any mentors while growing up?

19. What is your best memory growing up?

20. What is your worst memory growing up?

21. Are you married? For how long? Were you previously married?

22. Do you have children? How many? What are they currently doing?

23. What religion were you raised in as a child?

24. What religion do you practice today?

25. How frequently do you attend religious services?

26. Do you believe that a strong religious faith confers an advantage in business transactions? That is, do people who bring their personal religious beliefs to the office enjoy an edge?

27. What is your political affiliation (Republican, Democrat, or Independent)?

28. What is your political point of view (conservative, liberal, etc.)?

29. How were you taught to know right from wrong? How did you learn integrity, responsibility, forgiveness, and compassion? (This was asked of a majority of the pre-2009 CEOs. After 2009, we changed this to "Tell me a story about a time when someone demonstrated integrity, responsibility, forgiveness, or compassion.")

Sentence Completion

Before asking the CEO to complete this exercise, we explained that we wished to discover the individual's core convictions—the beliefs that individual expects to hold until his or her death. We suggested that the person identify the beliefs he or she wish to be associated with in others' memories. To collect this data, we provided the individuals with an internet survey form in which they were asked to complete a series of sentences beginning with the words, "I believe . . ."

Self-Assessment of Character Habits

We asked each CEO to rate the frequency (from "Always" to "Never") with which he or she demonstrated each of sixty-four behaviors. We created the behavioral items to reflect the four Keystone Character Habits of integrity, responsibility, forgiveness, and compassion. About half were phrased as positive statements and about half were phrased negatively. Following are sample questions:

- I will tell the truth unless there is an overriding moral reason to withhold it.

- In order to produce results, sometimes I am willing to mold the "truth" to fit the situation so that it works to my benefit.

- I own up to my own mistakes and failures.

- When things go wrong, it is usually because someone else has screwed up.

- I believe that people who make big mistakes deserve to be punished for being so stupid.

- I truly care about my people as people, not just as the "human capital" needed to produce results.

- I really don't care or want to know about what goes on in my people's personal lives.

Self-Assessment of Beliefs

We asked each CEO to rate the strength of his or her belief ("I always believe this" to "I never believe this") for a total of eighty-one belief statements representing seven categories of beliefs: fears, human nature, the world, family life, organizational life, role of the CEO, and personal purpose. Following are sample statements:

- I am afraid of change unless I'm in control.

- Most people want to work for a noble cause—for some purpose larger than their own self-interest.

- When it comes down to it, most people cannot be trusted.

- All businesses, no matter how large or small, share a responsibility to contribute to the common good.

- In the final analysis, the most powerful motivator is money.

- What drives me or gives me meaning is achieving financial security.

- What drives me or gives me meaning is to leave the world a better place.

Voting Record in US Presidential Elections

We presented the individuals with a list of the candidates in each of the US presidential elections for each election back to 1960. Nearly all of the CEOs in the study had voted in every election once they reached voting age.

CEOs' Workforce Data

How Employees Were Selected

In each company, we selected the employees at random from the company's e-mail roster. For the larger companies, some of the respondents had likely never met their CEO in person. Nonetheless, the CEO has a reputation that even the lowest-level person in the organization knows. When employees are properly polled, their collective judgments are usually very accurate. I applied the principles described by James Surowiecki in *The Wisdom of Crowds* and discussed by Daniel Kahneman in *Thinking, Fast and Slow*. About his own research, Kahneman says, "The procedure I adopted to tame the halo effect conforms to the general principle: decorrelate error!" He notes that when "the errors that individuals make are independent of the errors made by others and (in the absence of a systematic bias), they tend to average to zero."[2]

I understood that to be properly polled and guard against systematic biases, the employees we surveyed had to fully trust the process and have no fear of being identified. Secondly, their ratings needed to be made independently of each other. We met both of these criteria with our research surveys. We sent the surveys from the KRW Institute's e-mail address, not from the CEO's address. However, each employee received an e-mail from the CEO seeking their participation and stating that the employee's name had been chosen at random to respond to a research survey. We also assured each employee via our survey instructions that we would not reveal his or her individual responses to the CEO or anyone in human resources.

We received over eighty-four hundred employee survey responses for the eighty-four CEOs. The response rates averaged about 40 percent. We were pleased with this outcome, as in nearly all cases, it provided adequate sample sizes. Further, since these employees were told they would get nothing in return for their participation, we viewed this as an acceptable response rate. Each of them generously gave us their time and attention to participate in this research.

In most cases, we were provided with the e-mail addresses of three hundred employees (or in the case of a few smaller companies, the entire employee roster). Because the range and number of survey questions seemed to be too much to ask of any one employee, we randomly sorted the selected employees into three smaller groups and divided the questions among them.

The Surveys

We asked the three groups of employees to complete the following surveys:

1. **Group A**

    A. CEO character (the same 64 questions asked of the CEO)

    B. Workforce engagement (26 questions)

C. Satisfaction (1 question)

D. Open-ended questions:

- What does it feel like to work in this company?

- In what ways does your CEO demonstrate the qualities of integrity, responsibility, forgiveness, and compassion? In what ways does he or she lack these qualities?

2. *Group B*

A. CEO beliefs (we asked employees to rate how well the CEO's behavior aligned with each belief statement for the same 81 belief statements we asked of the CEO)

B. Company performance compared to competitors (6 questions)

C. Emotional atmosphere (6 questions)

D. Satisfaction (1 question)

E. Open-ended question: What does it feel like to work in this company?

3. *Group C*

A. Senior management character habits (21 questions)

B. The business model (clarity of vision and strategic focus, culture of accountability) and organizational dynamics (51 questions)

C. Business performance compared to competitors (1 question)

D. Satisfaction (1 question)

E. Open-ended questions:

- How would you compare your company's performance to its competitors? Why is it better or worse?

- What does it feel like to work in this company?

Appendix B

Research Findings

Academic Research

Experts in the world of accounting and economics have tried for years to identify the forces that account for business success. Specifically, they have focused on what accounts for the return on assets (ROA).

Academic scholars agree that the actions and decisions of the CEO and leadership team account for a significant portion of ROA. Research on the "CEO effect" covers a wide range of managerial characteristics. We have chosen to focus on CEO character, a previously unstudied dimension of leadership behavior. For a good overview of the academic research on ROA variance decomposition studies and the impact of CEO traits, the reader should consult the following articles:

- Bamber, L., J. Jiang, and I. Wang. "What's My Style? The Influence of Top Managers on Voluntary Corporate Financial Disclosure." *Accounting Review* 85, no. 4 (2010): 1131–1162.

- Bertrand, M. "CEOs." *Annual Review of Economics* 1, no. 1 (2009): 121–150.

- Bertrand, M., and A. Schoar. "Managing with Style: The Effect of Managers on Firm Policies." *Quarterly Journal of Economics* 118, no. 4 (2003): 1169–1208.

- Chatterjee, A., and D. Hambrick. "It's All About Me: Narcissistic Chief Executive Officers and Their Effects on Company

Strategy and Performance." *Administrative Science Quarterly* 52, no. 3 (2007): 351–386.

- Graham, J. R., S. Li, and J. Qiu. "Managerial Attributes and Executive Compensation." *Review of Financial Studies* 25, no. 1 (2011): 144–186.

- Jensen, M. C. "Integrity: Without It Nothing Works." *Rotman Magazine: The Magazine of the Rotman School of Management* (2009): 16–20.

- Malmendier, U., and G. Tate. "Superstar CEOs." *Quarterly Journal of Economics* 124, no. 4 (2009): 1593–1638.

- Mackey, A. "The Effect of CEOs on Firm Performance, Research Notes and Commentaries." *Strategic Management Journal* 29 (2008): 1357–1367.

These academic researchers agree that the creation of value for investors is dependent on three factors (illustrated in figure B-1):

1. *Macroeconomics.* Global macroeconomic forces can make or break a company. The results delivered by a business today, whether it is a small, family-owned company or a global corporation, can be affected by tsunamis, terrorist attacks, and the global financial markets, among other factors. These forces can swing both ways, eliminating weak players and strong companies alike and, occasionally, giving an unexpected (and unsustainable) tail wind to an otherwise floundering business.

2. *Business model.* Weak business models do not last. Strong business models, especially ones that create a new market (think Apple, Amazon, or Google), have an obvious advantage over the competition.

FIGURE B-1

The ROA equation

3. *The CEO effect.* The combined effect of macroeconomic factors and the business model, however, isn't the total picture. Analysis of the source of ROA points to a third factor: the "CEO effect."

Some studies report that the leadership of a CEO can contribute up to nearly 30 percent of the organization's ROA. See M. Bertrand and A. Schoar, "Managing with Style: The Effect of Managers on Firm Policies," *Quarterly Journal of Economics* 118, no. 4 (2003): 1169–1208.

CEOs may not always be able to create value because of forces beyond their control, but they can most certainly destroy value. While the CEO effect traditionally has been overshadowed by the more easily identifiable forces of the other two factors in this list, our research provides new insights on this effect and its impact.

What the academic studies have not articulated is this: *Just what is it about a CEO that enables him or her to create value?* Is creating value simply a skill gained from experience or is it more about who the CEO is as a person? Is savvy decision making mostly the result of business knowledge or life experience? What other factors might be important in shaping skillful leaders?

As noted in appendix A, our study began with a pilot project in 2006 and, beginning in 2007, ran for the next seven years. A little less than half (40 percent) of the Virtuosos entered the study before the 2008 collapse, compared to 60 percent of the Self-Focused CEOs. The timing of this major macroeconomic event, however, did not appear to be an important factor influencing the results of our study. The CEOs who entered the study after the financial collapse actually produced a marginally higher ROA than those who were in business before the collapse.

Our Sample Size

Our findings and conclusions about ROA are based on a sample of forty-four companies with over four thousand randomly selected employees providing their observations about the character of the CEO and the senior team. We were pleased to see that, as figure B-2 shows, the whole range of the Character Curve is well represented. That is, we obtained complete financial data on the Virtuoso CEOs as well

FIGURE B-2

CEO Character Curve

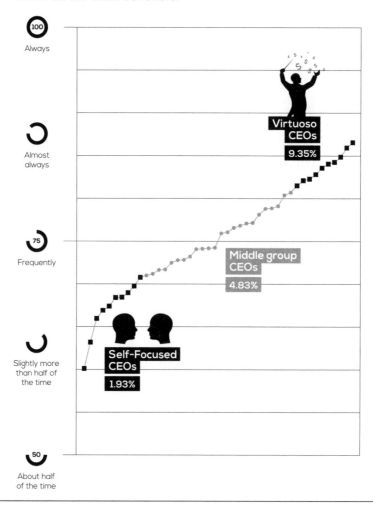

Return on Character score

CEO research subjects

The CEO and senior team demonstrate these behaviors:

100 — Always

Almost always

75 — Frequently

Slightly more than half of the time

50 — About half of the time

Virtuoso CEOs — 9.35%

Middle group CEOs — 4.83%

Self-Focused CEOs — 1.93%

as the Self-Focused CEOs *and* on a full range of CEOs between the extremes. The entire spectrum of the Character Curve is represented by this sample.

While admittedly this is a small sample, it is a much larger sample of real-world data than has previously been collected on this subject. Furthermore, we plan to add to our database as we continue this research and publish our findings on our website.

We expect to have these results confirmed. We fully expect to confirm that strong-character CEOs and their teams consistently deliver higher profitability to investors than the weak-character CEOs.

Our Data

See the following data tables so you can come to your own conclusions.

TABLE B-1

Combined CEO/senior team character score, Virtuoso

Number of CEOs	Type of organization	Business sector	Size of organization (number of employees)	CEO character	Senior team character	Combined CEO/senior team character	Workforce engagement	Average 2-year ROA
78	Private	Manufacturing	500–2,000	92	81	86.56	83.71	30.49%
99	Public	Financial services	<500	90	82	85.94	82.16	0.37%
88	Public	Retail	>10,000	90	79	84.87	77.64	5.47%
76	Nonprofit	Health care	>10,000	87	82	84.26	81.43	6.04%
70	Private	Media	500–2,000	89	79	84.06	78.09	−0.77%
6	Public	Retail	2,000–10,000	84	83	83.58	74.35	8.85%
28	Public	Aerospace	2,000–10,000	84	82	82.82	79.92	4.45%
73	Nonprofit	Health care	>10,000	83	81	82.28	78.59	16.70%
72	Public	Media	500–2,000	86	79	82.10	78.24	11.17%
37	Private	Financial services	<500	84	79	81.50	79.86	10.77%
MEAN				86.903	80.692	83.797	79.401	9.35%
N =	10	10	10	10	10	10	10	10

TABLE B-2

Combined CEO/senior team character score, middle group

Number of CEOs	Type of organization	Business sector	Size of organization (number of employees)	CEO character	Senior team character	Combined CEO/senior team character	Workforce engagement	Average 2-year ROA
82	Public	Computer software	<500	81	80	80.70	80.08	5.14%
101	Public	Insurance	500–2,000	85	76	80.39	77.92	0.42%
63	Public	Insurance	500–2,000	83	76	79.11	74.88	0.10%
94	Public	Food & beverage	>10,000	86	71	78.86	73.92	10.14%
75	Private	Financial services	<500	82	75	78.80	70.93	2.37%
80	Public	Retail	500–2,000	82	74	78.13	69.55	22.84%
79	Nonprofit	Other	<500	79	75	77.16	77.05	4.24%
103	Public	Food & beverage	2,000–10,000	80	74	77.09	75.81	4.20%
45	Public	Entertainment	500–2,000	77	76	76.83	72.63	−3.61%
8	Public	Pharmaceuticals	<500	79	74	76.58	68.93	−35.41%
77	Nonprofit	Professional services	2,000–10,000	78	75	76.06	73.70	11.37%
57	Public	Food & beverage	>10,000	82	70	75.93	66.71	9.12%
93	Private	Manufacturing	2,000–10,000	81	68	74.24	72.89	8.56%
96	Nonprofit	Health care	<500	82	66	74.17	64.39	7.22%
39	Public	Food & beverage	>10,000	76	72	74.11	67.47	17.97%
61	Private	Retail	<500	76	73	74.06	67.80	12.94%
95	Public	Manufacturing	>10,000	78	69	73.20	74.00	25.29%
7	Public	Food & beverage	>10,000	77	68	72.82	60.28	2.72%

(continued)

TABLE B-2 (*continued*)

Combined CEO/senior team character score, middle group

Number of CEOs	Type of organization	Business sector	Size of organization (number of employees)	CEO character	Senior team character	Combined CEO/senior team character	Workforce engagement	Average 2-year ROA
23	Private	Transportation	<500	75	70	72.78	57.71	2.84%
100	Private	Manufacturing	<500	76	69	72.47	69.45	11.14%
90	Nonprofit	Health care	<500	78	65	71.69	71.62	1.59%
85	Private	Professional services	500–2,000	74	70	71.64	68.82	2.09%
49	Private	Professional services	<500	76	67	71.19	66.53	−7.51%
50	Public	Computer software	<500	73	69	71.00	66.93	0.10%
MEAN				78.968	71.781	75.375	70.416	4.83%
N =	24	24	24	24	24	24	24	24

TABLE B-3

Combined CEO/senior team character score, Self-Focused

Number of CEOs	Type of organization	Business sector	Size of organization (number of employees)	CEO character	Senior team character	Combined CEO/senior team character	Workforce engagement	Average 2-year ROA
68	Private	Professional services	<500	69	73	70.78	70.49	−24.67%
17	Public	Computer hardware	500–2,000	73	67	69.76	61.58	−13.57%
67	Nonprofit	Social services	2,000–10,000	71	67	68.98	69.66	4.89%

(*continued*)

TABLE B-3 (*continued*)

Combined CEO/senior team character score, Self-Focused

Number of CEOs	Type of organization	Business sector	Size of organization (number of employees)	CEO character	Senior team character	Combined CEO/ senior team character	Workforce engagement	Average 2-year ROA
71	Private	Professional services	<500	71	66	68.46	65.44	26.07%
47	Public	Computer software	500–2,000	75	62	68.42	57.66	2.02%
11	Public	Financial services	>10,000	71	64	67.42	56.15	0.94%
86	Private	Professional services	<500	64	70	66.92	69.10	10.55%
102	Private	Transportation	<500	68	64	65.96	46.58	8.22%
65	Nonprofit	Social services	500–2,000	64	63	63.20	68.53	3.08%
69	Nonprofit	Government agency	500–2,000	58	62	60.13	66.31	1.80%
MEAN				68.316	65.687	67.002	63.150	1.93%
N =	10	10	10	10	10	10	10	10

TABLE B-4

Return on assets grouped by company size and character of CEO

Company size (number of employees)	Self-Focused CEOs	Virtuoso CEOs	Total ROA
<500	−1.67	+5.40	+2.12
500–2,000	+5.04	+13.63	+4.67
2,000–10,000	+4.89	+6.65	+7.05
>10,000	+0.94	+9.40	+9.12
Total ROA:	**+1.93**	**+9.35**	**+5.20**

Notes

Preface

1. Stephen Covey, *The 7 Habits of Highly Effective People: Powerful Lessons in Personal Change*, anniversary ed. (New York: Simon & Schuster, 2013).

Introduction

1. If you frequently feel overlooked and at the mercy of decisions imposed from above, you might buy a copy of this book and put it on your boss's desk. Or you might be more direct and ask your boss if the team could read the book and discuss its implications for your organization.

2. Jim Collins, *Good to Great: Why Some Companies Make the Leap . . . and Others Don't* (New York: HarperCollins Publishers, 2001), 35–38.

Chapter 1

1. Doug Lennick and Fred Kiel, *Moral Intelligence: Enhancing Business Performance and Leadership Success* (Boston: Pearson Education, 2005).

2. Edward O. Wilson, *Consilience: The Unity of Knowledge* (New York: Alfred A Knopf, 1985).

3. Donald Brown, *Human Universals* (New York: McGraw-Hill, 1991); and N. Roughly, ed., *Being Humans: Anthropological Universality and Particularity in Transdisciplinary Perspectives* (Berlin: Walter de Gruyter, 2000).

4. Steven Pinker, *The Blank Slate: The Modern Denial of Human Nature* (New York: Penguin Books, 2003).

5. W. Damon, "The Moral Development of Children," *Scientific American*, August 1999.

6. Lennick and Kiel, *Moral Intelligence*, 21.

7. Adam Smith, *An Inquiry into the Nature and Causes of the Wealth of Nations*, ed. C. J. Bullock, *The Harvard Classics*, ed. Charles W. Eliot (New York: P.F. Collier & Son, 1909–1914).

8. Adam Smith, *The Theory of Moral Sentiments* (North Charleston, SC: CreateSpace, 2013).

Chapter 2

1. Adam Smith, *The Wealth of Nations*, vol. X, ed. C. J. Bullock (New York: P.F. Collier & Son, 1909–1914; Bartleby.com, 2001).

2. Adam Smith's "invisible hand" as a positive force for humanity is not as dependable as the business press would lead you to believe. When business decisions are made based solely on investor return, sometimes there are coincidental positive side benefits, but the inverse is also true. Just as often, the invisible hand creates negative and unintended consequences. Smith assumed that most men were honorable and stated this view in his earlier and more popular book, *The Theory of Moral Sentiments*. One can easily imagine that any businessman in eighteenth-century Scotland who "colored outside the lines" quickly suffered negative consequences and social censure. Unfortunately, in today's global economy, the responsibility for the consequences of business decisions is most often disconnected from the business person who made the decision.

3. Lynn Stout, *Cultivating Conscience: How Good Laws Make Good People* (Princeton, NJ: Princeton University Press, 2011).

4. One of the most influential researchers and neuroscientists to explore and write about the human mind is Antonio Damasio. See Antonio Damasio, *Self Comes to Mind: Constructing the Conscious Brain* (New York: Pantheon Books, 2010). It is perhaps the best explanation of the human mind currently available.

5. Steven Pinker provides a thorough understanding of the genetic "givens" normal human infants possess at birth. See Steven Pinker, *The Blank Slate: The Modern Denial of Human Nature* (New York: Viking Press, 2002).

6. Daniel Kahneman, *Thinking, Fast and Slow* (New York: Farrar, Straus and Giroux, 2011). This is by far the best compilation of research on how our minds work. Kahneman, a social psychologist, won the Nobel Prize in Economic Science for his analysis of risk and decision making. While I have reviewed the work of many other researchers who also describe the fast and slow brain, Kahneman's work is the most complete; I have drawn extensively from his book. Other authors are Keith Stanovich, *Rationality and the Reflective Mind* (New York: Oxford University Press, 2011); and Sheena Iyengar, *The Art of Choosing* (New York: Hachette Book Group, 2010). Two pioneering researchers published a landmark article in 1999. See John A. Bargh and Tanya L. Chartrand, "The Unbearable Automaticity of Being," *American Psychologist* 54, no. 7 (July 1999): 462–479.

7. Another problem is that, developmentally, our slow brain doesn't begin to even wake up and smell the roses until about age three, and it doesn't become fully engaged until near the end of the third decade of life. This means that we go through roughly the first third of our lives without a fully developed brain. No wonder teenagers make so many impulsive decisions and are frequently confused.

8. E. O. Wilson, professor emeritus at Harvard University, is the father of social biology. He is a world-renowned biologist and the foremost expert in the study of ants. But perhaps his greatest contribution is on the biological basis of human social behavior. His work provided the foundation for the works of Jonathan Haidt on moral intuitions and Paul Lawrence and Nitin Nohria on motivational drives. Major works by these authors are: E. O. Wilson, *On Human Nature*, rev. ed. (Cambridge, MA: Harvard University Press, 2004); Jonathan Haidt, *The Righteous Mind: Why Good People Are Divided by Politics and Religion* (New York: Pantheon Books, 2012); Jonathan Haidt, *The Happiness Hypothesis: Finding Modern Truth in Ancient Wisdom* (New York: Basic Books, 2006); J. Haidt, "The Emotional Dog and Its Rational Tail: A Social Intuitionist Approach to Moral Judgment," *Psychological Review* 108 (2001): 814–834; Paul R. Lawrence and Nitin Nohria, *Driven: How Human Nature Shapes Our Choices* (San Francisco: Jossey-Bass, 2002); and Paul

R. Lawrence, *Driven to Lead: Good, Bad and Misguided Behavior* (San Francisco: Jossey-Bass, 2010).

9. Ibid., Haidt.

10. Lawrence and Nohria, *Driven*.

11. Lawrence, *Driven to Lead*.

12. Two journalists have done a great job of taking a reader on an excursion through the Big Five model of personality theory. Hannah Holmes combines sophisticated science reporting with a novelist's writing style in *Quirk: Brain Science Makes Sense of Your Peculiar Personality* (New York: Random House, 2011). David Brooks has gone one step further and written a novel of sorts, describing two individuals from before birth through their respective lives and finally the end of life, in his 2011 book, *The Social Animal: The Hidden Sources of Love, Character, and Achievement* (New York: Random House). The academic literature is rich with many articles on this subject. A relatively recent book that does a good job of summarizing the research on the Big Five model is by Samuel Barondes, *Making Sense of People: Decoding the Mysteries of Personality* (Upper Saddle River, NJ: FT Press, 2012).

Chapter 3

1. Daniel J. Siegel, in his book, *Mindsight: The New Science of Personal Transformation* (New York: Bantam Books, 2011) has provided an excellent chapter on the importance of one's life story. See chapter 9, "Making Sense of Our Lives," 166–189.

2. John Lennon, "Beautiful Boy (Darling Boy)," *Double Fantasy* album, April 1981, on the Geffen Records label.

3. Attachment theory was put forth in the last half of the twentieth century to explain the necessary conditions for a human infant to develop socially and emotionally. Several authors have written on the subject. The pioneer in the field is psychologist Mary Ainsworth. Her 1978 book (written with three coauthors) is generally accepted as the classic publication on the subject. See M. Ainsworth, M. Blehar, E. Waters, and S. Wall, *Patterns of Attachment* (Hillsdale, NJ: Erlbaum, 1978). See also, Jude Cassidy and Phillip R. Shaver, eds., *Handbook on Attachment: Theory, Research, and Clinical Application*, 2nd ed. (New York: Guilford Press, 2008). More recently, see Siegel, *Mindsight*, for an excellent chapter dealing with the impact of attachment patterns on adult behavior. I have drawn from Siegel's book for much of my analysis of the early life histories of the CEOs in our study. Attachment theory claims that an infant's experience with its primary caregiver from birth to about age two has a major impact on the child's adult relationships. Extensive empirical research has been conducted over the past three decades, and it is generally accepted in the scientific community that there are four discernible attachment patterns (secure, avoidant, ambivalent, disorganized) depending on the behavior of the caregiver: (1) a caregiver who is sensitive to an infant's bids for connection, reads the infant's signals, and then effectively meets the infant's needs is providing a *secure* attachment pattern; (2) the *avoidant* pattern is the result of a caregiver who is indifferent to or ignores the infant's signals and bids for connection; (3) the *ambivalent* pattern is when the caregiver is inconsistent— sometimes warm and sensitive and other times unpredictably cold and indifferent; (4) the *disorganized* pattern is present when the caregiver is frightening to the infant and shows a severe lack of concern or connection to the infant. According to

Siegel, infants develop organized strategies for dealing with the first three patterns, but when faced with a frightening or hostile caregiver, attachment strategies collapse. Each pattern has a predictable impact on the infant in later life. The impact is certainly not an absolute. People can remake their life stories, and frequently do.

4. Charles Duhigg, *The Power of Habit: Why We Do What We Do in Life and Business* (New York: Random House, 2012).

5. Steven N. Kaplan, Mark M. Klebanov, and Morten Sorensen, "Which CEO Characteristics and Abilities Matter?" *Journal of Finance* 67, no. 3 (June 2012): 973–1007. They describe their paper as follows: "We exploit a unique data set to study individual characteristics of CEO candidates for companies involved in buyout and venture capital transactions and relate these characteristics to subsequent corporate performance. CEO candidates vary along two primary dimensions: one that captures general ability and another that contrasts communication and interpersonal skills with execution skills. We find that subsequent performance is positively related to general ability and execution skills. The findings expand our view of CEO characteristics and types relative to previous studies."

These researchers concluded that the no-nonsense approach to being a CEO is more effective than being a good listener or team leader. It seems strange to me that these researchers selected these two variables that they identify as "hard" versus "soft" skills, as if they are opposites on some kind of continuum. In our study, the Virtuoso CEOs are individuals who are both execution focused and are good team leaders, good listeners, and care for people. Virtuoso leaders have both hard and soft skills. One without the other seems to us to be a liability.

In our study, the variables that are most critical to creating value are the character habits of the senior team. My guess is that the tough, no-nonsense CEOs they had in their study might have lacked some of the softer skills, but might have been coupled with senior teams who did possess good communication skills and team leadership skills. Overlooking the impact of the senior team in measures of the subsequent CEO performance seems to us to be a major flaw of this study.

We also looked carefully at the CEO behavior they measured and I see no attention given to behavior that would demonstrate the character habits of forgiveness and compassion. They measure interpersonal dimensions such as "shows respect" and "develops people," but they really miss the whole dimension of forgiveness and caring for people as people.

Our hypothesis is that Kaplan and colleagues measured only one part of the elephant. I believe they depended on an incomplete assessment of CEO leadership behavior and also completely missed the importance of the senior team. Thus, based on incomplete data, they came to an erroneous conclusion.

These authors regard Jack Welch and Steve Jobs as the best examples of the highly effective CEO. I know that they rode the crest of a wave of admiration, but I think Welch and Jobs succeeded for a host of reasons that overshadowed the negative impact of their personal styles. I think they succeeded in spite of their personal characteristics.

Our data is consistent with Kaplan and his colleagues that general abilities, resoluteness, and execution skills are highly predictive of CEO success. Our Virtuoso CEOs all created organizations with a high "Execution Readiness" score. We would also agree that CEOs who are just nice people with great interpersonal skills, but lack general abilities or resoluteness and execution skills are destined to fail as CEOs.

Is there not a more nuanced way of looking at CEO effectiveness? I wonder how much more effective the CEOs in the venture capital and private equity world that Kaplan and colleagues studied could be if general ability and execution skills were combined with caring for people as people, forgiving well-intentioned mistakes, owning up to mistakes, and so on.

6. For a thorough review of this subject, I encourage you to read: Ajit Varki and Danny Brower, *Denial: Self-Deception, False Beliefs, and the Origins of the Human Mind* (New York: Hachette Group, 2013).

7. When I served as an adviser to CEOs, I would nearly always insist that we gather data from his or her coworkers. It always amused me when a CEO client would ask with great concern about how I would protect the confidentiality of his data. Of course, we routinely were very careful to do so, but what amused me was that it was apparent that the CEO was the only person who didn't know these facts. This was hardly confidential information.

8. When KRW began this research program, I assumed that most of the decisions and choices we all make on a daily basis about how to behave are influenced by our consciously held beliefs. In early 2005, I had stated this observation in an opinion piece, by writing: "Our research suggests to us that a leader's behavior is the expression of a set of underlying beliefs and that all behavior is aligned with a corresponding belief. We believe that this is part of an individual's 'moral compass,' which contains a relatively short list of beliefs about human nature, the world and how to best influence people—[in other words] one's worldview. These beliefs inform one's decision making and drive behavior."

I also assumed that with a little digging, each of us could accurately describe our worldview. I figured we could state what our core convictions are—the beliefs we hold near and dear to our hearts that guide our decisions in daily living, including our moral decisions about how to treat other people. Of course, I recognized the existence of our subconscious mind (I am a psychologist, after all). But my early training was as a behaviorist and I never delved very deeply into that realm. My conception of the subconscious was that it was sort of like a storage bin for ideas and beliefs that could influence behavior when called on. With just a bit of digging, one could bring these beliefs into consciousness and either reaffirm them or discard them. This makes so much sense. I just wish it were true.

We asked the CEOs in our study to tell us their "top-ten" beliefs. We have nearly eight hundred spontaneous statements about what these leaders claimed to be their core convictions—the beliefs they hold near and dear to their hearts. We wanted to discover the worldviews of our research subjects. We have sorted and resorted these statements, looking for some kind of theme that would differentiate a high-character CEO from a Self-Focused CEO. But we have found nothing that is worth reporting. All of the CEOs in our study report a list of admirable beliefs, all very reasonable and socially desirable. But we cannot tell whether a belief statement belongs to a high-character CEO or a low-character CEO.

Unfortunately, I think humans are rarely driven by beliefs. Most often we respond to our gut intuitions or simply respond automatically with a habit and then pull up a belief statement from the storage bin to justify our behavior. I can find no strong evidence in this research that one's stated beliefs drive much behavior. Instead, intuitions and habits drive most behavior, including important moral and business decisions made by the CEO. The single critical exception to this principle is the power of aspirational beliefs. These beliefs do drive behavior.

9. Robert Kegan and Lisa Laskow Lahey, *Immunity to Change: How to Overcome It and Unlock the Potential in Yourself and Your Organization* (Boston: Harvard Business School Publishing, 2009). Kegan and Lahey describe the levels of mental complexity in detail. They also offer a tool for assessing the level of mental complexity called the "Subject-Object Interview" (22ff). According to Kegan and Lahey, most adults achieve one or more of these three levels of mental complexity over time: (1) *The Socialized Mind.* Kegan cites extensive research, which reports that approximately 60 percent of the general population operates at this level of mental complexity. People at this level tend to align their ideas and beliefs with those of others around them, and they are especially likely to adopt the worldviews of the leaders and influential people in their social group or "tribe." The identity of people at this level is tied to their relationships with others in their local culture, and they become loyal, unquestioning followers of people in authority. (2) *The Self-Authoring Mind.* People at this level of mental complexity are able to distinguish their opinions from others and are more likely to create, rather than adopt, their worldview. At this level, people typically are self-directed, thinking for themselves and acting in what they see as their own best interests. While studies show that only about 35 percent of the general population operates at this level of mental complexity, I believe that all of the Self-Focused CEOs who participated in our study demonstrate a Self-Authoring mind. They form their opinions and ideas, and then are unlikely to ever revisit them, question them, or test their accuracy. (3) *The Self-Transforming Mind.* This is the highest level of mental complexity. People operating at this level can assess their own ideas, abandon or adapt them, and accept that more than one view or position can be accurate. The Self-Transforming Mind is continually aware of not knowing everything—of understanding that every worldview is incomplete and we can never know everything there is to know about anything. This highest level of mental complexity tends to develop as we age. Kegan and Lahey state only around 7 percent of people achieve this level of mental complexity, although it was demonstrated by all of the Virtuoso CEOs who participated in the ROC study. These individuals strive to be inclusive and open-minded, thinking in terms of "both/and" versus "either/or."

10. Ibid.

Chapter 4

1. As we began to accumulate data during the first two or three years of the ROC research, we realized that we needed to refine our research design to include more detail about what leaders actually do. This forced us to review the literature as well as to draw from our own experience as leadership consultants. These Keystone Skills emerged for us when we asked ourselves, "What is it that the leader does that is unique to that role? What does the leader do versus what does the leader's team do?" We began to gather data on four of the five Keystone Skills when we were halfway through the research. The importance of decision making was not discovered until near the end of the research when it was too late to gather quantifiable data about the CEO's decision-making skill. Thus, our comments about decision making are based on interview data and are anecdotal.

2. A list of leadership skills is usually called a competency model. The most comprehensive work on this subject was published over two decades ago. See

Lyle M. Spencer Jr. and Signe M. Spencer, *Competence at Work: Models for Superior Performance* (New York: John Wiley and Sons, 1993). Most leadership competency models are mind numbing. I recently came across one adopted by a *Fortune* 100 company. It is eight pages long. It has four major categories and seventeen subcategories and three or four dimensions in each subcategory. The multi-rater assessment tool based on this list included over two hundred items. This model is thorough, but is so intricate and complex that I believe it is useless in any practical sense. The Virtuoso leadership competency model is quite simple. ROC research suggests that a leader who has strong character habits and makes disciplined business and people decisions (decisions about vision, strategic focus, the executive team, and accountability) will be a Virtuoso leader.

3. When weighing a broad range of facts, Nate Silver points out that it is "crucial to develop a better understanding of ourselves, and the way we distort and interpret the signals we receive, if we want to make better predictions." See Nate Silver, *The Signal and the Noise: Why So Many Predictions Fail, But Some Don't* (New York: Penguin Press, 2012), 231. The human brain is really great at finding patterns in data, but can be really poor at coming to accurate conclusions when we consider a range of facts. Our biases can distort the meaning of the data—we can easily confuse the "signal and the noise."

4. I have drawn extensively from four works for my description of disciplined decision making: Daniel Kahneman, *Thinking, Fast and Slow* (New York: Farrar, Straus and Giroux, 2011); Sheena Iyengar, *The Art of Choosing* (New York: Hachette Book Group, 2010); Keith Stanovich, *Rationality and the Reflective Mind* (New York: Oxford University Press, 2011); and Chip Heath and Dan Heath, *Decisive: How to Make Better Choices in Life and Work* (New York: Crown Business, 2013).

5. "Flaws in Strategic Decision-Making," *McKinsey Quarterly*, November 2009, 3.

6. Malcolm Gladwell, *Outliers: The Story of Success* (New York: Little, Brown and Company, 2008).

7. John P. Kotter and Dan Cohen, *The Heart of Change: Real-Life Stories of How People Change Their Organizations* (Boston: Harvard Business School Publishing, 2012), 62.

8. Bill Hybels, *Courageous Leadership* (Nashville, TN: Zondervan Publishing Group, 2002), 31–33.

9. Researchers at the University of St. Gallens in Switzerland have pioneered the measurement of organizational energy and its impact on organizational performance. Their research is reported in: Heike Bruch and Bernd Vogel, *Fully Charged: How Great Leaders Boost Their Organization's Energy and Ignite High Performance* (Boston: Harvard Business School Publishing, 2011). CEOs who try to make a furious pace "the new normal" fall into what these authors call the "acceleration trap," 139ff.

10. Roger Martin and A. G. Lafley, *Playing to Win: How Strategy Really Works* (Boston: Harvard Business Review Press, 2013).

11. Lawrence A. Cunningham, *The Essays of Warren Buffett: Lessons for Corporate America*, 3rd ed. (Durham, NC: Carolina Academic Press, 2013), 77–78.

12. These differences are statistically significant at the .05 level—they are not likely due to chance but are real differences.

Chapter 5

1. Tragically, most people go to work every day and fail to find it rewarding or engaging. North America leads the world in having engaged workers, according to Gallup research, with a paltry 29 percent saying that they are engaged. The remaining 71 percent are not engaged or actively disengaged. Gallup's worldwide results revealed that only 13 percent of workers claim to be engaged. See http://www.gallup.com/poll/165719/northern-america-leads-world-workplace-engagement.aspx?ref=more.

2. This model is usually referred to as the GRPI model, an acronym for Goals, Roles, Processes, and Interpersonal relations. It was first introduced by Richard Beckhard in "Optimizing Team Building Effort," *Journal of Contemporary Business* 1, no. 3 (1972): 23–32. A classic on this subject that has stood the test of time is Jon R. Katzenbach and Douglas K. Smith, *The Wisdom of Teams: Creating the High-Performance Organization* (Boston: Harvard Business School Press, 1993).

3. Perhaps the most soundly researched organizational development system is one created by Elliott Jacques. A core premise of his theory is that nearly all organizational dysfunction can be traced to poor structure and systems, not deficient employees. He did not assess the impact of weak character in accounting for organizational dysfunction. However, given that the leadership of an organization is composed of individuals of strong character, I agree that most dysfunction should be first dealt with by improving the structure and systems. For more on this theory, refer to Elliott Jacques, *Requisite Organization: A Total System for Effective Managerial Organization and Managerial Leadership for the 21st Century: Amended* (Arlington, VA: Cason Hall and Company, 2006).

4. Embedded in our research survey are the following four items that reflect how well the organization structure supports execution effectiveness: (1) I am given the freedom and authority to make necessary decisions and take action in a timely manner. I feel empowered; (2) In my areas, we are flexible and respond quickly to changing requirements; (3) Departments in this organization function as silos—they operate within their own world, often unaware of their effect and connection to other departments; and (4) We share information across different departments. I recognize that organizational structure dimensions are more complex than these four items indicate, but in the absence of more robust data, we have used these four items to assess the organizational structure. The scores obtained by the Virtuoso CEOs versus the Self-Focused CEOs are statistically significant. The Virtuosos score higher.

Chapter 6

1. One needn't look far to uncover stories of such CEO chicanery, but I can point you toward two: "Top 10 Crooked CEOs," *Time*, 2009, http://content.time.com/time/specials/packages/article/0,28804,1903155_1903156_1903160,00.html; and Susan Adams, "The Worst CEO Screw-ups of 2013," *Forbes*, December 18, 2013, http://www.forbes.com/sites/susanadams/2013/12/18/the-worst-ceo-screw-ups-of-2013/.

2. I encourage you to visit the Barry-Wehmiller website, http://www.barry-wehmiller.com, where you can learn more about the company's message, culture, and commitment to principled leadership. There, you also can link to Bob Chapman's blog, *Truly Human Leadership*, and the company's YouTube site, *leaders@work*.

3. Brad Stone, "Costco CEO Craig Jelinek Leads the Cheapest, Happiest Company in the World," *Bloomberg BusinessWeek* online, June 6, 2013, http://www.businessweek.com/articles/2013-06-06/costco-ceo-craig-jelinek-leads-the-cheapest-happiest-company-in-the-world#p2.

4. Ibid.

5. Austin Smith, "An Interview with Costco CEO Craig Jelinek," *Motley Fool,* August 1, 2013. http://www.fool.com/investing/general/2013/08/01/an-interview-with-costco-ceo-craig-jelinek.aspx.

6. Trefis Team, "How Costco Has Maintained a Steady Growth Rate in the U.S.," November 14, 2013, http://www.trefis.com/stock/cost/articles/214922/how-costco-has-maintained-a-steady-growth-rate-in-the-u-s/2013-11-14

7. Smith, "An Interview with Craig Jelinek."

8. Trefis, "How Costco Has Maintained a Steady Growth Rate in the U.S."

9. American Customer Satisfaction Index, Benchmarks by Company list, http://www.theacsi.org/index.php?option=com_content&view=article&id=149&catid&Itemid=214&c=Costco+.

10. Renee Dudley, "Customers Flee Wal-Mart Empty Shelves for Target, Costco," Bloomberg.com, March 26, 2013.

11. Adrian Campos, "Why Costco Is Beating Wal-Mart," USAToday.com, December 2, 2013, www.usatoday.com/story/money/markets/2013/12/02/why-costco-is-beating-wal-mart/3691555/.

12. Daniel Ferry, "What Makes Costco One of America's Best Companies," *Motley Fool,* February 27, 2013, http://www.fool.com.

13. Wal-Mart, "2013 Diversity and Inclusion Report," http://corporate.walmart.com/global-responsibility/diversity-inclusion/.

14. After ten years with the company, Sheahan left Patagonia in January 2014. See Clare O'Connor, "Outdoor Gear Titan Patagonia Names Rose Marcario CEO as Company Bets on Sustainable Food," *Forbes,* January 23, 2014.

15. For the reports, see http://www.rei.com/stewardship/report.html.

16. For Patagonia's environmental initiatives reports, see http://www.patagonia.com/us/environmentalism.

Chapter 7

1. The story of Mark that I've used in this chapter is based on the collected experiences of selected clients my colleagues and I have served over the years at KRW International. I've changed the names and other details to create this composite story and protect the privacy of KRW's clients.

2. You can read Tech Crunch reporter Darrel Etherington's story of the event at http://techcrunch.com/2013/08/13.

3. If you are courageous and would like to compare your self-assessment to the observations of a large sample of family, friends, and work colleagues, we offer you the opportunity to find out your ROC Virtuoso Similarity Index—a score that, like a credit score, varies from 0 to 1,000. Your score will show you how similar you are to the Virtuoso CEOs who score at 825 and above. You will also be able to view your score on each of the Keystone Character Habits. You can register at our website www.returnoncharacter.com and then invite people who know you well to anonymously send us their observations of the strength of your character habits. No report will be generated until at least fifteen people have entered their ratings. At that time, you will receive a PDF report showing how your self-observations

compare to those who know you well. If the disparity between your self-rating and the combined ratings of others is large enough, this may become your invitation to change.

4. Daniel J. Siegel, *Mindsight: The New Science of Personal Transformation* (New York: Bantam Books, 2011).

5. Ibid., 173.

6. If you decide to probe this part of your personal history, you should seek the help of a wise friend, mentor, or an experienced consultant. Digging into one's early years can elicit some unexpected emotional responses, and having a friend help you make sense of these memories provides a level of security.

7. Even if you don't find that mindfulness training leaves you with more self-awareness about what you want to change in your life, you'll receive valuable additional health benefits from the practice. Mindfulness training is well documented as a means for lowering blood pressure and providing overall benefits to your physical and mental health.

8. Interestingly, willpower is typically strongest at the beginning of the day and wanes as the day progresses. So using it to accomplish something important in the evening is a dicey proposition at best.

9. In addition to my own years of experience in advising leaders in the personal change process, I've also drawn from three excellent sources in describing this step in the personal change process: Siegel, *Mindsight*; Robert Kegan and Lisa Laskow Lahey, *Immunity to Change: How to Overcome It and Unlock the Potential in Yourself and Your Organization* (Boston: Harvard Business Review Press, 2009); and Ronald A. Heifetz, Marty Linsky, and Alexander Grashow, *The Practice of Adaptive Leadership: Tools and Tactics for Changing Your Organization and the World* (Boston: Harvard Business Press, 2009).

10. Brain science is a hot topic, so new research is constantly underway, followed by new publications of brain research findings. While you should always explore these new publications, I have found two sources very helpful in understanding just how the human brain works and changes itself: John Medina, *Brain Rules: 12 Principles for Surviving and Thriving at Work, Home, and School* (Seattle, WA: Pear Press, 2008); and Sharon Begley, *Train Your Mind, Change Your Brain: How a New Science Reveals Our Extraordinary Potential to Transform Ourselves* (New York: Ballantine Books, 2007).

Chapter 8

1. John P. Kotter and Dan S. Cohen, *The Heart of Change: Real-Life Stories of How People Change Their Organizations* (Boston: Harvard Business School Press, 2002).

2. Ibid, 84.

3. A complete discussion of the Execution Readiness model can be found in KRW Research Institute, "Execution Readiness: Effectively Executing the Business Plan," White Paper No. 103 (2009).

4. Bill Bojan is the CEO and founder of Integrated Governance Solutions. Prior to forming this organization, he was the chief risk and ethics officer for a *Fortune* 25 company and witnessed first-hand how an out-of-balance "eco-system" could result in disaster for a company. See http://www.integratedgovernance.com.

5. Jack Lederer has a depth of experience in advising boards and has also witnessed first-hand what can happen when a board fails to govern effectively. See http://www.jlboardadvisors.com.

6. John P. Kotter, "Leading Change: Why Transformation Efforts Fail," *Harvard Business Review*, March-April 1995.

Conclusion

1. Daron Acemoglu and James A. Robinson describe in vivid detail the consequences of the Economic Human model and how societies remain stuck in poverty when Self-Focused leaders create extractive political institutions and economies. When economic and political power becomes concentrated among an elite group, the whole society suffers. See Daron Acemoglu and James A. Robinson, *Why Nations Fail: The Origins of Power, Prosperity, and Poverty* (New York: Crown Publishing, 2012).

2. Kishore Mahbubani, *The Great Convergence: Asia, the West, and the Logic of One World* (New York: Public Affairs, Perseus Books, 2013). This author provides a non-Western view of geopolitical and economic forces. It is, in my opinion, a balanced position. He acknowledges the severity and depth of the world's problems, but also offers concrete solutions and optimism. Mahbubani writes from the perspective of a native Asian. He grew up in Singapore and has served two terms as the Singaporean ambassador to the United Nations. He is currently the dean of the Lee Kuan Yew School of Public Policy at the National University of Singapore.

3. I am indebted to my friend, Phil Styrlund, for coining this term.

4. My data on the millennial generation was obtained from a Pew Research Center report, "Millennials in Adulthood: Detached from Institutions, Networked with Friends," March 7, 2014.

Appendix A

1. Dan Strumpf, "U.S. Public Companies Rise Again: Stock-Market Listings Grow for First Time Since Internet Boom," *Wall Street Journal*, February 5, 2014.

2. Daniel Kahneman, *Thinking, Fast and Slow* (New York: Farrar, Straus and Giroux, 2011), 84.

Index

Note: Page numbers followed by *f* refer to figures; page numbers followed by *t* refer to tables; page numbers followed by n refer to notes.

Acknowledgments

I've been blessed over the years with many people who volunteered hours of their time to make this research a reality and also provided me with encouragement and support.

This is only a partial list of those deserving my thanks:

- **Norbert Berg,** retired Vice Chairman of the Control Data Corporation, who mentored me and gave me my first leadership development contract in 1976. This serendipitous event changed my career. Thank you, Norb.

- **Doug Lennick,** my coauthor on *Moral Intelligence 2.0* (2011). Without Doug's generosity with both his time and his money, we never would have published our first book, *Moral Intelligence,* which provided the foundation for the ROC research. Thank you, Doug.

- **Kelly Garramone,** KRW's Managing Partner, who has supported me and approved my significant use of KRW's resources to conduct the many years of this research. Kelly carried the load of leading and managing KRW while I turned my attention to this project. Without her help, I would not have completed it.

- **Nikky Heidel,** my trusted research assistant. She maintained a masterful control over the many megabytes of data we collected and has always been able, on short notice, to provide detailed answers to esoteric questions.

- **Marsha Nater,** my long-suffering administrative assistant, who so skillfully arranged introductory appointments with potential CEO research participants. Thanks, Marsha, for the years of loyal service.

- **Kim Merrill**, KRW Partner, who gave of her time and energy to pioneer the application of ROC in a real-world situation and also conducted some of the interviews.

- **Richard Aldersea**, a trusted adviser who provided support when I sorely needed it. If not for Richard's support, I would have scuttled this project when the going was tough.

- **Kathryn Williams**, the "W" of KRW and a cofounder, thank you for your support and your willingness to open doors.

- **Eric Rimmer**, the "R" of KRW and also a cofounder, thank you for your enthusiasm and support in founding our practice nearly thirty years ago.

- **Bob Kaplan**, one of the early thought leaders on senior leadership development, who invited me to join the adjunct faculty at the Center for Creative Leadership in 1988. This led to many good opportunities. Thank you, Bob.

- **Brent Walsh**, KRW's newest partner, who brought a mission-driven passion to our desire to change the world.

- **Gayle Bunge** and **Heather Richetto-Rumley**, both KRW Associate Partners, who introduced me to several participating CEOs, gave of their time and energy in the first application of ROC, and have been steadfast in their support.

- **Thom Walters**, who contributed a significant amount of time and thought leadership to the early organizational application of our research findings.

- **Peg Howell**, who provided invaluable thought leadership and came up with the observation (after applying ROC to an executive team) that ROC is the "source code" for leadership.

- **Randi Birk, Nancy Bologna, Tom Ferguson, John Swain, Brian Brittain, Stephanie Parry,** and **Mike Meyer**, all KRW consultants who provided support for the research in various ways.

- **Heather Smallman, Cari Tongola,** and **Anya Cleaver,** all KRW associates who conducted telephone interviews and helped keep me on schedule.

- **Anna Martin,** who helped in data analysis and interviewing.

- **John Moore, Freda Kiel,** and **Gina Peterson,** interns who worked diligently to uncover analytic trends.

- **Mark Edwards, Alison Sharpe,** and **all of the other KRW alumni** who influenced the success of this project by providing their positive energy and outlook.

- **Josh Birkholz,** who provided his expertise in statistical analysis and predictive analytics. Josh and I met on an airplane—another serendipitous event.

- **Shane Dikolli, PhD,** Associate Professor of Accounting at Duke University, who reviewed our results and helped me understand the ROA variance decomposition studies.

- **Mark Gorman,** whose expertise in big data has been so useful and valuable in planning for the future.

- **Dick Harrington,** who had great insights about how we could gain clarity about our business plan and operations.

- **Kyle Markland,** who, over several months, generously gave his time and helped open doors for us in his world.

- **Angie Franks,** who provided a much-needed reminder not to forget our heritage and, instead, to enrich our historical service offerings by adding ROC to them.

- **Tama Smith,** who introduced me to interested CEOs and supported and encouraged me over the years.

- **Meg Armstrong,** thank you for all your engaging conversations with me over the years and for reminding me that leadership really is a performing art.

- **Marcus Heidler,** who offered enthusiasm and support and introduced us to experts in technological applications.

- **Jack Lederer,** who has brought clarity to how we express our mission and achieve positive business results at the same time.

- **Martin Harder** and **Christoph Epprecht,** my European colleagues, who have consistently provided support and advice.

- **Donna Zajonc,** who so generously volunteered many weeks of her time during the pilot project phase. Donna spent many days at both Costco and Weyerhaeuser gathering data from senior executives.

- **Kari Glover,** who provided great advice and also volunteered her time to conduct interviews.

- **Sandra Underbakke,** who did a great job setting up the database at the start of the project.

- **Charlie Zelle, Steve Woelfel,** and **the entire workforce at Jefferson Lines,** for agreeing to serve as our original R&D site.

- **Keith Michaelson,** who gave his time and energy to brainstorm with us on how to combine "head" and "heart" solutions to execution issues.

- **Paul Harris,** who encouraged me thirty years ago to attend a spiritual retreat weekend that changed my life forever.

- **Phil Styrlund, CEO of the Summit Group,** who at dinner one night said, "You should call the book *The Return on Character.*"

- **Esmond Harmsworth,** my literary agent, who continued to convince me, when I was wavering, that this could be an important book.

- **Pat Francisco,** my writing coach, who helped with the book proposal. Thanks, Pat—it worked.

- **Lorna Gentry,** my developmental editor/writer, who revised my first manuscript and did an excellent job in helping me discover my "voice."

- **Miguel Trindade,** who was always gracious in dealing with demanding deadlines while producing the wonderful graphics in this book.

- **Jeff Kehoe** and his team at Harvard Business Review Press, who made this whole process pleasant and successful.

- **Kelly, Amy, Bryn, Anna, Jordan,** and **Freda,** my wonderful children, who understand and support for my life's work and often serve as character models for me.

- **My Lanesboro friends,** Wayne and Joni; Keith and Kitty, Mary and Joe, Mark and Marsha, and Vern and Jennifer, who reviewed early manuscripts and consistently unanimously encouraged me to continue.

I wish to give special acknowledgment to **Sandy,** my life partner for thirty-five years, who helped me grow up. If not for her loyal, loving support, constructive criticism, and encouragement, I would have crashed and burned long ago. She's the best friend I've ever had.

This project would not have gotten off the ground if not for the participation in our pilot project from the CEOs and executive committees at **Costco Wholesale** and **Weyerhaeuser.** From them we learned how to define and measure character.

Most of the CEOs who participated in this research preferred to remain anonymous, but the following provided either their verbal or signed consent to be listed as participants:

- Scott Armstrong, Group Health Cooperative

- Gary Bhojwani, Allianz Life Insurance Company of North America

- Archie Black, SPS Commerce

- David Brandon, Domino's Pizza

- Bob Chapman, Barry-Wehmiller Companies

- Joe Dedin, Eagle Bluff Environmental Learning Center

- Lon Dolber, American Portfolios

- Jeff Ettinger, Hormel Foods

- Bill Evans, AmeriPride Services

- Jeff Hamiel, Metropolitan Airports Commission

- Jon M. Huntsman, Huntsman Chemical
- Sally Jewell, REI
- Kim Jordan, New Belgium Brewing
- Dale Larson, Larson Storm Doors
- Kyle Markland, Affinity Plus Credit Union
- Jeff Noddle, SuperValu
- Will Oberton, Fastenal Company
- Mark Peterson, Lutheran Social Service of MN
- Chris Polinsinski, Land O'Lakes
- Bill Ptacek, King County Library System
- Bruce Reese, Bonneville International
- Jim Sinegal, Costco Wholesale
- Sally Smith, Buffalo Wild Wings
- Jeff Smulyan, Emmis Communications
- Charles Sorenson, Intermountain Healthcare
- Peter Ungaro, Cray Computers
- James Whitehurst, Red Hat, Inc.
- Charlie Zelle, Jefferson Lines

Finally, I wish to acknowledge the following authors, whose thought leadership has been so central to my work:

- Donald Brown, *Human Universals* (1991)
- James Q. Wilson, *The Moral Sense* (1997)
- Edward O. Wilson, *Consilience: The Unity of Knowledge* (1998)
- Paul R. Lawrence and Nitin Nohria, *Driven: How Human Nature Shapes Our Choices* (2002)
- Paul R. Lawrence, *Driven to Lead: Good, Bad, and Misguided Leadership* (2010)

About the Author

FRED KIEL, PhD, and the KRW research team have drawn international attention to the critical issue of leadership character, which is the source code of organizational success. Fred's team's groundbreaking research on the connection between the character of senior leadership and profitability is resetting organizational expectations. The associated data measurement and predictive analytic tools that have sprung from this research are used worldwide by both executive teams and corporate boards.

For more than thirty years Fred has guided *Fortune* 500 companies in their journey to accelerate business success through principled leadership. The foundation of KRW International's model is a rigorous data-gathering and customized development process designed to provide transformative insight and growth. As a result of his work, Fred is recognized as one of the pioneers in the field of executive coaching.

Fred is cofounder of KRW International, coauthor of the influential book, *Moral Intelligence*, and a speaker whose popular TEDxTalk, "Psychopaths in the C-suite," has drawn international attention to the critical issue of leadership character.

Fred believes in a world where leadership character is fundamental to business education programs and performance evaluation processes . . . a world where *who* a leader is receives as much attention as *what* the leader is trained to do.

Inquiries

For information about consulting services, please contact:

Heather Smallman, Director of Client Services
KRW International, Inc.
612-338-3020
clientservices@krw-intl.com

Professionals interested in joining KRW's Consultant Member Group should contact Kelly Garramone, Managing Partner and CEO: garramone@krw-intl.com

To e-mail the author: kiel@krw-intl.com

Follow on Twitter: @fkiel

For an assessment of the strength of *your* character habits, go to www.returnoncharacter.com